abc English
Phonics

Level 2

abc English Phonics, Level 2
Systematic Phonics Lessons for Adult & Adolescent English Language Learners

Copyright 2021, abc English
abceng.org
Jennifer Christenson

R230711

ISBN 9798771049946

Image licensing: istock.com

Teachers: Slideshow lessons and teacher instructions to accompany this book can be found at abceng.org/library.

Contents

Alphabet and Short Vowel Review

6 L Blends

7 R Blends

8 S Blends

Words with -ing

Vowel Teams: ay & igh

Compound Words

"When 2 vowels go walking..."

 -er and -ing endings

Silent e

Vowel Teams with o

More Sounds of oo

R-Controlled Vowels

L-Controlled Vowels

-er and -est endings

36 Decodable Stories

Teachers:
Slideshow lessons to accompany this book
can be found at abceng.org/library.

Alphabet Sounds

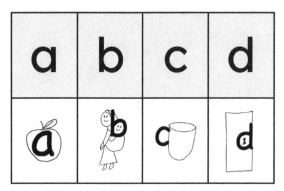

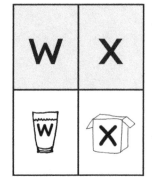

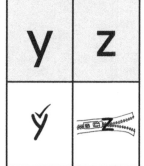

2

a - apple	n - nose
b - baby	o - October
c - cup	p - pencil
d - door	q - quiet
e - elephant	r - run
f - fish	s - snake
g - glasses	t - table
h - hand	u - umbrella
i - inside	v - visit
j - jump	w - water
k - kick	x - box
l - light	y - yes
m - mama	z - zip

ch - chair

sh - shirt

th - thank you

5 Vowels

Letter names:

a	e	i	o	u

Letter sounds:

a	e	i	o	u

What sound?

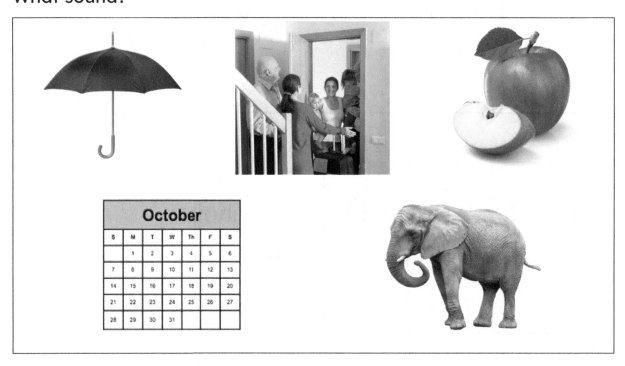

What sound?

1. a e a e a

2. a i a i a i a

3. a o a o a

4. a u a u a

5. e i e i e i e

Short Vowel Sounds

a	e	i	o	u

man   bad   cat

sun   bus   cut

red   bed   ten

jog   top   hot

sit   lip   hit

lip	cut	top	bed

Vowel Teams

ee	oo

meet	room	boot
feet	soon	pool
need	noon	teen
see	moon	keep
week	food	beet

moon	meet	pool	see

6 L Blends

bl	cl	fl	gl	pl	sl

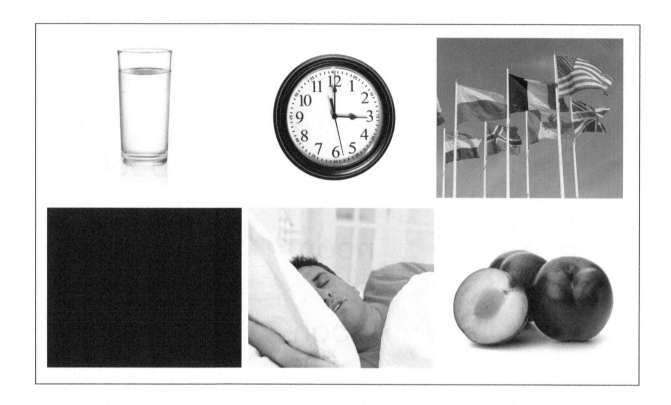

bl, bl, black   gl, gl, glass

cl, cl, clock   pl, pl, plum

fl, fl, flag   sl, sl, sleep

6 L Blends

bl	cl	fl	gl	pl	sl

slip	class	glass
sleep	clap	glad
slug	clip	plug
flag	black	plus
clock	bleed	plum

plug	slip	clip	plus

The Flag

Look at the flag. Is the flag black? No, it is not black. The flag is red.

Flip Flops

I have flip flops. Flip flops are good. Flip flops are good if it is hot. I have flip flops for my feet.

The Wet Floor

See the floor. The floor is wet.
You can slip. You can slip on the
wet floor. Look! Don't slip!

Sentences

1. The class is at six.

2. They clap and clap.

3. What is ten plus ten?

4. I need to plug it in.

5. Do you see the slug?

br	cr	dr	fr	gr	pr	tr

br, br, brother

cr, cr, cry

dr, dr, drive

fr, fr, friend

gr, gr, grapes

pr, pr, pray

tr, tr, tree

7 R Blends

br	cr	dr	fr	gr	pr	tr

frog   crib   grass

free   drop   green

brush   drum   truck

broom   dress   trash

crash   drip   tree

dress	broom	crash	drum

Green Grass

The grass is green. The tree is green. He can cut the grass. The grass will get cut every week.

The Crib

She is in the crib. The crib is big. The crib can help mom. Do you have a crib?

Drip, Drip, Drip

The sink has a drip. I need to fix the drip. The drip will not stop. Can you fix the drip?

Sentences

1.   Dad can brush.

2.   Tap, tap on a big drum.

3.   It is a big green frog.

4.   The truck was in a crash.

5.   I like this dress.

8 S Blends

| sl | sm | sn | sc | sk | sp | st | sw |

sc, sc, school   sn, sn, snake

sk, sk, skirt   sp, sp, spoon

sl, sl, sleep   st, st, stop

sm, sm, smell   sw, sw, swim

8 S Blends

sl	sm	sn	sc	sk	sp	st	sw

smell	spill	skin
slip	spoon	stop
sleep	speed	stick
snap	scab	swim
snack	skip	sweep

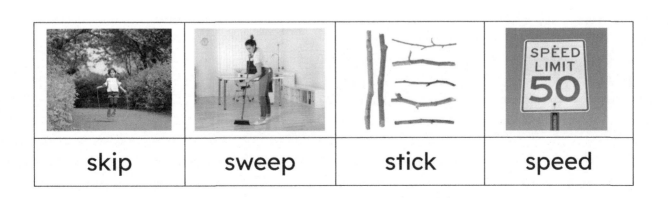

skip	sweep	stick	speed

Milk

Milk is in the cup. She can drink the milk. The cup can spill. Don't spill the milk.

Flowers

Her dad has flowers. She can smell the flowers. The flowers smell good. Thank you for the flowers!

Friends at School

She is Stef. He is Brad. They are friends. They have class. They go to school. They are friends at school.

Sentences

1. Snap, slap, and clap.

2. Scott has a scab on his skin.

3. I can smell a snack.

4. Stop, look, and cross.

Words with -ing

sleep	sleeping
brush	brushing
bleed	bleeding
clap	clapping
dress	dressing
drip	dripping
swim	swimming
sweep	sweeping

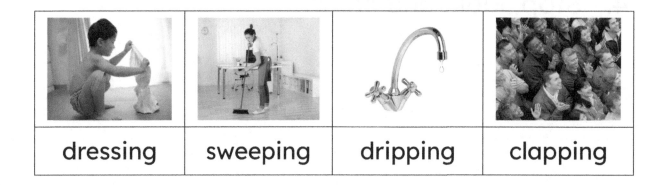

dressing	sweeping	dripping	clapping

Sentences

1. They are swimming.

2. He is sleeping.

3. He is brushing his teeth.

4. She is sweeping. He is mopping.

5. She is bleeding a bit.

Vowel Teams

ay	igh

day	light	tight
pay	night	sight
play	fight	way
tray	right	pray
stay	bright	say

pay	tray	night	sight

Sentences

1. They play and they fight.

2. The sun is bright today.

3. Go right.

4. Go that way.

5. Don't go right.

Left or Right

The pen is in his left hand.

The pen is in his right hand.

He can kick with his right foot. She can kick with her left foot.

Do you like right or left?

Will you go?

Will you go shopping today?
Will you go? Yes or no?

Maybe. I might go. I might
go today. I might go tonight.

If I don't go today, I will go
next Monday.

High School

They go to high school. They
have English class every day.
They have math class every day.
A class in high school can be
difficult. It is difficult, but they
will stay and finish high school.

Word Grid

he	his	do	have
she	her	don't	be
they	you	like	next
I	or	go	every

Which one is different?

big	way	night
will	day	light
kick	stay	fight
with	can	fit
pin	play	bright
pen	pay	right
bill	say	tight

Compound Words

freeway　　　　highway

paycheck　　　nightstand

light bulb　　　subway

payday　　　　midnight

playroom　　　stoplight

paycheck	midnight	stoplight	playroom

Sentences

1. I need to get a light bulb.

2. Do you like the freeway?

3. Go to the stoplight. Then go right.

4. The nightstand is in the bedroom.

5. She will go on the subway.

"When 2 vowels go walking..."

ai	ea

rain	meat	seat
pain	clean	heat
wait	teach	eat
train	team	chair
hair	read	stairs

| pain | hair | team | heat |

Sentences

1. He can teach me to read.

2. Wait for the train.

3. They are waiting in the rain.

4. Do you like to eat meat?

5. He can go up the stairs.

Braid

Can you braid? Can you braid hair?

Yes, I can braid hair.

I can not braid. Can you teach me?

Yes, I can teach you. It is not too difficult. I will teach you.

Too Much Rain

We had a lot of rain. Rain, rain, and more rain.

We had rain for ten days. We had a lot of rain for ten days.

The truck got stuck. We had to get help.

Meat

Do you eat meat? I eat chicken. I eat beef. I eat fish. I don't eat pork.

He eats pork, chicken, and beef, but no fish. They don't eat meat. No meat!

What meat do you eat?

Word Grid

he	we	do	too much
they	you	don't	a lot
I	yes	what	more
me	no	was	of

Which one is different?

meet	rain	meat
met	pain	clean
green	pan	teach
teen	wait	team
feet	train	ten
beef	braid	read
see	paid	seat

Words with -ing and -er

teach	teaching	teacher
read	reading	reader
speak	speaking	speaker
paint	painting	painter
wait	waiting	waiter
rain	raining	
clean	cleaning	

| raining | painting | speaker | waiter |

Sentences

1. He is a good teacher.

2. She is a good reader.

3. The waiter is giving them food.

4. It was raining a lot when I was waiting for the bus.

5. He is a painter.

Compound Words

mailbox	wheelchair
hairbrush	fingernail
paintbrush	hairnet
teacup	earplug
teaspoon	seat belt
upstairs	seafood

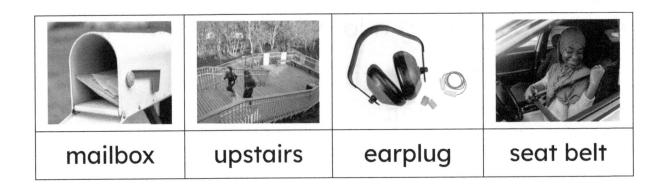

| mailbox | upstairs | earplug | seat belt |

Sentences

1. The painter has a paintbrush.

2. She is cleaning her fingernails.

3. You need a hairnet for this job.

4. He has a wheelchair.

5. I need a teacup and a teaspoon.

"When 2 vowels go walking..."

oa	ie	ue

oa	ie	ue
goat	tie	blue
boat	pie	glue
road	lie	true
coat	coach	suit
soap	load	fruit

goat	road	tie	glue

Sentences

1. I see a goat and a boat.

2. Do you want to eat pie?

3. His coat is blue and green.

4. I like to eat fruit.

5. Please help me load the truck.

Clean with Soap

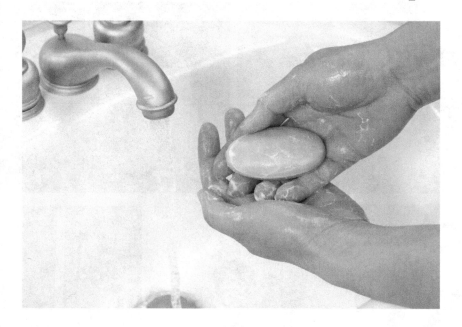

Clean your hands with soap. Clean hands can help you to not get sick.

Clean your hands with soap before cooking. Clean your hands before eating. Clean your hands after the bathroom.

Don't get sick. Clean with soap!

A Good Coach

They are a team. They like to play together. They are training to play well. They train on Monday, Wednesday, and Saturday. They run together. They kick together. They kick the ball in the goal.

They have a good coach. They have a good team.

A Suit and Tie

He wants to get a suit. Maybe a black suit, maybe a green suit, or maybe a blue suit.

He also needs a tie. Which tie? A red tie, a blue tie, or a yellow tie?

He gets a black suit and a blue tie. He looks good.

Word Grid

he	with	are	get
they	before	like	gets
you	after	want	need
your	don't	wants	needs

Which one is different?

road	sun	sick
coach	run	tie
toast	rug	fish
soap	bug	dig
got	bus	big
goat	glue	sit
boat	cut	with

Compound Words

raincoat	goalkeeper
soap dish	sailboat
oatmeal	necktie
cupboard	hair tie
blackboard	bluebell
clipboard	blueprint

oatmeal	sailboat	bluebell	blueprint

Sentences

1. The doctor has a clipboard.

2. She has a raincoat and an umbrella.

3. The cup is in the cupboard.

4. He is a good goalkeeper.

5. The teacher is at the blackboard.

Silent e

| a_e | o_e |

name	home	smoke
same	nose	stove
late	close	store
lake	vote	plate
take	rope	plane

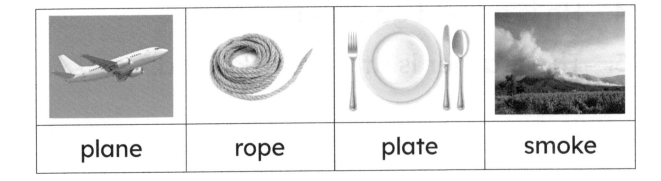

| plane | rope | plate | smoke |

Sentences

1. They ate cake and also had coke.

2. They are playing a game.

3. I hope the red team wins.

4. Those twin sisters look the same.

5. I will go home at 3:00.

Home Alone

Can they stay home alone? She is 4 and he is 3. It is not safe for them to stay alone when mom and dad are not home.

If they are six can they stay home alone? No, it is not safe. Is it OK for a teen to stay home alone? Yes, that is OK.

Which kids can stay home alone?

The Lake

We are going to the lake. We can swim. We can get in a boat. We can go on a rope. We can jump.

We can fish from a boat. We can fish from the shore. Do you like going to a lake?

What do you see?

I see a rake. I see a hose. I see grapes. I see a rose. I see a gate. I see stones and plants and flowers.

I see them dig a hole. I see them plant a tree.

I like this garden!

Word Grid

we	she	when	this
you	are	what	old
they	do	which	older
he	like	them	if

Which one is different?

rake	home	pay
gate	stone	day
plate	hole	home
grape	hose	stay
lake	lone	way
like	smoke	play
safe	lane	clay

Silent e

i_e	u_e	e_e

five	cute	drive
time	cube	wife
bike	use	nine
like	June	Pete
lime	tune	Steve

bike	lime	cute	cube

Sentences

1. What is the time?

2. What is the date?

3. He likes to use the computer.

4. Who will win the game?

5. I hope the white team wins.

Ways to Go

How do they go? She can ride a bike. She can drive a car. He can get a ride. They can take the bus.

She can take a plane. They can take the train. They can take the subway. They can go on foot.

How do you like to go?

The Dentist

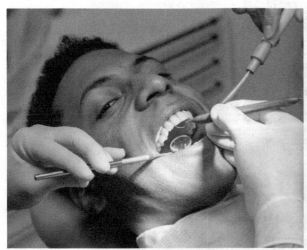 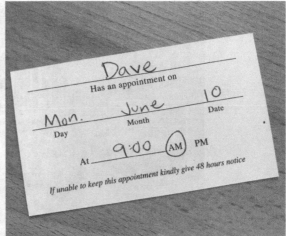

He will go to the dentist. He needs to have a checkup. The dentist will check his teeth to see if they are OK.

What is the time? Nine o'clock. What is the day? Monday. What is the date? June 10th. What is the name? Dave.

Don't be late!

Call for Help

If you see smoke, or if you see a fire, call for help! Get everybody away from the fire. Get everybody safe. I hope the fire truck will get here fast.

They may need a ladder. They may need a hose. The firefighters can help.

What number can you call for help?

Word Grid

his	have	every	if
how	needs	everybody	or
do	don't	away	for
are	be	here	from

Which one is different?

ride	cute	name
bike	cut	late
like	cube	Dave
time	June	smoke
drive	tune	same
fire	rude	lake
name	tube	take

Compound Words

notebook	daytime
airplane	night time
pancake	bedtime
fire truck	name tag
bookcase	inside
bookstore	website

pancake	bookcase	website	daytime

Sentences

1. What is a good bedtime for kids?

2. I am going on an airplane.

3. I am looking for my notebook.

4. He is inside. She is not inside.

5. I have a name tag for my job.

Vowel Teams with o

ou		ow

mouth	now	town
south	how	couch
out	cow	flour
cloud	down	mouse
loud	brown	house

| flour | cow | loud | town |

Sentences

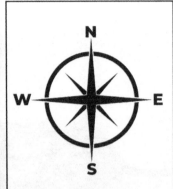

1. How are you? I'm fine.

2. Is your house east, west, or south?

3. Ouch! I hit my finger.

4. They shout! They are loud.

5. I see a brown cow and a black cow.

A Mouse

I have a mouse in my house. I don't like it. I don't like it in my house. I need a trap.

I will go to the store to get a trap. I will catch the mouse. Get out of my house mouse!

Clouds and Rain

Look up. See the clouds. I see a lot of clouds. It is cool. It is not hot. If the clouds are black, maybe it will rain.

I like to go out when it is cool. I like clouds and rain. That is good for me. It is the best.

A Couch

I am looking for a couch. I need it for my house. When they come to my house they can sit.

I want a cheap couch. I want it for less than $100. Where can I get a couch for $100?

Word Grid

I	go	are	where
my	and	is	that
have	if	will	than
don't	it	when	for

Which one is different?

mouth	now	smoke
south	how	hope
couch	cow	hop
loud	town	home
out	down	stove
house	dine	note
moon	brown	stone

Vowel Teams with o

oi		oy

oi	oy
oil	boy
boil	toy
foil	joy
coin	soy
join	Roy

boil	foil	joy	soy

Sentences

1. I like to cook with oil.

2. I need to get foil.

3. She will boil the egg.

4. They have 2 boys.

5. Please join the meeting at 2:00.

Cooking

I like to cook. I cook with oil. I cook fish in oil. Maybe I will boil it.

I like to eat it with soy. It is good. I like to make a lot so I can eat it again tomorrow. If I have more, I will keep it in foil.

A Toy

He has a toy. It is a toy train. He likes to play with the toy. He plays with it every day. He enjoys it a lot!

The toy was a gift. It was a gift from his mom and dad. He got the gift when he was 1.

What does it mean?

What does it mean?

- <u>Joy</u> is the same as happy.

- <u>Enjoy</u> is the same as like.

- <u>Boil</u> is a way to cook.

- A <u>coin</u> is money.

- A <u>toy</u> is for a baby.

- <u>Oil</u> is for cooking.

- <u>Soy</u> is for cooking.

Word Grid

with	he	from	for
a lot	the	when	a
so	every	does	in
again	was	money	it

Which one is different?

oil	boy	light
boil	soy	night
join	joy	seat
coin	Troy	bright
can	toy	sight
toil	Roy	right
foil	say	tight

More Sounds of oo

room	book	/or/
		door
moon	look	
		floor
spoon	cook	
		poor
tooth	good	
		/u/
food	hood	blood
broom	foot	flood

spoon	hood	poor	blood

Sentences

1. Look at the moon.

2. I need a broom to clean the floor.

3. We had a big flood in June.

4. This cookbook has good food.

5. Sounds good. See you soon!

Compound Words

downtown	outdoors
outside	indoors
housekeeping	doorstep
keep out	download
townhouse	cowbell
mousetrap	cowboy
lighthouse	soybean
boyfriend	soy milk

mousetrap	download	soybean	cowboy

Sentences

1. I like milk from a cow, not soy milk.

2. They like to run indoors and outdoors.

3. She has a boyfriend.

4. The box will be outside on your doorstep.

5. She has a housekeeping job.

R-Controlled Vowels

er	ir	ur

er	ir	ur
her	bird	hurt
herd	shirt	church
fern	skirt	turn
clerk	girl	nurse
serve	third	purse

fern	bird	hurt	purse

Read

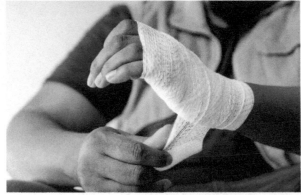 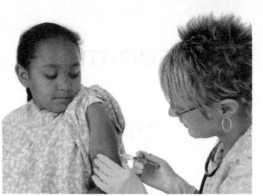

1. a girl, a skirt, a shirt

2. first, second, third

3. first floor, second floor, third floor

4. I hurt my hand.

5. The nurse is giving her a shot.

R-Controlled Vowels in Multisyllable Words

sister	September
letter	hamburger
winter	internet
summer	yesterday
finger	Thursday
silver	Saturday
pepper	birthday
hammer	girlfriend

silver	pepper	letter	hammer

Sentences

1. Do you like winter or summer?

2. Her birthday is next Thursday.

3. He will eat a hamburger.

4. She cut her finger.

5. He has a girlfriend.

R-Controlled Vowels

ar	or

car	fork	short
star	pork	sport
cart	corn	born
park	north	arm
dark	storm	March

park	dark	fork	corn

Sentences

1. She was born in March.

2. Those cars are going north.

3. When it is dark, I can see the stars.

4. Do you eat pork?

5. It looks like it will be a big storm.

R-Controlled Vowels in Multisyllable Words

market	mentor
marker	tractor
farmer	apartment
barber	important
garden	carpenter
corner	landlord
doctor	kindergarten

| marker | barber | corner | landlord |

Sentences

1. I will go to the farmer's market.

2. My sister is a doctor.

3. They are in kindergarten.

4. She has an important letter.

5. A barber can cut hair.

My Apartment

My apartment is on the third floor. I have to go up six sets of stairs. We don't have an elevator.

When I have a lot of stuff to take upstairs, it's a pain! Next time, I will look for an apartment on the first floor.

Farmer's Market

This is a farmer's market. They have it every Saturday in the summer. It is an outdoor market in the park.

You can get fresh fruit and a lot more. Last Saturday I got some good stuff. I got fresh corn and a big watermelon. It was so good!

A Broken Arm

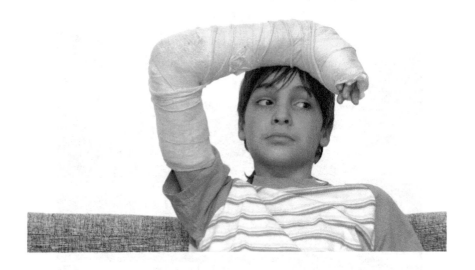

His name is Porter. He is thirteen. He was playing in the park with a friend. He fell out of a tree.

After 3 days, his arm still hurt a lot. His mom took him to an appointment at the clinic. The nurse took an x-ray. The bone has a crack. He has a broken arm. He needs to have a cast for six weeks.

Word Grid

my	we	don't	will
on	I	have	for
go	they	when	this
was	you	it's	a lot

Which one is different?

park	for	bird
dark	fork	first
March	north	big
car	pork	skirt
far	lock	shirt
fat	corn	third
star	born	girl

L-Controlled Vowels

al	ol

salt	hall	old
bald	wall	cold
all	tall	gold
fall	call	fold
ball	small	roll

salt	hall	old	roll

Sentences

1. She is painting all of the walls blue.

2. She is helping her grandmother fold the towels.

3. Did she fall down? Yes, she fell down.

4. He has no hair. He is bald.

5. I will call you tomorrow.

-er and -est

big	bigger	biggest
small	smaller	smallest
fast	faster	fastest
old	older	oldest
short	shorter	shortest
tall	taller	tallest
hot	hotter	hottest
cold	colder	coldest
cheap	cheaper	cheapest

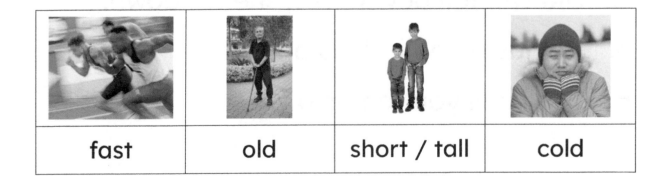

fast	old	short / tall	cold

Sentences

1. My sister is older than me.

2. He is the fastest runner.

3. The green couch is cheaper than the black couch.

4. Which is colder?

5. Which is the coldest?

Brothers & Sisters

I have 3 brothers and 1 sister. My sister is the oldest. Her house is near my house. My older brother is next. He also lives near me.

I have 2 younger brothers. Both of them live far away from me. My younger brother lives in Texas. The youngest brother lives in Japan.

A Used Car

I want to get a car. I don't have much money, so I want to get a used car that is cheap. It's OK if it is an older car. It's OK if it has some small problems. I just need a car that can get me to work and back home.

It will help me a lot. I'm going to go shopping for used cars on Saturday. I hope I can get a good used car for cheap.

Gold & Silver

 She likes gold and silver things. It is expensive, but she likes it a lot. She likes to get gifts, and also likes to go shopping herself. She has rings. She has earrings. She has something for her neck, and something for her arm, and something for her feet.

 Silver is cheaper than gold. Gold is the most expensive. She likes all of it!

Word Grid

used	old	young	expensive
cheap	older	younger	herself
problems	oldest	youngest	something
just	near	far away	most

Which one is different?

salt	old	older
bald	fold	younger
fall	rock	cheaper
cat	cold	taller
tall	mold	shorter
small	told	biggest
call	sold	faster

Appendix

Appendix

Vowel Chart

Short Vowel Sounds

a	e	i	o	u

Letter Names

a	e	i	o	u

Vowel Teams

ay	ee	igh		oo

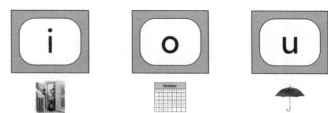

"When 2 vowels go walking…"

ai	ea	ie	oa	ue

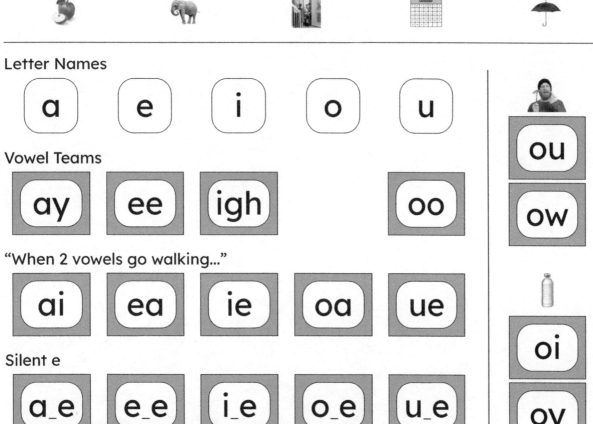

ou

ow

Silent e

a_e	e_e	i_e	o_e	u_e

oi

oy

R-Controlled and L-Controlled Vowels

er

ir

ur

ar	or
al	ol

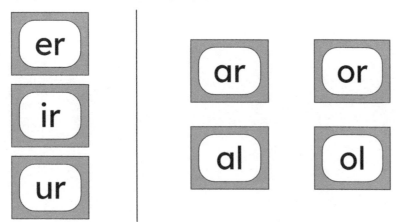

3 Ways to Spell /ā/

Color code or cut & sort:

day	rain	name
same	pay	pain
wait	late	play
tray	train	lake
plane	pray	hair

3 Ways to Spell / ī /

Color code or cut & sort:

night	bike	bright
time	light	like
tie	pie	lie
drive	right	lime
fight	nine	sight

 9

3 Ways to Spell /ē/

Color code or cut & sort:

feet	meat	green
clean	Pete	teach
week	here	meet
team	Steve	read
see	eat	tree

4 Ways to Spell /ū/

Color code or cut & sort:

cute	blue	moon
room	suit	cube
flute	glue	spoon
broom	fruit	use
June	true	pool

2 Ways to Spell /ō/

Color code or cut & sort:

home	coat	rose
boat	nose	goat
stone	road	rope
soap	close	coach
bone	goal	hose

Certificate of Achievement

awarded to

for successfully completing

abc English Phonics Level 2

Teacher Signature

Date

Made in the USA
Monee, IL
15 May 2024

58501071R00070

Upon a Spring Breeze

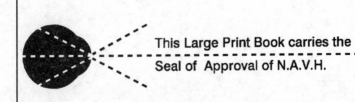

This Large Print Book carries the
Seal of Approval of N.A.V.H.

UPON A SPRING BREEZE

KELLY IRVIN

THORNDIKE PRESS
A part of Gale, Cengage Learning

GALE
CENGAGE Learning·

Farmington Hills, Mich • San Francisco • New York • Waterville, Maine
Meriden, Conn • Mason, Ohio • Chicago

Copyright © 2017 by Kelly Irvin.
An Every Amish Season Novel.
Scripture quotations marked NIV are taken from The Holy Bible, New International © Version ®, NIV ®. Copyright © 1973, 1978, 1984, 2011 by Biblica, Inc. ® Used by permission of Zondervan. All rights reserved worldwide. www.zondervan.com. The "NIV" and "New International Version" are trademarks registered in the United States Patent and Trademark Office by Biblica, Inc. ®
Also quoted: The ESV3 Bible (The Holy Bible, English Standard Version®), copyright © 2001 by Crossway, a publishing ministry of Good News Publishers. Used by permission. All rights reserved.
Any Internet addresses (websites, blogs, etc.) and telephone numbers in this book are offered as a resource. They are not intended in any way to be or imply an endorsement by Zondervan, nor does Zondervan vouch for the content of these sites and numbers for the life of this book.
Thorndike Press, a part of Gale, Cengage Learning.

LIBRARY OF CONGRESS CATALOGING-IN-PUBLICATION DATA

Names: Irvin, Kelly, author.
Title: Upon a spring breeze / by Kelly Irvin.
Description: Large print edition. | Waterville, Maine : Thorndike Press, a part of Gale, Cengage Learning, 2017. | Series: An every Amish season novel ; #1 | Series: Thorndike Press large print Christian romance
Identifiers: LCCN 2017008909| ISBN 9781410499721 (hardcover) | ISBN 1410499723 (hardcover)
Subjects: LCSH: Amish—Fiction. | Large type books. | GSAFD: Christian fiction. | Love stories.
Classification: LCC PS3609.R82 U66 2017b | DDC 813/.6—dc23
LC record available at https://lccn.loc.gov/2017008909

Published in 2017 by arrangement with The Zondervan Corporation LLC, a subsidiary of HarperCollins Christian Publishing, Inc.

Printed in the United States of America
1 2 3 4 5 6 7 21 20 19 18 17

For Mary Sue Seymour,
my friend, mentor, and agent
who guided me down this road.
We'll talk about books and writing and
grandbabies again one day in heaven.
Until then, peace be with you.

I have told you these things,
so that in me you may
have peace. In this world,
you will have trouble.
But take heart! I have
overcome the world.

JOHN 16:33 NIV

DEUTSCH VOCABULARY*

aenti: aunt
bopli: baby
bruder: brother
daed: father
danki: thank you
dawdy haus: grandparents' house
dochder: daughter
doplisch: clumsy
eck: married couple's corner table at wedding reception
Englischer: English or non-Amish
fraa: wife
Gelassenheit: fundamental Amish belief in

*The German dialect spoken by the Amish is not a written language and varies depending on the location and origin of the settlement. These spellings are approximations. Most Amish children learn English after they start school. They also learn high German, which is used in their Sunday services.

yielding fully to God's will and forsaking all selfishness

Gmay: Church District

Gott: God

grandkinner: grandchildren

groossdaadi: grandpa

groossmammi: grandma

guder mariye: good morning

gut: good

hund: dog

jah: yes

kaffi: coffee

kinner: children

lieb: love

mann: husband

mudder: mother

nee: no

onkel: uncle

Ordnung: written and unwritten rules in an Amish district

rumspringa: period of running around

schweschder: sister

suh: son

wunderbarr: wonderful

JAMESPORT, MISSOURI
FEATURED FAMILIES

The Weavers:
Solomon and Mattie
Caleb and Bess
Elijah
Luke and Jane Weaver and their son: William
Ruth and Seth Byler
Sophie and Obediah Stultz and their children: Esther, Lewis, Martin, and Angela
Hazel and Isaac Plank and their children: Rachel, Sarah, Levi, and Gracie
Leah and James Lowman

The Grabers:
Aidan (bachelor)
Henry (married with a son: Matthew)
Paul (bachelor)
Timothy and Josie Graber and their children: Samuel, Robert, Vera, and Nyla
Jennie Troyer (widow, husband was Atlee)
Matthew

11

Mark
Celia
Cynthia
Micah
Elizabeth
Francis
Mary Katherine Ropp (widow, husband was
  Moses)
Children still at home:
Angus
Beulah
Barbara
Laura Kauffman (widow, husband was Eli)

Children all grown
Freeman and Dorothy Borntrager (Bishop)
Cyrus and Josephina Beachy (Deacon)
Iris
Joseph
Rueben
Samuel
Carl
Louella
Abigail

Haven, Kansas
Jeb and Judith Shrock (Bess's parents)
Mercy
Grace

Christopher (married to Anna)
Jasper (married to Diana)

ONE

Heaven must smell like bread baking. Bess Weaver inhaled and smiled. The heat from the oven felt good on her cheeks.

Caleb liked his bread fresh and hot on the supper table. She'd learned that during their first year of marriage. And so many other things. The way he liked for her to sit across the table from him so he could watch her eat and see his reflection in her eyes.

Leastways that's what he'd told her as he sopped up the last dollop of fried chicken gravy with a hunk of bread clutched in his mammoth, callused fingers. His *daed* snorted and his brothers snickered, but Caleb didn't care.

Such a flight of fancy from a farmer. Bess chuckled to herself and began to chop carrots for the vegetable stew, enjoying the clatter of knife against the wooden cutting board in a staccato-laden song of contentment. A delicate flutter tickled her midsec-

15

tion. She paused, knife poised in the air. Baby thought Daed was funny too. Boy or girl? Either suited her fine. She and Caleb would have plenty more. The house they were building down the road from her in-laws would have half a dozen bedrooms. Their children would be snug as bugs two or three to a room. *Gott* willing. The flutter increased to a kick. Little kick-ball player wanted her attention.

"Settle down in there, little one." She patted her belly with her free hand. "You stay put for at least one more month, you hear me?"

"Who are you talking to?" Mattie trotted into the kitchen, weighted down with a stack of large bath towels in her stubby arms. Bess's niece, Sarah, skipped in behind her grandma, singing a tuneless song that sounded a bit like something she'd heard in church. Mattie sidestepped her little shadow and frowned. "Is the bread burning? It smells burnt. You haven't forgotten about it, have you?"

"The baby kicked, that's all." Bess dropped the knife on the counter and turned to the wood-burning stove. She was used to her mother-in-law's implied criticisms. Mattie meant well. She'd raised six *kinner*. She thought of Bess as the baby of

16

the family.

Bess used a dish towel to tug the bread from the oven. The top was a beautiful, perfect golden brown. The scent enveloped her, bringing back the contentment not even Mattie could dispel. "It's just right. See? Not burned at all."

Mattie's *harrumph* mingled with the crackle and pop of the wood burning, its smoky scent an acrid complement to the bread's. Still, she said nothing more, which with Mattie, was a triumph.

"I want a cookie. I'm so hungry." Sarah's missing two front teeth gave her a funny little lisp. "I need a cookie."

Bess set the pan on the counter and dropped the dish towel. She broke a huge peanut butter cookie in half and bent over eye level with the six-year-old. "Here you go. I don't want you to spoil your supper so I'm giving you half." She patted Sarah's cheek. With her chocolate brown eyes, dimples, and wide smile, she looked so much like her uncle Caleb. "Now run get Rachel and you two can bring up a jar of green beans and a jar of corn from the basement so I can add them to the stew. Be careful you don't drop them."

Sarah planted a kiss on Bess's nose, turned, and scurried away. "I want the other half for Rachel when we come back," she yelled through a full mouth. "She'll be hungry too. Supper is too far away." Supper sounded like *thupper*.

Smiling, Bess turned back to the counter. Rachel was a year older than Sarah, but most of the time they seemed like twins. They were so similar and so inseparable. Bess couldn't wait to bake cookies for her own kinner. She wanted at least eight. Or however many Gott decided she and Caleb should take care of for Him.

Enough daydreaming. Time to get the carrots into the pot on the stove. Movement outside the window above the sink caught her gaze. "Oh, look, it's snowing."

"Again?" Mattie struggled to stuff the towels onto a shelf along the far wall. "We've had more than our fair share this winter. It's January. Enough is enough."

Ordinarily, Bess would agree. But snow this afternoon meant Caleb, his father, Solomon, and his brothers might come back from Aidan's farm early. They were helping Aidan Graber build yet another shed for his pullets. Caleb's best friend was doing well with his business of selling chickens to the company that processed them for sale at grocery stores. Meat from his chickens was being sold all over Missouri and right here

18

in the Jamesport supermarket. Caleb would work for Aidan until he could get a harvest out of his own. At any rate, they had plenty of work to do. Having the men home early for supper would be a treat.

Still, she would never argue with her mother-in-law. "Those are bath towels. Don't you want to put them in the laundry room, next to the tub?"

Mattie gave her a blank look, something she did a great deal of late. Followed by irritation. She snatched the towels back from the shelf with another *harrumph* and stomped across the room. "Best set a place for Aidan. He's got no hot meal waiting for him at home."

That was the thing about Mattie. She might be a cranky, persnickety old soul, but she had a heart under that crusty exterior.

"I'll have the girls do it."

"I'll do it when I get back."

That was the other thing about Mattie. She had to have the last word. Bess didn't mind. Nobody worked harder than Mattie, and sometimes age deserved the last word.

"Bess."

As if saying his name could make Aidan appear. Chuckling at this new flight of fancy, Bess turned at the sound of their friend's voice. He strode into the room and skidded to a stop on those long legs that made him the best kid to have on the baseball team at school. He was the opposite of Caleb in every way, tall and skinny to his best friend's short and stocky. Hair the color of toast that seemed peculiarly at odds with his gray eyes. Caleb had warm almond-brown eyes and hair. Opposites in looks and temperament. The same in their love for Gott, family, land, and animals, in that order.

"I figured you would come in early with the snow, but —"

"Bess." Aidan's voice sounded odd. Hoarse. Probably the cold air aggravated his throat. He'd been down with pneumonia right after Christmas — a fact that surely could be attributed to not having a *fraa* to care for him. "Caleb. He's . . ."

"Caleb's what?" Mattie stomped across the room and picked up a stack of plates from the shelf, her perpetual frown deepening. "You're dripping on the floor. And look, you've tracked in mud."

"It's Caleb. He's gone."

The anguish in Aidan's voice sent a fierce pain burrowing into Bess's chest. Comprehension tried to follow after it. She shoved it away. *Nee. Nee.* Her legs wavered under her. "What do you mean, he's gone? Where?

20

He better get himself back here right now. It's starting to snow, and we're having stew for supper. He loves stew. I made bread and peanut butter cookies, his favorite."

Aidan's arms came up, whether to stop the flow of words or to defend himself, Bess couldn't say. "There was an accident. The roads were slick from the snow. A pickup truck hit his buggy right where the dirt road meets the highway. He was almost home. He died."

The bare recitation of the facts ended suddenly. Silence fell. The battery-operated clock on the pine table ticked. The wood in the fire crackled, no longer a comforting, familiar sound.

"Nee." She didn't recognize her voice. It sounded high and breathless like it belonged to a little girl who'd been twirling around and around in circles until she fell to the ground. "The bread is hot. It's ready. The stew will be ready when he comes home."

"He's gone." Aidan took a step toward Mattie, who stood frozen in the center of the room. "I'm sorry. He's gone."

The plates fell to the wooden floor and shattered. Why did she have plates? She knew they were having soup. Soup bowls were needed. Why think about plates at a time like this? Broken plates seemed of

21

paramount importance in this moment when Bess didn't want to think of anything else. Why didn't Mattie clean up her mess? The kinner were barefoot. They would cut their toes. There would be blood.

Blood everywhere.

Mattie didn't seem to think of this. She didn't move. Her mouth fell open, but no sound came out. Solomon appeared in the doorway. Caleb's brothers Elijah and Luke followed. They stood, silent, faces etched with grief, as their father slipped past Aidan and went to his fraa. The stoic set of his shoulders matched the firm, straight line of his mouth.

"Come. Sit." He led her to a chair at the table. She stumbled and sobbed. The sound reverberated in Bess's heart, bruising it over and over again. Solomon put his arm around Caleb's mother. "Hush, woman, Gott took him home."

Gott did this? Gott wouldn't do this to Bess. Or to Mattie. Nee, He wouldn't.

"I don't understand." Bess became aware of her breathing, her heart pounding, the beat pulsing in her ears. Caleb no longer breathed the same air. "It can't be."

"I tried to help him." Aidan's hands fisted and unfisted. They were stained red. "I tried to make him keep breathing, but he wouldn't. He just wouldn't."

Red.

A tiny sound escaped her mouth, a half-formed thought that became a sigh before she could bear to say the words.

A rust-colored smudge on Aidan's whiskerless cheek made her want to wipe at it like a mother cleaning her child's face. She teetered toward the pile of broken dishes and knelt. A shard bit into her finger. Bright-red blood appeared.

Aidan knelt next to her. His big fingers tugged the shard from hers with a gentle but deft touch. She stared at the rust-colored smudge on his cheek. His face held the very pain that emanated from the marrow of her bones. "Leave it."

It took every ounce of strength she had, but Bess tore her gaze from him as if not looking at Aidan would somehow postpone the inevitability of the truth in his eyes.

Caleb had left her.

Two

Digging a grave in the winter was not a task for the faint of heart. Aidan's shoulders and his back ached, but he welcomed the pain. The rest of him seemed numb from his brain to his heart to his hands out in the cold too long.

The graveside service had been as short as the service at the house, but by no means painless. Watching Solomon's stoic face, alongside his remaining five children, had allowed Aidan to steel his own heart and maintain a brave front throughout Freeman Borntrager's message. Watching white clouds puff from the bishop's mouth, warm air against cold, mesmerized Aidan until he could force himself to pick up the shovel and turn the dirt back into the hole on the coffin he'd built himself only the day before.

He'd said his good-byes, climbed into his buggy, and driven to Solomon's house with every intention of making this equally quick.

Instead, he waited and waited some more, loathe to interrupt tradition. Food had to be served, guests fed, visiting done. Caleb's grown brothers and sisters, their spouses, dozens of grandchildren, in-laws. So many loads had come from as far away as Iowa and Nebraska. Distant family of the Weavers. Even second cousins from South Texas. It wasn't his place to interrupt.

So here he stood. The heat of Solomon's fireplace felt good, but what man wanted to feel good on the day he had laid his best friend to rest in a tiny, snow-dusted cemetery that held the graves of his *mudder* and daed. The tasks Aidan didn't want to do weren't complete. He had to talk to Bess. They hadn't spoken since that day in the kitchen when he delivered news that would end their lifelong friendship. He'd allowed her husband, his best friend, to die.

Nothing could change that, but he had to try to fix it, for the sake of Caleb's only child. He owed it to Caleb to watch over his wife and child. Aidan had promised as he held Caleb in his arms when he drew his last breath. But it wasn't that promise that drove Aidan to the house this cold, blustery day. It was his own selfishness. He couldn't bear not to see her.

Yet the last thing any man wanted to do

25

was tromp into a kitchen full of women. It appeared Aidan would have no choice in the matter. He could ask her father to go in and get her, but from the looks of Jeb, standing at the window staring at something far away, he had no desire to tangle with a bunch of grieving women either. Still, Bess seemed to have no intention of coming into Solomon's front room. Aidan had to see her and give her the seed packets with his assurance that something good would grow from them. She loved to garden. Digging in the dirt and planting the seeds would give her hope that joy would grow in her again.

He believed that. So would she.

Winter would end. It did every year. Spring came. They could count on it, just as they counted on Gott for all their needs. It could be hard to understand His plan, but what did they expect with their walnut-size brains?

Contemplating his options, he rubbed his burning eyes. If anyone should ask, they were red from lack of sleep, not unshed tears. He could leave the flower seeds with Solomon or one of Caleb's brothers. But they wouldn't explain the gesture properly. Would she understand? Would she even care?

"You catching a cold?" With a grunt, Jeb

Shrock turned and lowered himself into the hickory rocking chair in front of the fireplace so close to the blaze it would be a wonder if a spark didn't catch his pants on fire. "Standing out there at the service in that cold wind is enough to give a person a severe chill."

"Nee, not sleeping good." Aidan stuck his hands out toward the fire, looking anywhere but at Bess's father. "Wind kept me up last night."

Howling winds that sounded like a woman sobbing. That and no one to whom he could talk about losing a friend dearer to him than a brother. The only person closer to Caleb was Bess and she wasn't talking. To anyone, but especially not to Aidan.

"Wasn't your fault." Jeb had a habit of getting to the point that Aidan had always liked, until now. "And done is done. I reckon Caleb ain't fretting over it."

What was this life compared to an eternity with Gott? Aidan believed that. So had Caleb. But Aidan had been the one to ask his friend to go into town for that generator part. If he had gone himself, likely Caleb would be here now with his fraa, looking forward to the birth of his first child and finishing his house down the road so he could move in with his growing family. "I

27

know but —"

"No buts. Our puny brains can't understand, but Gott has His plan."

"If it were your *suh* or your fraa, would you be able to say that?" The question was out before Aidan could squash it, like an annoying mosquito on a humid summer night. "They only had a year and then there's the *bopli.*"

"We lost two boplin before they were a year old, one before he was born." Jeb rocked faster, the rocker making a clacking noise on the hardwood floor. "I ain't saying it's easy, but a man learns . . ."

Jeb's gaze wandered over Aidan's shoulder. He turned to see what the other man saw. It was Judith, Bess's mudder. She had an arm around Bess and the two seemed headed for the stairs. Her *kapp* askew over her blonde hair, Bess plodded along, heavy with child and grief, her head down as if trying to make sure her feet still moved, one in front of the other.

"Bess."

She looked up. Their gazes connected. Recognition, followed by what he most feared. Anger. Pain. Despair that darkened her already deep-blue eyes.

"Bess's not up for company. She needs a little nap." Judith's sad smile matched her soft voice so full of compassion. It reminded Aidan of his tenth birthday when he fell off a horse and broke his leg. The next best thing to having his own mudder there. "Maybe tomorrow."

He'd never been considered company before. Determined not to lose his nerve, he stepped forward and held out the seed packets of coneflowers, bluebells, and black-eyed Susans. Three packets held together by a green rubber band. "When the weather's nice I thought we could plant them around his grave. Brighten the place up."

She might think it a fanciful idea. The bishop surely would. They would plant them first and ask forgiveness later.

Her gaze went to the packets, but she didn't raise her hand to take them. Nor did she speak.

After a few seconds, Aidan lowered his hand. "Spring will come. We'll plant them then. You like to garden."

Her eyes vacant, she kept walking. He couldn't look away. She was as beautiful in sorrow as she was in joy. As beautiful as a mother-to-be as she'd been as a short, skinny, teenage girl with freckles on her face and a bandage on her nose from when she fell from a sycamore tree. She'd shinnied up there to try to get the momma cat to come down after Caleb's ornery, old dog Boo scared it. Being a girl in a dress never stopped her. She was a force of nature — something Jeb and Judith seemed to understand and accept about their oldest girl.

Seeing her up in that tree, legs dangling, sunburned face split with a grin, served as one of his best memories of her. Even with the scolding her mudder had given her.

Bess didn't know how he felt, because he'd never told her. And he never would. She'd been Caleb's special friend and then his fraa. No one had ever expected otherwise, least of all Aidan.

"Leave them on the table. I'll make sure she gets them." Judith gripped her daughter's arm as she looked back at him. "They'll be pretty in the spring. She'll like that."

Judith understood. He nodded, sure the band around his throat would strangle him.

Jeb rose and stood next to him to watch the two women make their way up the stairs. It was a laborious process, much like the earlier funeral procession along muddy back roads dark against snow that sparkled in those brief moments when the sun fought its way through morose clouds that hung around like guests who lingered long after the frolic was over. "We've been talking about her coming home with us to Haven.

She'd have her *schweschders* to help her through this. And us. We've made a good life in Kansas with Christopher and Jasper and their fraas. She can too."

Aidan's heart skidded across his chest and slammed into his rib cage. Jamesport had been Bess's home her whole life. His home. It wouldn't be home without her. Even if seeing her amounted to watching her trudge across the fields, picnic basket in one hand, cooler in the other, to feed her *mann.* "I reckon Solomon and Mattie will want her to stay here." He managed to keep his tone on the right side of neutral. He didn't have a horse in this race. Not so anyone would notice. Or so he hoped. "They'll want Caleb's only child close to home."

"She needs to be with family. Mercy and Grace miss having their older sister around. The only reason she stayed here in the first place was Caleb." Jeb pulled at his whiskers, his expression dour. His tone said it all. Mattie and Solomon would never be Bess's family. "She'll need a fresh start. She's young. She'll marry again. Haven has its share of men in need of fraas."

Marry again. Aidan swallowed against the fierce, strange anger those words brought. *Jah,* she would marry again. It would be expected. But not with her mann's best friend. Nee, it would be wrong. *Gott, could it be wrong to love my friend's fraa, in his painful, permanent absence?* On the other hand, leaving her to fend for herself with Mattie and Solomon seemed a shame too. He was being selfish, only thinking of himself. Mattie wasn't an easy woman, and with her son gone, she most likely would be more cantankerous than ever.

Her querulous voice at the cemetery demanding to know who'd died echoed in his head. Gott bless her shattered soul. Her confusion seemed to grow in direct proportion to Solomon's refusal to acknowledge it. Difficult days lay ahead for the Weaver household. "Bess should go. She could go for a while, until she has a chance to feel better, then come back to give Solomon and Mattie time with their grandbaby."

"Coming back would be too hard." Jeb's head shake made his beard bounce. "Like tearing the scab off the wound for a second time."

"She's a strong girl. She'll buck up." Bess had her faith. Her *rumspringa* had been short. She'd had no qualms about baptism. He couldn't be sure, though, if it was faith or hurry to become Caleb's fraa. He would buck up too. He would be her friend. She would need a friend, not a lovesick suitor.

32

"She'll have the bopli to think about."

"Gott's blessing, to be sure. All this won't be decided tonight. One thing at a time. If she digs in her heels, we'll let her spend some time here. She'll come around after a bit." Jeb lifted his Sunday-go-to-church hat and settled it on ragged tufts of silver hair. The words left unsaid crowded the air between them. Time spent with Mattie and Solomon would send her to Haven in short order. "I best bring the buggy around. Judith wants to spend the night with Mary Katherine."

"Not here?" Aidan wanted the words back as soon as he said them. Judith might want to be close to her daughter's side, but while everyone knew Solomon and Mattie Weaver lived in the *dawdy haus* on their property now, they were still involved in every decision made by their son-in-law Isaac Plank and daughter Hazel. The older couple wasn't the most hospitable in the community. No sense in talking about it. "Of course Judith will want to see her best friend while she has a chance."

"They'll be up gabbing half the night, Mercy and Grace with them." Jeb limped to the door, his bad leg dragging behind him. No amount of willpower or gumption could change the effects of a stroke two years back. "Being a widow herself, Mary Katherine will have all manner of advice. She might be able to convince Bess what's best for her and the bopli is to come to Haven and leave all these memories behind. Family is what she needs now."

How could a person leave behind the memory of a beloved husband and a marriage so sweetly short, it hurt to think of it? Those memories would stay with Bess no matter where she went and no matter what man longed to step into the big boots left by a decent man who would've been a good father.

"Family is important, but so is experience. Mary Katherine could guide Bess if she stayed here."

"She could." Jeb paused at the door and looked back. "There's that possibility too, I reckon. You could help as well."

"Me?" Sudden heat blistered Aidan's face. His gut heaved like it did when the waves on Stockton Lake pounded their fishing pontoon during a sudden, unexpected storm. "What can I do?"

"Your secret isn't as secret as you think." Jeb jerked open the door, letting in a blast of frigid air that took what little breath Aidan had left. "A parent knows these things. A father knows them. I never said

34

anything, not even to my fraa. I'm telling you now 'cause I know you feel guilty about what happened. Gott doesn't make mistakes. His plan unfolds before our eyes. We need only step up and do our part when the time comes."

"I'm . . . I have a —"

"A special friend?" Jeb grunted. He didn't seem to be the least bit embarrassed to talk about these private matters with Aidan, but then Aidan had always felt like the man was closer than his own father, who had never been much for talk or show of affection. "But you haven't married Iris. There's a reason for that. Ever asked yourself why you haven't taken the next step? I reckon because Gott knew your time would come."

When exactly would that be? After his best friend died and left the woman he loved a widow heavy with child? "She blames me." Aidan's throat tightened. *Gott, don't let me embarrass myself in front of this man.*

He shouldn't be having these thoughts. Until a few days ago he'd been determined to ask Iris to be his fraa. She wanted it, even though she never said a word. He could see it in the wistful way she watched other couples. He swallowed. "She's right to blame me."

"A truck hit my son-in-law's buggy. Not

35

you." Jeb turned his back and moved through the door. His voice faded into the wind. His words swirled, soft but clear, around Aidan. "You're still here. Marriage is hard enough. Don't marry for anything less than love. In the meantime, watch out for my *dochder* and be ready when Gott's plan unfolds. Be patient, but be ready."

He looked back just before the door closed. "For her daed, if not for yourself."

THREE

The pillow beckoned to Bess. She would put it over her face and block out all light and sound and feeling. She waited like a compliant child while her mother pulled down the quilt and flannel sheets on the bed Bess would share with Caleb no more. It smelled of her husband, or was it a cruel trick of a body that craved that smell and that touch with a ferocity that made her bones ache?

"Go on, get yourself in there. You'll be toasty warm in no time." Mudder held the sheet up higher. "Listen to that wind blow. I think it's snowing again."

Wind or no wind, Bess would never be warm again. She stood, unable to make her muscles comply with the desire to seek warmth. The cold that had seeped into the marrow of her bones as she stood in the cemetery, feet frozen blocks of ice, would remain there until the day they slipped her coffin into a gaping black hole next to the one that now held her beloved. Dry eyed, determined, she'd listened to each word that came from Freeman's mouth, nodding as if she agreed. As if she understood.

She did not understand. She could not.

"In." Mudder tugged at her arm with a firm grip. Her fingers were warm through the flannel of Bess's nightgown. "Your skin is like ice. Let's get you under the covers, and I'll bring you a cup of chamomile tea with honey and lemon. You'll sleep."

As if hot tea could heal her wounds like it did a nasty winter cold. As if saying it could make it so. She hadn't slept in days. "It's okay. Go on with Daed. You two must be tired too after the long drive yesterday and what with the cooking and such today."

"We're fine, your daed and me. Don't you fret." Mudder smoothed the blankets and eased onto the edge of the bed, her bony frame barely registering against the mattress. "I want to talk to you without everyone hanging on to every word. Such a lot of busybodies in that kitchen."

"They mean well."

"They do." Mudder pushed her silver wire-rimmed spectacles up her nose with more force than necessary. Her blue eyes were bright with an animosity that surprised

Bess. Her mudder liked everyone and never uttered a bad word about a soul. She had plenty to say, but she said it with kind abandon. "But they'd do well to remember that only Gott our Lord knows what's best for you now."

Gott and Mudder, if the look on her face told Bess anything. When Mudder decided to have a word, nothing on Gott's green earth could stop her. For a tiny woman, she packed a powerful punch of words, thoughts, and deeds. Bess rolled over on her side and put her hands under her cheek like a little girl preparing to pray. Mudder would know what to do. She always did.

"Daed and I, we've been talking."

They talked and talked and talked. That's what they did. Bess had never seen a couple more tuned in to each other. They started the day at the breakfast table wrangling over what to have for supper and ended the day in front of the fireplace dissecting every scribe's article in *The Budget* and talking of trips they wanted to take to places they hadn't yet seen. "This is not news."

"Funny girl. See there, you haven't lost your sense of humor. You'll be fine." Mudder slipped Bess's kapp from her head and began to undo her bun. Bess leaned into the feel of her sturdy, sure fingers doing

39

something she used to do only on the rare occasions when Bess was sick and staying home from school. "Daed thinks it's best if you come on to Haven with us. You can get a fresh start. Be surrounded by family when it's time."

Time for the bopli to show his face. Or her face. The baby moved. A sharp, well-placed kick in her midsection as if to say, *I'm still here. I have a mind of my own, thank you very much.* Bess's hands went to her stomach and rubbed as if of their own volition. She couldn't fathom a world where she would be a mother to a baby who had no father. A baby who would remind her every single day of the absence of one Caleb Weaver, who skipped out on this life before he could do one of the most important things a man did. Be a father.

She couldn't think. Haven had never been her home. Her parents moved there to live in the dawdy haus at Christopher's farm when Caleb had begun to court Bess in earnest. She'd stayed with her friend Martha's family, helping Martha with her jams and jellies and baby quilts until the wedding. Going back to live with her brother and her parents was not a fresh start. It was returning to a place that she had long vacated — daughter and little sister to

40

brothers who liked to tease her as if she were still a twelve-year-old who liked the barn better than the kitchen. Would she attend singings and take walks with her sisters, dispensing sage advice about first kisses and declarations of love? Who was she to give advice when she had walked that path and it had led her here?

Nee. "*This* is home. Haven is not home."

"It can be. It wasn't for us until we picked up and moved. That's the whole point. A fresh start."

"I love you and Daed and Christopher and Anna and the rest of the bunch." She stopped. Her family — most Plain families — didn't declare their feelings on a regular basis. It was a given. They loved each other. No reason to get sappy about it. "It wouldn't be right to leave when Solomon and Mattie just lost their son. They'll want to be close to their grandbaby too."

Mudder shivered. She picked up the covers. "I'm coming in. My feet are like ice cubes."

She slipped into the bed. Despite her words, her body was warm and wiry, a pier unmoved in crashing waves. Bess moved so she could lay her head on her mother's lap. Mudder stroked Bess's hair, her hands so sure, yet so soft. "Close your eyes, sweet

41

dochder. It's been a long, difficult day, but tomorrow the sun will shine and Gott will bless us just as He has done every other day of our lives."

Not on January tenth, He hadn't. That was no blessing, no matter what Scripture said, no matter what Freeman said, no matter what anyone said. Bess would not be convinced that a plan that included Caleb's eternal absence was a good one.

"Close your eyes. Think of spring. Think of the tulips blooming and the roses. Think of how they will smell as fragrant as any perfume the *Englisch* ladies buy in their fancy stores. Think of the warm sun on your face while you plant in the garden. We'll plant tomatoes and cucumbers and peas and eggplant and green peppers and onions and corn."

Bess did as she was told, letting her mother's words run like a gentle stream over her, lulling her. Her mind drifted. Imagines of white gravestones barely discernible against the snow, dark, bleak trees naked of leaves against the lead-gray skies filled her mind. Freeman's red lips moving, moving, moving, wisps of steam floating, then dissipating with words she couldn't understand. She jerked her eyes open against the unbearable dark.

"Solomon and Mattie have grandbabies galore. They'll come to Haven and we'll come here. They'll see the bopli plenty."

Bess burrowed closer to her mother. "I can't go."

"You can."

"It would be wrong." Her protest sounded weak in her ears. "Wouldn't it?"

"Nee, it would be what's best for you." Mudder patted her cheek. "I'll go now so you can rest. I'll check on you by the by with the tea."

She slipped out of the bed, so very careful not to let in the cold air. She stood and tugged the blankets up over Bess's shoulders until she was covered in downy softness up to her chin. "We'll talk in the morning. Right now, sleep is the best medicine. You'll be a mudder soon. Sleep while you can."

"I'll think about it."

"You do that and then we'll take you home and things will be better for you. Gott's plan is to prosper, not harm you. Remember that."

Bess wrapped her arms around a pillow and clasped it to her aching chest. The shadows in the room rocked as Mudder picked up the kerosene lamp and slipped out the door. "Sweet dreams, my sweet child. Gott bless you and keep you until

43

morning."

The door closed and darkness descended.

Gott surely stayed. He hadn't abandoned her. So why did the dark feel so cold and empty?

Because Caleb wasn't in it.

"I'm not leaving, Caleb. I'm not leaving you."

She felt silly, talking aloud into the darkness. Her eyes adjusted and she could see the chair where he sat to take off his boots. Where he snapped his suspenders and waggled his bushy eyebrows as if to say *Get over here, fraa.* She would go, obedient wife that she was. She'd sit on his lap and he would take her kapp from her head, his thick, callused fingers deft and nimble in his delight. They would move on to her nightgown, the smile on his face lighting every corner of the room. They had no need of a lamp. Their love provided all the light they needed or wanted.

Her throat ached with a pain worse than any she'd ever felt. She inhaled his scent on the pillow. It enveloped her in the sheets and the quilt, his very essence taunting her, telling her he was still here but just beyond her reach, just beyond her sight.

"I'm here, Caleb. Where are you?"

The silence echoed with his un-answer.

"I promise. I'll never leave you."

Not the way he left her.

The door creaked, but no lantern lighted the hallway. Bess lifted her head. "Mudder, that was quick."

"Caleb?" Mattie's voice rasped, heavy with unshed tears. She teetered at the edge of the room, her face hidden in the darkness. "Caleb, are you there?"

Bess's heart wrenched like a tree pulled from the ground, roots and all, by a violent wind. "Mattie, Caleb's not here. You know that."

A light flashed and the smell of phosphorus, acrid and sharp, burned her nose. A candle flickered, sending shadows dancing across the floor. Mattie held it high, her features harsh and wrinkled in the flame. "This is Caleb's room. What are you doing in here?"

"It's me. Bess. You know me. Caleb's wife."

"Where is he?" Her tone became plaintive, like a naughty child denied a hug in punishment for her crime. "I can't find him. It's a terrible night. The wind is howling and it's snowed a good four inches since darkness fell. He shouldn't be out on a night like tonight."

Bess slipped from the bed and grabbed

her heaviest wool shawl. "It is a terrible night, but don't worry. Caleb is in good hands. He's well taken care of by our Lord and Savior."

The words came easily. She'd heard them hundreds of times over the years. Mattie's frown eased. She nodded. "Our Lord and Savior has a good wool coat to give my suh, then?"

No matter how sad Mattie might be, she still had that sharp way with words. Bess tightened her shawl around herself, chilled by the image of Caleb, cold and wet, in need of a coat on this January night. "He's not cold. Not anymore."

"I don't understand what you're saying." Mattie's voice rose. "I don't understand anything."

"Mudder, Mudder, it's fine. It's fine." Hazel. Thank Gott. Hazel hustled into the room. She slid an arm around her mother and held tight. "I wondered where you'd gone to. You told me you were going to the dawdy haus, but Daed said he hadn't seen hide nor hair of you."

"I'm here. Where else would I be? This is our home, isn't it?" The candle's flame trembled and dipped. Hazel rescued it from her mudder's hand. Mattie wrapped her arms around her middle. "It's a simple question. Cat got both your tongues?"

"It is your home and my home and Bess's home."

"Everyone but Caleb's?" Mattie began to keen. Tears streamed down her wrinkled face. "I know his days are done, but I would like mine to be done likewise."

"Don't talk like that. Gott's will for you is that you stay put right here and take care of Daed just like you have for the last forty-six years." Hazel drew Mattie toward the door. "And soon you'll have another grandson to think about and help Bess care for. Won't that be fine?"

Mattie's tears subsided. She craned her head and looked back at Bess. "Jah, it will be fine. I look forward to that day when Caleb's bopli arrives."

"Soon." Bess managed one syllable. She clamped her mouth shut. Did one month qualify as soon? Too soon or not long enough, she couldn't be sure. "You'll be one of the very first to hold him — or her — and see how much the bopli looks like your suh."

Hazel nodded and mouthed the words *sorry* and *thank you.* Her expression begged Bess not to say anything to the others. They wouldn't understand. Plain folks didn't get all tied up in knots over death. They simply accepted it as Gott's will. To do otherwise showed a sinful lack of faith.

This little scene in the bedroom would be their secret. Mattie wasn't the only one struggling to understand and accept. Bess finally had something in common with her mother-in-law.

No way she could up and leave for Haven.

No way at all.

FOUR

Getting down on the floor was one thing, but getting up quite another. Her knees complaining of the hard, packed earth of the barn floor, Bess contemplated her options. Lean back and stick a hand on the pine bench or twist and turn so she could get both hands there. Her girth didn't allow for much else. She could simply stay kneeling until the service was over, but then someone was likely to notice.

She could feel Mattie looking at her. And Leah, Ruth, Hazel, and Sophie, all Caleb's sisters. Solomon and Caleb's brothers on the men's side. And then the aunts and cousins and sisters-in-law. Everyone watching her and waiting for her to get up and get on with it. In more ways than one.

Only Hazel seemed to understand. She was more than a sister-in-law; she was a friend. Amusement in brown eyes wide behind her thick, dark-rimmed glasses, she

49

gripped Bess's arm. "Let me help you." Her whisper contained a hint of laughter. "You're top heavy. I don't want you to topple over."

It wasn't that funny. If this baby didn't come soon, Bess wouldn't be able to waddle from the bedroom the necessary five times a night. Nee, she wouldn't think about the bedroom. She simply would not think about it here and now. That empty bed she faced every night for the last month. To her eternal embarrassment, tears formed.

Stop it. Chin up. That's what her daed would say. She should've stayed home. She shouldn't have allowed Hazel to talk her into returning to church for the first time since Caleb's death. Her first outing of any kind in a month.

"It's okay." Hazel tugged, a knowing look on her face. She leaned closer. "Everyone understands. It'll get easier."

Willing herself to smile, Bess tottered to her feet, inhaling the scent of hay, horse, and man sweat. The smells were so familiar, so like Caleb, she wanted to draw them around her like the old quilt she and her husband had huddled under the night before his death, giggling at some silly thing she'd said, tickling each other and pretending to argue over who would change the diapers and walk the floor with a fussy baby in a few months.

The others didn't understand. Mudder and Daed had gone home with the promise to return soon. They still wanted her to move to Haven, but they relented when Bess described Mattie's anguish and her desire to be close to Caleb's only child. They would be back after the birth "to give her another chance," as Mudder had put it.

Mattie and Solomon had returned to their regular routines the week following Caleb's funeral. Not a word had been uttered about Mattie's strange late-night appearance in Bess's bedroom after the funeral. His name had not been spoken once at the supper table in an entire month. Mattie remained dry-eyed through the sorting of his clothes and his boots and his hats and his simple toiletries. They'd been handed out to brothers and cousins and friends with little commentary.

It was expected. It was done. Only Bess seemed afflicted with this peculiar flu-like ache that refused to dissipate. She sucked in air and focused on Bishop Freeman. Surely something in his message would help her understand why she seemed to be the only one still grieving.

Nothing. A long, seemingly endless discourse on forty days in the wilderness. Jah, she found herself wandering in the wilderness now, but that was because she hadn't been a slave before. She'd been happy. Content. Certain of Caleb's love and Gott's love. She wanted that certainty back. She wanted her blanket — woven with tight, colorful strands of joy and love and happiness — back. The gray, tattered pieces of her life weren't enough to wrap around her shoulders and give her warmth.

She seemed to be the only one who couldn't accept this as Gott's will. Where was His compassion, His unfailing wisdom? Taking her mann at the age of twenty-two showed neither. How could these people worship a Gott so cruel?

How could she dare to question Him? He would strike her with a bolt of lightning and she would deserve it. She would welcome such a cruel ending if it meant being reunited with Caleb. But it wouldn't. He was good. She fell into the "O ye of little faith" category. Where she would end up, only Gott knew.

"Bess, we're done."

She looked around. The men were moving to the yard to talk weather, crops, and horses, the women to Ellen and Roy Miller's house to fix the sandwiches and bring out the potato salad and pies to the front room where they would eat in shifts. Some would brave the chilly February air to eat outdoors. The thought of food made Bess's stomach churn. Still, she didn't dare avoid the kitchen. Mattie would notice.

Hazel jerked her head toward the crowd that flowed around them. She clutched Gracie on one wide hip and had little Levi's hand in hers. "Can you get Sarah and Rachel? I don't want them running off. I need to feed Gracie before she starts squalling."

"I've got them." She corralled the two girls before they could shoot between the adults and head for the trampoline in Roy and Ellen's backyard. It drew the kinner like a magnet, especially after a long winter. They moved so fast they rarely noticed the cold. A line would form in no time. "Eat first and then you can play."

Sarah grinned, displaying the progress she'd made in having her missing teeth grow about halfway in. "I want an egg sandwich. Do you think Ellen made egg sandwiches?"

"I want peanut butter." Rachel shook a small finger at her sister, the picture of her mudder making a point. "We have to get the same thing. We're sisters."

"No we don't. We don't, do we, *Aenti*?"

Bickering of this sort filled most days at

the Weaver house, but it didn't bother Bess. She sought it out like gauze and ointment for her wound. She wouldn't have it with her own kinner, but these two, they were so close. Sarah had Caleb's eyes and Rachel, his nose. Would this bopli in her belly look like his daed?

She swallowed the lump drier than week-old bread that lodged in her throat. "How about one-half of each. Variety is *gut.*"

The girls nodded, their matching smiles more balm. She would make a good mother. She would keep telling herself that, each morning when she arose and each night when she slipped under the quilt that still held that lingering, musky Caleb scent and forced herself to say her prayers.

They followed Hazel through the barn doors into the open yard where the brisk wind took Bess's breath away. The sun blinded her for a few seconds. A dark shadow stepped in front of her. She blinked. *Caleb?* Not Caleb. Too tall. Aidan.

"You're here. How are you?"

His voice sounded as if he'd not used it in a while.

"I'm here. I'm gut." Without thinking, she let go of the girls' hands. They scampered toward the house, still discussing the pros and cons of egg salad versus peanut butter.

"And you?"

"Gut. A lot of work." He shoved the hat farther down his forehead. "I talked to Solomon every day, so he let me know how you were doing. I was waiting for you to . . ."

His voice trailed off as if he'd lost his train of thought. Their neighbors continued to pass by, their happy chatter like the gurgling of a stream flowing around them. Bess forced herself to look at him. The brim of his black hat hid his eyes. His fair, clean-shaven cheeks reddened in the cool air. He looked thinner, gaunt, and tired. The image of the flower-seed packets that lay on the fireplace flittered in her mind's eyes. Something about planting them in the cemetery. She hadn't moved the packets and neither had Mattie, who seemed to have lost interest in dusting and sweeping the front room.

She wouldn't think about the way a faint-hearted sun had struggled to filter through the bare elm tree branches as they planted the plain pine box in the ground. "I have to get to the kitchen."

"It's gut to see you back in church." He cleared his throat. His Adam's apple bobbed. "You've been missed."

"It was time." She brushed past him. "Everyone said it was time."

It wasn't time for her. She prayed once

again that Gott wouldn't strike her dead for lying. Aidan bore no responsibility for Caleb's death. Her husband's days on earth were done, pure and simple. Bishop Freeman had said so. Aidan couldn't have known what would happen that day when he asked Caleb to go to town for the generator part. It was an innocent request. So why did he have guilt written all over his face?

"Bess, wait."

Angst and pleading gave his words a sharp edge that pressed against her heart, threatening to cut the tenuous threads that prevented the broken pieces from scattering to the ends of the earth in the blustery breeze. She bowed her head and kept walking. "I should help out in the kitchen."

"If you need anything, I'm here."

Need anything? She needed Caleb. A sad refrain reverberated in her head. *I need Caleb. I need Caleb. You're selfish. You're selfish.*

The second verse brought her up short. She stumbled and caught herself. Caleb and Aidan had been closer than brothers their entire lives. Aidan likely missed his friend almost as much as she missed her husband. He looked so lost and tired. He looked like she felt. Her face hot with shame, she stopped and turned. Aidan stood in the same spot, big hands loose at his sides, staring at her, his pewter eyes dark with tethered emotion.

"I'm sorry." She tossed the words on the breeze, hoping they would reach him. She couldn't go back. No one could. "I'm so sorry."

He started forward. Iris Beachy scurried across the yard, her hand to her forehead to shield her eyes from the sun. "Aidan, I've been looking for you. Mudder wants to know if you're still coming for supper tonight." She glanced toward Bess. "How are you, Bessie? It's so nice to see you again. I brought snickerdoodles. You like them, don't you?"

Bess could only nod. Iris was a year older and the kindest of girls. She was the only one in the world to call her Bessie. When they were in school she was the one who always took care of the little ones if they had cuts on their fingers or scratches on their knees. She was apprenticing with the district's midwife to take over when Laura retired from such doings.

She looked so stricken now, as if thinking of what Bess must be going through. Bess had seen that look of pity multiplied a hundred times in the last month. She didn't need it. It didn't help. Looking at Aidan was harder still. His guilt and grief were etched on his face like an open wound. Aidan's attention seemed swallowed up in Iris. The guilt drained away, replaced by something that could only be relief. Iris had rescued him from his obligation to talk to the wife of his dead friend.

Bess turned back toward the house. Only sheer willpower — and the weight of her unborn child — kept her from breaking into a trot the last few yards to the steps and the door that would take her from Aidan's sight. He had someone from whom he could seek comfort. That was good. She needn't worry about him. He would be fine. She would be fine.

I don't feel fine, Gott. Help me be fine.

Breathless, she grabbed the railing and hoisted herself up the steps. Ellen Miller opened the screen door and held it for her.

"There you are. We were afraid you'd run off."

"Run off? I can barely walk." Still gasping for breath, she squeezed past Ellen and marched toward the kitchen. "Did Sarah and Rachel come in?"

"They did. They're arguing over gingersnaps or snickerdoodles. I reckon they'll stuff their faces with one of each. Little piglets." Ellen passed her by. "Everyone's so glad you came this morning. We were beginning to think something was wrong."

"Wrong? Caleb —"

"What I mean is, wrong in the sense that you weren't getting better." Ellen's face turned the color of the radishes Mattie loved to plant in her vegetable garden every year. "Mattie and Solomon and the *bruders* and schweschders, they've all been coming, so it seemed like you should too."

Breathe. Breathe. Bess steered past the Miller sisters busy stacking sandwiches on plates. "What can I do to help?"

"Cut the pies." Ellen paused in the middle of the kitchen, hands on her hips, kapp askew, a smudge of mustard on her cheek. Two-year-old Lilly wrapped her arms around her mother's leg and hid her face in her apron. "Then start washing dishes, will you? No point in sitting around feeling sorry for yourself."

"I'm not —"

"Bess's not like us. The Shrocks have always been a bit on the melancholy side." Sophie sniffed as she dumped a paper bag full of gingersnaps into a chipped ceramic serving bowl. Unlike Hazel, she looked nothing like Caleb. She had Mattie's blue eyes, long nose, thin lips, and all of her

59

mudder's attitude. "I reckon it's poor stock."

"We do not have poor —"

"Or just a weak constitution." Ruth chimed in, her words half muffled by a big bite of potato salad. "She'll come out of it as soon as she has the baby. Babies make everything better."

Ruth's expectation was understandable. She and Seth Byler had been married three years and no boplin in sight. It must be like a constantly repeating knife prick to see Bess carrying Caleb's baby so soon after marriage.

"I'm fine." She managed to fall short of shouting at them. They meant well. All of them meant well. "My constitution is fine. I'm just a little tired. It'll pass."

"Jah, as soon as that baby passes."

The younger girls tittered. Sophie shrugged. "It's true."

"Don't you miss your bruder?"

Silence descended, broken only by the low murmur of people in the front room moving the benches together.

"Jah, I do." Sophie's lips pinched tight in a long, thin line for a few seconds. Her hollow cheeks darkened to a dusky rose. She wiped at her face with her sleeve. "But I don't see a reason to dwell on it. His days

60

on this earth were done. Freeman said so. He's gone home. Blessed be."

The women stared at Bess as if she were the meanest woman ever to walk the earth. A rattlesnake discovered in a place none expected to find it, coiled and ready to strike. A flush of shame billowed through her. "You're right. Freeman is right. I didn't mean anything by it. I'm tired, that's all."

"We better get these sandwiches out to the front room." Ellen scooped up Lilly under one arm and grabbed a plate. "Let's go. Ruth, bring the pickles. Sophie, cookies. Jane, potato salad."

No job for Bess. She turned to the cabinet and picked up a knife. The ache where her heart should be made it impossible to draw a deep breath. *What is wrong with me, Gott? Help me to get on with it. Please.*

"Don't mind them." An arm settled over her shoulders and squeezed. Jennie Troyer handed her a napkin. "They haven't had to walk a mile in your shoes."

"No, but that's no excuse for being mean to Sophie. She's hurting over Caleb too." Bess blew her nose in the napkin. The loud *honk* caused heat to rush to her face. She ducked her head. "I have no right to think my loss is greater. It's selfish. She's being strong and relying on her faith. I should be

61

doing the same."

"It's easier for some people to hide their feelings and fill up their days with work and more work so they don't have to feel. I have walked the road you're on. Still do." Jennie's tone was matter-of-fact. "No one knows until she sets foot on our road how she will react. We all like to think we'll be strong. We have faith. We believe. Then that unthinkable thing happens and we're tested."

Grimacing, she grunted and popped the lid from a new jar of mustard. "I'd have to say we're usually pretty disappointed in how we do. Leastways, I know I am."

"How long did it take you to get over it?" Get over it wasn't the right phrase. Jennie's husband, Atlee, had been gone about three years, trampled by his own team of horses. "I mean, how did you learn to accept it?"

Emotions Bess couldn't read flitted across Jennie's face. Sadness, for certain, but others, darker and mixed, as well. Bess wanted her words back. She had no right to force Jennie to retrace her steps on such a hard road. "I don't mean to pry. If you don't feel like talking about it, I understand. Believe me, the last thing I want to do is stand around and jaw about something that can't be undone."

"It's not that. I really don't know the answer to your question. Some days I'm fine. I go hours, even an entire day, without thinking about Atlee." Jennie slathered mustard on the thick, crusty homemade bread. She held up the knife as if examining it for spots. "Then suddenly it hits me, *pow,* right in the stomach, and I want to throw up. He's gone. Forever and forever. He's never, ever coming back."

A strange light flickered in her pale-blue eyes. "I ask myself when that happened and how. And how will I raise seven kinner by myself? How will I feed them and clothe them and work the land, sow and reap, and sew and cook and clean and teach right from wrong . . . ?"

The sentence petered out as if she had lost all breath.

"I can't imagine. I don't know how you do it with seven kinner. I'll have just the one bopli." Bess choked on the last word. Such a lovely word. She'd always liked it. She liked the plural much better. She tossed her knife on the counter. It clattered to the floor. "I'm sorry. I know we are expected to do what is necessary."

"I have friends and family who help me. And Gott." Jennie bent over and picked up the knife. She laid it on the counter and turned to Bess. "Go home. Don't let anyone tell you when you should be ready to get on with your life. It's your life. When you feel like getting out, come see me. A few of us get together in the evenings to sew and talk. Laura and Mary Katherine. You'll find no judgment there."

"I feel like something's wrong with me." She wrapped her arms around her swollen belly. "I keep seeing his face and hearing his voice. I can smell him on everything."

"It'll get better." Jennie's eyes were wet with unshed tears. She shoved stubborn curls of sandy-blonde hair under her kapp with shaky fingers. "There's nothing wrong with you. Come see me after you have the baby. Promise me you'll come or I'll come drag you out of there. I know you want out of Mattie's house."

A giggle burbled up in Bess. She snorted, a most unwomanly sound. "How did you know?"

"Because I know how I'd feel." Jennie patted Bess's shoulder. "Go, before she comes looking for you. Get some rest before that bopli comes. You won't be sleeping once he gets here. It'll be okay. I'll be praying for you."

Bess nodded. Hope lived in Jennie's face. The hope that things could get better. A person could learn to go on. Jennie propelled her toward the door with more force than such a slight woman should be able to muster. "You have a way home?"

"Hazel brought me in the second buggy. She can go in the wagon with Isaac, Mattie, and Solomon and the kinner."

"Go with Gott."

Gott hadn't been on her side so far, but Bess clamped her mouth shut. Jennie had managed to hang on to her faith. No sense in poking holes in it with her pitchfork tines of anger, despair, and bitterness.

FIVE

Running after Bess would only have made a scene. Plain people didn't make scenes. Aidan gripped his hat to keep it from sailing away in the breeze, while keeping a grip on his emotions proved to be so much more difficult. Bess blamed him. It was obvious from the look on her face. No way to undo that look. He'd been waiting for a month, knowing she labored only a few miles down the road from him.

No more dinners at the Weaver house. No more evenings chewing the fat with Caleb and Solomon on the front porch, listening to the steady *click-clack* of the treadle sewing machine inside. Making clothes for the baby, last time he remembered hearing it. He'd prayed and he'd given her time to heal. Everyone had said it was time for her to get on with life. The rest of Caleb's family had. But Bess's face told a different story. She hadn't forgiven him.

He ducked his head so Iris couldn't see his face, focusing instead on Ram, his *hund,* who kept nudging his hand with his long, dark snout, looking for a treat. Ram went where Aidan did, even if it meant sleeping outside the barn during the long church services. "Quit it. I don't have anything for you." He ruffled the German shepherd's black-and-tan fur. The dog smelled of whatever road kill he'd rolled in while waiting for the service to end. "Go hunt something to eat, you lazy old hund."

"Are you coming to supper?" Iris ran her hand over Ram's head before he bounded away. She was an animal lover too. "We'll set you a plate, if you can make it."

"I'll come if I can. My sow may have that litter any day now." It was true. The sow could deliver her piglets without his help, but he couldn't afford to lose any of them. Things were tight. Keeping his father's farm going got harder with each passing year. "Tell your mudder I'm looking forward to her pot roast and potatoes. I've had enough chicken to last me a few years."

"I'll say my prayers for a healthy litter." Iris's tone was soft, a balm to his aching heart. She had a way about her that always soothed him. "You've been working hard, and knowing you, you've forgotten to eat —

67

even the chicken."

"Nee . . . Well, I'm sure I ate yesterday. I just can't remember what." More than likely, he'd sank into his bed without eating. It seemed like too much trouble most of the time. "Mostly, I'm not hungry and there's so much work to do."

"Not eating won't bring Caleb back. You haven't been to the house in ages to have supper with us. Mudder misses your compliments."

Sweet could be Iris's middle name, but she also had a wisdom usually reserved for much older folks. Another thing he appreciated about her. "I eat plenty." He patted his flat gut. "I'm getting fat."

"Nee, you aren't. You need to eat. Hazel makes the best potato salad this side of the Mississippi. Go, sit, and I'll bring you a plate."

"Truth be told, you *should* be serving and not nagging me."

She smiled. *Lord, have mercy.* When Iris smiled, her slim face glowed. She had dimples and even white teeth and eyes as blue as Stockton Lake in spring. Her hair — what he could see of it — was the color of honey. Her neck was nice too. She had curves in all the right places, and she had a heart for babies and kinner. She would soon be delivering boplin on her own, once her apprenticeship with Laura ended and the older woman retired, finally.

So why hadn't he asked her to be his fraa? Was Jeb Shrock right? Iris was a good cook. She liked to sew. She rarely complained and she didn't have a mean or lazy bone in her body. What was he waiting for? Nothing. He would ask her. Soon.

"Are you trying to get rid of me?"

"People will talk."

She laughed, that sweet, light laugh of a simple person. "The only thing they're talking about is why we're getting old and gray instead of married." She halted. Her hands fluttered in the air. Her eyes widened. "I can't believe I said that out loud. Forget I said it."

"It's okay."

"Nee, it was forward of me, and the last thing I want to do is pressure you into doing something you don't want to do."

Thankful the crowd had thinned, and everyone was deep in conversation elsewhere, Aidan sucked in a breath. "It's not that I don't want to do it —"

"You don't owe me an explanation. I understand how you feel."

"You do?" How could she? Was Jeb right? Did his feelings for Bess show on his face?

69

"I don't even know how I feel."

"When Esther died of leukemia, it was a terrible shock. I prayed and prayed, Thy will be done, Gott. His will was to take her. I wanted my way. It hurt." Kindness shone in Iris's face, mixed with the lingering sadness of having lost a cousin a few years earlier. Not a hint of judgment or anger. "You lost your best friend. It's natural that it would take you some time to get back to normal."

She was talking about Caleb. Not Bess. Caleb. "I'm fine."

"Iris, over here."

He looked over Iris's shoulder. Her father, looking like an overstuffed chair in his heavy wool coat, sat on a picnic table bench near Solomon's porch. Aidan's father had built that bench the year before he died of a sudden heart attack at the age of forty-six, one of dozens he had fashioned over his years as a farmer who doubled as a carpenter to make ends meet. He had shown his sons how to do what it took to provide for their families. "We'll talk later."

"You'll come for me?"

The hope that washed over her face met him in wave upon wave. He hadn't driven his buggy up to her house in two months. "I'll try. Soon."

Her mouth opened, then closed. She nodded and slipped away. For a second, he thought he'd made it through. Then she glanced back. "Don't keep me waiting forever. All right?"

"Understood."

He almost choked on that single word. He understood what it was like to wait for someone to recognize and acknowledge love. He'd been waiting his whole life.

Six

Idle hands led to an idle mind. Sunday evening stretched before Bess. She took her time washing the dishes. She had no sewing to do. No holey socks to mend or pants torn by wire. Making biscuits for breakfast would take all of half an hour. Her girth made it almost impossible for her to sleep — that and the thoughts running around and around like chickens spooked by a coyote every time she closed her eyes.

How would she raise this child without a mann? How would he — or she — grow up without a father? Plain families had fathers and mothers. Manns were the head of the house. Women cooked and cleaned. Men worked the fields. Everything had its place. In her new world, everything was topsy-turvy.

The water had cooled to lukewarm. She poured more hot water from the kettle on the stove into the tub. Better to cut through the grease on the skillet in which she'd fried the potatoes and onions. The hot water felt good on her hands. A chill seeped through the crack under the back door. The steady patter on the roof of rain mixed with sleet told her the weather had grown inhospitable. She should count her blessings: a warm home, a full belly, family who cared.

Gott, forgive me for this discontent, this fear, this lack of faith in Your plan.

She'd sent the girls to play checkers in front of the fireplace. Elijah had gone to the singing. Hazel and Mattie were likely sewing. Bess preferred it this way. She didn't have to make conversation as if everything was fine. They all acted as if everything was fine, when really nothing at all seemed fine.

"Have you seen Mudder?" Hazel stuck her head in the door, her knitting needles dangling from one hand. "She said she wanted to finish putting that puzzle together we started last week."

One-thousand tiny pieces that all put together would reveal a lovely painting of a herd of horses in a meadow dotted with wildflowers. Bess would like to escape into that meadow and lose herself there. "I haven't seen her since supper. I thought she went back to the dawdy haus."

"Nee, she said she was going upstairs to

borrow one of my sweaters, but she's not up there now." Hazel dropped her knitting on the table and rubbed her red, chapped fingers together. "She's been disappearing a lot lately."

"Have you seen your mudder?" Solomon strode into the kitchen. His hat was lopsided and as usual, he'd forgotten about the stub of a pencil behind one ear. His black-rimmed glasses matched his daughter's, except they rode perpetually low on his long nose. "She's not at the dawdy haus."

"I just asked that question. Bess hasn't seen her."

Father and daughter had the same look on their faces, as if they were trying to hide something. The image of Mattie, candle dipping and wavering in her hand the night of the funeral, marched across Bess's mind's eye. It hadn't been repeated. Had it? "She probably went to the basement to get a jar of molasses for breakfast. I'm making biscuits."

"Nee. I checked." Solomon shifted from one foot to the other, his gaze fixed on a spot over her shoulder. "You didn't see her go out the back door?"

"Nee. What's going on?"

"Mudder has been doing some wandering —"

74

"Hush now." Solomon's frown deepened, along with the row of wrinkles on his forehead. "If she wants to take a walk now and again, why shouldn't she?"

His devotion to his fraa after all these years touched Bess. However they might see Mattie, Solomon saw the woman he'd loved for a lifetime. "It's icy cold and sleeting. Surely she wouldn't wander around outside."

Solomon shoved his hat down on his head and grabbed his coat from a hook by the back door. "I'll just take a look-see."

"Isaac and I will go too." Hazel whirled and headed toward the front room. "I'll get my shawl."

"Nee." He jerked open the door. "No sense in us all getting wet." The door slammed behind him.

"Wait. What's going on?" Bess dried her hands as she strode after her sister-in-law. "Why does Solomon look so worried? You both do."

Hazel took off her glasses. Her chocolate-brown eyes were big under long, dark lashes. "You've been so wrapped up in your situation with the bopli coming and all. We didn't see a need to bother you with it."

"I'm not family, I realize, not really. Not anymore." Bess corralled her voice, forcing a softer tone. "With Caleb gone, I can see how you might feel that way, but Mattie is my family too. She's Caleb's mudder and the bopli's *groossmammi.*"

"You are still family. That's not it. I didn't want to worry you. You seem as lost as Mudder sometimes." Hazel wrapped a strand of gray wool around the long green knitting needle, an absent look on her face. "Caleb is with Gott. I know it. You know it, so it's hard to see you and Mudder so out of step with your faith."

"I'm not out of step. I believe . . ." She did believe. She simply couldn't understand why Gott's plan for her involved being alone. "I do. I'm just sad."

"I know. So is Mudder. I'm not trying to be mean." Hazel didn't have a mean bone in her round body. Another thing she had in common with her brother. "She hasn't been herself. She's been wandering around the house at night in the dark. This is the first time she's left without saying anything — I think."

"She never says a word. I thought she was doing fine." Bess wanted to sink through the floor and disappear. Never once had she offered a word of support or encouragement to her mother-in-law. She hadn't seemed to need it. "She told everyone it was Gott's will. I thought I was the only one having trouble with it."

"She would tell you or any of us she's fine. But she's not."

Bess grabbed her black bonnet and wool shawl from the hook by the front door. "I can talk to her. I know how she feels."

"Nee, Daed won't want you to go."

"I'll explain to him. I can talk to her easier than a man." She tucked the shawl around her shoulders. "Make some hot cocoa, why don't you? I'm sure we'll be right back."

"You shouldn't be out this weather so close to your time. You'll slip and fall in the mud and ice." Hazel clutched her knitting to her chest. "I should be the one to go."

"I'm fine. Solomon told you to stay. He won't be cross with me."

"He's cross with everyone right now."

Undoubtedly, his way of dealing with it.

Bess pulled the bonnet over her kapp and tied the strings tight under her neck to keep the wind from sending it sailing. She opened the door and stepped out into the icy night air. It felt good. Tiny sleet arrows pinged against her cheeks. She tightened her grip on her shawl and heaved herself down the slick, wet back stairs one careful step at a time. Solomon was nowhere in sight. The barn seemed like the most likely place to find Mattie. She wouldn't go far in this weather.

Bess's sneakers sank into the mud with a squelching sound. The moisture would bring green grass and flowers and feed the streams come spring. Spring couldn't be far off. Winter had languished long enough, hadn't it? New life would flourish.

Gott, I know You're good. I know it. Please forgive me. Have patience with me. I'm trying.

The sound of raised voices broke her reverie. She tugged the barn door until it rolled to the side. The light of a lantern tilted and swung, making shadows jump and sway. "Solomon? Mattie?"

"What are you doing out here?" Solomon turned, one hand on Mattie's shoulder. "You didn't need to come."

"We were worried."

Mattie wriggled from her husband's grasp. She grabbed the railing on the buggy and hoisted herself onto the seat. "I'll bring him back, don't you worry."

"Fraa." Determination danced with despair in Solomon's voice. "Get down. Now."

"The weather's bad. Those boys never know when to quit. They won't catch any fish in this weather."

"Caleb isn't fishing."

"Well, then where is he? If you don't wear

78

out his behind in the woodshed, I will." Mattie wrapped her arms across her chest, her chin lifted. She huffed a gusty sigh. "It's late. He missed supper again and I won't have it."

"I've explained this before." Solomon trudged to the other side of the buggy and dragged himself into the seat next to her. "Caleb isn't coming home. He's with Gott now."

Mattie frowned and shook her finger at him. "Whatever are you talking about, mann?"

"He died. In January." Solomon covered her outstretched fingers with his hand. His hoarse voice shook. His Adam's apple bobbed. "We buried him. You were there."

Mattie shook her head so hard her bonnet slid back. Her hands fluttered. "I'll find him."

"The horses aren't even hitched."

"Then hitch them."

"You're cold and wet. Come inside. Hazel is making hot cocoa." Bess couldn't bear the look on Mattie's face. It seemed so familiar. Like seeing herself in the small cracked compact mirror she kept in the box under the bed with other remnants from her rumspringa. "She's waiting to work on the puzzle with you. You've almost got the horses done."

"Who are you?" A person couldn't miss the note of hostility in her mother-in-law's voice.

"You know me. I'm Caleb's fraa. Bess."

"You took him from me."

"Nee, Gott took him from both of us."

"Is that what you think?" Solomon's voice boomed louder than the thunder. "Hush your mouth, girl. You'll make this worse."

It hadn't been her intent. The words had slipped out. "I only meant —"

"Go help Hazel with the cocoa. Leave my fraa to me. And don't you be saying anything about this to the others. She's fine. She'll be fine."

Mattie was many things, but she was no more fine than Bess. "I'm sorry."

"Go."

Bess turned around at the door. The look of profound grief on Solomon's face took her breath away. She put a hand to her mouth to stop the sobs determined to break free. Solomon gently guided his fraa from the buggy. He put his arm around her and Mattie collapsed against him, her face buried in his chest. Bess turned away. They deserved their privacy.

They had each other. How she longed for such an embrace.

Seven

All that grunting and groaning had paid off. Aidan squatted next to the sow and counted. A nice litter of ten good-looking piglets. Two, maybe two-and-a-half pounds, a piece. He smoothed the sparse white hair that covered the sow's head. She raised it a second, her broad-dished face illuminated in the lantern light. She looked proud. He was sure of it.

Aidan stood and stretched. The stench of pig and farrowing smelled sweet to him, the piglets' high-pitched squeals music to his ears. Pigs equaled meat equaled food on the table for his brothers' and sisters' families. Bacon, ham, pork chops, pork loin, sausage, canned meat for casseroles. He might not have his own kinner, but he could help out the others.

His boots crunched on the hay as he strode to the edge of the stall and reached for the lantern. If he'd had his druthers, he might have been a hog farmer instead of a chicken farmer. Both stank, to be sure, but chickens were so silly. Hogs were smart and curious and not dirty like some folks tried to say. They rolled in the mud because they couldn't sweat. They knew how to cool themselves off. His daed had gone with chickens. So chickens it was.

"She did the deed, then?"

Aidan jumped and nearly dropped the lantern. Timothy chortled and stomped up to the stall, looking so much like their daed Aidan did a double take. He looked cold and wet, yet cheerful as always. "What are you so jumpy about?"

"It's not funny. I wasn't expecting company."

"I'm not company, I'm your bruder." Timothy's frown bunched up round cheeks under blue-green eyes. No hair peeked from his straw hat. His shiny bald pate had to be hidden from the sun at all times. It was prone to sunburn year-round. "I figured you could use some help if momma pig decided to make a night of it."

"She did what comes natural." Hogs had a gestation period farmers could set a calendar by. Another thing Aidan liked about them. They could have two or three litters a year. "Three months, three weeks, three days, as usual."

Timothy swung one long leg up and then the other, until he perched on the stall railing, his chubby cheeks puffing out with the effort. He took off his straw hat and brushed away droplets of rain that glistened in the lantern's light. "How many?"

"Ten."

"Those Yorkshire are the best for big litters. Just make sure she doesn't lie down on them."

"I got it set up so they have room to move." This wasn't his first go-round, but Aidan knew his big brother had to give advice. It was his way of showing he wanted to help. Even if Aidan didn't need it. "I'm thinking I may expand on my hogs. There's a decent wage to be made there."

Timothy nodded, his forehead wrinkled in thought. "Takes longer to get them grown to size you can take to market, but the money's decent from what Abraham says."

Abraham raised hogs and sheep. He would know. "With six or seven females, I could have ninety to a hundred pigs a year to sell."

"Diversify."

"Doesn't seem like a good idea to put all my eggs in one basket, even if that's what Daed did."

"Daed was stubborn that way."

In every way. A moment of silence acknowledged the shared thought. Aidan brushed off his pants and his hands, brushing away memories of his daed's tirades about newfangled farming ideas and the evils of technology. They all agreed on the latter, but the former would keep them from losing their farms to the big commercial operations that were more efficient and had huge profit margins. "But you didn't come all the way out here to talk swine."

"Me and Josie ate supper with her family tonight." Timothy crossed his arms across his chest. From the looks of his potbelly, he'd been sampling quite a lot of his own wife's cooking. He had bread crumbs in his long, bushy beard — or maybe they were cookie crumbs — as added proof. "I got the impression they expected you to be there."

Having a sister-in-law who was cousin to the woman with whom Aidan had taken a few buggy rides made the grapevine mighty short in his way of thinking. "I told Iris I'd try, but if the sow decided to farrow tonight, that was that."

"Josie and the womenfolk got to jawing about how you don't eat and you don't sleep."

"How do they know? I don't see any of them following me around the house." He wiped his hands on an old towel with more force than necessary. He took a breath, trying to curb irritation born of lack of sleep, a long day, and no food. Timothy was more right than Aidan cared to admit. "I'm a grown man. I can take care of myself. Been doing it a while now."

"No need to get crabby with me." Timothy hopped from his perch and followed Aidan to the door. "Iris made a plate for you. I set it on the kitchen table before I came out here."

Aidan shrugged on his coat and took his time buttoning it. "That was nice of her."

"Her mudder insisted. She said you're starting to look like a scarecrow."

"I'm not." He had noticed his pants wanting to fall down around his knees lately. He stalked through the barn door. Good, the soupy mixture of rain and sleet had stopped. He swerved toward the poultry houses. From squeal to squawk. His day in a nutshell. Ram unwound himself from his spot by the porch, stretched, and trotted toward Aidan, a rumble in his throat, his long tail swishing back and forth. A skinny stray tabby who had decided to make his porch her home followed suit. They were as much company as Aidan needed these days. "I'm fine."

"Everyone misses Caleb."

Aidan plowed to a stop. His short parade of animals did their own version of the two-step. "Sorry, you two. You've already been fed so stop following me around." He took in a breath, determined to rein in his irritation with his brother. The man meant well, but the last thing Aidan intended to do was talk about Caleb. "You planning to help me with the birds or what?"

"You spend more time with those animals than you do people, Bruder. Something's wrong."

"Animals tend to be better company. Nothing more."

"You should talk to Freeman. Or Cyrus, if you feel more at ease with him."

The bishop or the deacon. Nee, Aidan simply needed for people to quit picking at him. He would work things out in his time, at his own pace. If there were things to work out, which there weren't.

He propped himself against the pullet house and tugged his long rubber boots over his muddy work boots. Ram took a hint and plopped down. He knew he wouldn't be allowed inside. He liked chasing chickens a little too much. Cat, on the other hand, wound her way around his leg, forcing Aidan to hop on one foot. Her high-pitched meow sounded anxious. Aidan settled into the boots and took the time to smooth her ruffled fur. "Stay with Ram. You'll not have my birds for an evening snack."

"You take on any more strays, and you'll have to add a room to the house for them."

Ignoring that ridiculous statement, Aidan opened the door and entered the first poultry house. His feet sank into the thick layer of sawdust. The smell of ammonia wasn't too bad with the steady breeze that blew through the open windows. He would close them before going back to the house. The noise rolled over him. One thing about chickens, they never shut up. A bit like his brother.

"The birds have feed." Timothy had caught up with him. "They have water. Knowing you, you shoveled the floor as soon you got back from church."

"I want to check on the little ones." As usual he'd received his biweekly shipment of six hundred chicklets on Friday. Now three days old, the babies were still fragile. It would take eighteen to nineteen pounds of feed in the next seven to nine weeks to get each one of them to full weight for sale. He couldn't afford to lose any of them. "You can go home. I don't need your help."

"Don't be so contrary. Everyone can use help."

Such a philosopher, his brother. "I reckon your fraa could use your company on a Sunday night."

"More likely she's breathing a sigh of relief that I'm not sitting around the house irritating her." Timothy grinned. Everyone knew he and Josie were still two peas in a pod after ten years of marriage. "Like you said, it's Sunday. A day of rest."

It didn't matter what day of the week it was. Eventually someone would eat these birds, but in the meantime, they deserved a decent life. "Some of them haven't been right the last few days."

Timothy stomped a few more feet, then halted and surveyed the long rows dotted with red feeders and water nipples. "Not right how?"

"Coughing, sneezing, wet eyes. Droopy, I guess." He slid his hat back on his head and contemplated the flock. "Almost like a cold, but they've been huddling and their feathers are ruffled."

"Droopy?" Timothy scratched at his beard. "Are their faces bloated?"

"A little." Filled with the gnawing sensation something was amiss that had been eating at him for a while, Aidan studied the masses of white Cornish Cross birds with their red combs and wattles. Hundreds of identical twins. He pointed his finger toward the far wall. "What's that?"

"I don't see anything." Timothy squinted. "The pile of feathers? Maybe they've been picking on that one bird again."

Chickens could gang up on the weaker birds. Once it started, it was almost impossible to stop unless he separated them into different flocks. Daed had said it was survival of the fittest, but Aidan found it cruel and too similar to the way humans bullied each other.

Holding a lantern high, he slid past his brother and strode toward the end of the first row. The birds trotted after him, carrying on as if they expected him to feed them again. They were bred to eat, eat, and eat some more so they could gain weight fast. The lantern swung in his hand, creating a dizzying effect until it struck the mounds of white feathers he sought. He stopped and squatted.

One, two, three. Three dead birds flopped over side by side as if they'd had a powwow and simply succumbed as a group exercise. He started to reach, then held back. "Get me some rubber gloves from the box."

Timothy didn't question the command.

He was back in three shakes. He donned a pair as well. "What do you think happened?"

Aidan pulled on the gloves, took a breath, and lifted the closest bird. Its face was swollen, but he saw no signs of pecking or injuries of any sort.

A bird in the corner started toward the wire mesh. It weaved side to side, its beak opening and closing as if gasping for air. Halfway there, it stopped, squatted, and hung its head, still gasping.

Timothy sighed. "You best get down to the phone shack and call Doc Carter."

"You go. Be sure to hose down your boots. I don't want to track anything outside the shed." He could try to be an optimist and assume the flocks in the other buildings were uninfected. It wouldn't matter. The entire operation with six thousand birds would be quarantined and all of them euthanized, sick or healthy. "Call Solomon, will you? Everyone with backyard flocks will need to know. And we'll need help digging the trenches so we can start burying the carcasses."

"Maybe they won't make you get rid of all of them."

"They can't take a chance. If it spreads to the bigger commercial farms, it affects the economy of the entire state."

He'd read in the newspaper about the impact on the huge commercial farms in Iowa and Nebraska. At one farm, more than one-and-a-half-million egg-laying birds had been destroyed. His small flock grown for their meat would be quick work for the state officials here.

"I don't understand. You're so careful. How do you think they got it?"

It had nothing to do with being careful. Like everything else in his life, he had no control over bird flu. "They say it's migrating birds — ducks, geese, something passing through. It comes from their droppings."

"I'm glad I grow crops." Timothy walked backward part of the way as he talked, then turned toward the door. "Don't worry, everyone will help. I'll be right back. You know Isaac and Paul and Henry and all the rest will be right behind."

Timothy took off as fast as his big, hulking frame would allow.

Aidan rose and straightened. There wasn't any hurry, really. The vet would come. He would take samples and send them to a lab. Then he would call the Missouri Department of Agriculture.

Tomorrow the decontamination would begin.

It didn't matter how many birds were already dead. If bird flu had invaded his flock, they would all be dead soon. Taking with them Aidan's livelihood.

His dream of marrying and starting a family, the day Bess learned to love him as he loved her, laid to rest with them.

EIGHT

This baby simply didn't want to come out.
That would be fine with Bess if it weren't
for the pain. The pain needed to stop.
Twelve hours of labor and counting. The
light in the afternoon sky had died. Dusk
had turned to deep night. Bess clamped her
lips together tight, determined not to let the
moan escape. Her dry throat ached. From
the pain, true, but also from unshed tears
that couldn't be allowed to fall. The birth of
a baby brought tears of joy. Not of grief and
despair. Sweat dampened her dress despite
the cool breeze from the window Hazel had
opened. Bess could hear the drip, drip of
water as yesterday's sleet melted.

Her sister-in-law wiped Bess's forehead
with a dry washrag. "You're doing fine. This
is a stubborn little bopli, no?"

"He'll come when he comes." Laura
Kauffman pulled up a stool at the foot of
the bed. Her cheerful tone soothed Bess's

weary soul. The great-grandmother of who knows how many kinner knew of what she spoke. She'd been delivering boplin for years. She'd delivered Bess's little sisters Mercy and Grace. They'd come out fine. One a little lazy. The other a terrible cook, but that couldn't be blamed on Laura. "Let's see what we can see. It should be time to push."

A powerful contraction ripped through Bess, forcing all thought from her mind. Only pain existed. She closed her eyes and willed the tears to subside. Maybe this baby knew his daed didn't wait in the front room, pacing, wondering when he would hold his firstborn child.

His only child.

"Push now. Push." Laura's warm hand touched Bess's knee. "You can do it, my girl. You can do it."

Bess had no choice. The baby had made up his mind to make an appearance after all. She could tell from the pressure. As much as she wanted this baby to stay inside her, she simply had no choice. Just as Bess had no choice but to get up each morning and go on. The families in this community where she'd lived her entire life expected it. Gott expected it.

He should know better.

Three pushes. Four. Then the cry said it all. Strong. Peeved.

"A son." Laura sounded satisfied as if she herself had done this thing. "He has ten fingers and all ten toes."

She laid him in Bess's arms, wrapped tight in a faded towel. She dropped a kiss on Bess's forehead. "Take joy in this, child, as hard as it is, seek the joy in it. There *is* joy in the pain."

The gesture surprised Bess. Laura had been a fixture in her life as long as she could remember. A friend to her groossmammi before she passed on. A friend to Mudder until she and Daed moved to the dawdy haus on Christopher's farm in Haven, Kansas. The ache blossomed until it was all Bess could do to hold back the tears. "I'll try."

"What will you name him?"

They hadn't talked about names. There hadn't been time. "I don't know."

"He looks like Caleb." Hazel had given into her tears. Her nose was red and her eyes swollen behind black-rimmed glasses. "He has his cheeks and all that wooly brown hair."

Bess forced herself to look down at the tiny bundle in her arms. Her son did indeed have his daed's face. Brown, inquiring eyes

95

peered up at her. His tiny mouth formed an
o that expanded as he yawned. Another
piercing shriek followed. He was not happy
with his new surroundings.

"May I take him to Mudder and Daed?"
Hazel wiped at her face with her apron.
"They'll want to see him."

They would. Neither had said a word the
next day about the encounter in the barn.
Mattie appeared to join them for breakfast
as if nothing had happened. The same cross,
plain-spoken woman she'd always been.
She'd fried eggs and toasted bread as if
nothing had changed in their lives. Bess
begged to differ, if a simple Plain woman
were allowed to do such a thing. She handed
her son to Hazel and closed her eyes,
submitting to Laura's ministrations.

"Let's get you a clean nightgown. I'll bring
you a bowl of soup in a bit. You have to keep
your strength up." Laura pattered on as she
bustled about the room. "That little one is
depending on you from now on."

Bess rolled to her side and put her hands
under her cheek. She couldn't imagine the
days to come. Most days she could hardly
think from one hour to the next. "He may
wish he hadn't come out at all."

Laura eased her round frame to the edge
of the bed as she rubbed her wrinkled hands

together. Her knuckles were swollen with arthritis and her skin chapped from hot water and soap. "You know I lost my Eli two years ago?"

"Jah." On Christmas Eve. Where was Gott's hand in that?

"So I know how your heart aches."

"It's different."

"Because I had forty-one years with my Eli and nine kinner?" Laura shook her head. Tendrils of iron-gray curls that matched her gray eyes escaped from her kapp. "I still get up each morning wondering how I'll get through the day and go to bed each night, hoping Gott will take me in the night like He did my mann."

"But you have kinner and grands and even great-grands."

"With lives of their own. They've no need of an old woman."

"I'm sure they —"

"Say differently? They do. They want me to sit by the fire and read and sew baby blankets. I'm an old woman, after all, what more do I need?"

Bess knew what she needed. She needed her Caleb back. She needed her life as a fraa back. She'd waited nineteen years to be that woman, fraa to her mann. To have it taken after one year, how could Gott be so cruel, so devoid of compassion? "What do you do then?"

"I'll keep doing this as long as my body allows. My little contribution to bringing new life into the world." Laura splayed her swollen fingers in her lap. "And I'll pass the evenings sewing and playing checkers with Mary Katherine Ropp. Sometimes Jennie Troyer comes by or we go to her house if her kinner can't be left on their own."

All fraas who'd lost their manns. "Jennie invited me the other day after church."

"And now I'm inviting you. You're not alone." Laura stood, her knees making a creaking sound. She put her hand on her lower back and rubbed. "Mooning around doesn't help. The wound can't heal if you spend all your time picking at the scab. Come over. Bring the boy. We miss having boplin to rock and hug and coo over."

Maybe. The thought of loading herself into a buggy and driving anywhere seemed too much right now. Her muscles were tired. Her heart, exhausted. She had no more strength than a newborn kitten. "Joshua. His name is Joshua."

Caleb had liked the name Joshua. It was his *groossdaadi*'s name.

"We'll take turns spoiling him and then send him home with you."

"I'm fine."

"You will be." Laura patted Bess's shoulder. "We all will be. Gott has a plan. I'll bring you some soup."

Bess didn't respond. She didn't dare. How could she tell this woman that she hadn't liked Gott's plan so far and she didn't see how it could get any better?

NINE

The dusty, dark Suburbans lined the dirt road that meandered from Aidan's house to the first pullet shed. He heard the footsteps but leaned harder in to the shovel. Digging trenches was easier than thinking about the birds that would all be dead in short order.

"Mr. Graber, can I have a word?"

Aidan knew without turning that the gravelly smoker's voice belonged to Joe Spano from the MDA. Aidan wiped at his forehead with the back of his sleeve, slammed the shovel into the dirt, and turned to face the man. "It's Aidan."

"Aidan, call me Joe, will you? The tests were positive. A quarantine has been set up in a six-mile radius around the farm. No poultry moves in or out of that grid." Joe looked like an overstuffed pillow in his down-filled blue jacket that stretched too tight across his paunch. His florid face darkened as if thinking about errant birds making a run for it and crossing the line. He scrubbed at his face with his coat sleeve. The man looked tired. He surely didn't get into the ag business to spearhead wholesale killings of domesticated birds.

"We'll start testing any chickens on farms around here. Even backyard flocks. Let your neighbors know. The state vets will supervise. You understand that the depop will have to start stat. Our goal is to end the threat within twenty-four hours of identifying the infected flock."

Depop short for "depopulation." A sanitary way of saying all the birds would be killed. "How do you do it?" He swallowed against sudden emotion that shamed him to the core. He cleared his throat. "I mean, kill them?"

"Well, we like to use foam. It suffocates the birds, but it's too cold. The hoses don't function well with the cold. They want to freeze up. We're going with carbon dioxide. Co_2. Gas. It's more humane and a lot faster than killing them manually, I promise." Kindness suffused the words. Depop might be the man's mission on this particular day, but he took no pleasure in it. He hadn't lost sight of his humanity. "We'll do it quick, no lingering."

Nothing humane could be found in killing

fowl that had contracted a disease through no fault of their own, but Aidan understood what he meant. They would not suffer. "Then what?"

"Then we have to decontaminate every inch of this place." Joe stuffed his hands into the pockets of his too-tight suit pants. He rocked on his muddy, scuffed boots as if warming to his favorite subject. "Every car in and out of here has to be washed down before it leaves. We'll bury all the birds on-site. We don't want to take a chance of spreading the disease through transport."

"We don't have a lot of cars in here. Mostly buggies." His farm would become a burial site, a cemetery for birds that would've been his livelihood. He had tromped about at his brother's farm, at Solomon's, at every farm where church was held. Had he spread this misery to their backyard flocks? They might not grow them for sale, but they raised plenty of chickens for eggs, even sold some at market. "How else is it spread? Could I have already spread it without knowing it?"

Joe nodded, his dark five-o'clock shadow not masking his empathy. "The virus lives up to 105 days, so it is super easy to spread via clothes or boots. The problem is that the birds get the virus, but they still look healthy. You could be spreading it before you realize your flock is infected."

The air was heavy on Aidan's shoulders. The day seemed dark despite the sun filtering through the branches of the sycamore trees in his yard. "Are my other animals at risk? I have hogs, horses, a few cattle, a dog, and a cat."

"No worries on the other animals, or the two-legged variety for that matter. It's not communicable that way, and once the chickens are dead the decomp and heat kills the virus."

Together, they turned to watch as men in puffy white contamination suits and masks over their mouths carried tanks into his pullet sheds. They looked like space men or aliens from movies he'd seen at the St. Louis metroplex movie theater during his rumspringa. That could've been a hundred years ago. Aidan forced back a sigh. "How long?"

"Until you can start again?"

He nodded, afraid his fear would stain any words he uttered.

"Six months after decontamination is completed."

Six months with no income. He nodded.

"The USDA can help, you know."

The United States Department of Agriculture. A governmental agency that helped would be a novelty in Aidan's way of thinking. Around here, most farmers saw it that way. Aidan had seen how government controlled and tried to change Plain ways when it came to everything from building standards and plans and smoke alarms to disposal of human waste that had once been used as manure for their farms. "How?"

"They pay farmers for the birds that die from the flu and even the ones that have to be euthanized just in case."

He would have to talk to Freeman and the others about it. Accepting government assistance would be a rare occasion in most Plain communities. Certainly in this one. "I'll keep that in mind. Thank you."

Joe looked back, his pudgy face creased with surprise. "No need to thank me. I know this is a nightmare for you. Don't be too hard on yourself. There is nothing you could've done to stop it from happening any more than you can stop birds from migrating every year. This isn't your fault."

Two men in protective suits plowed through the open door of the first pullet shed, dead chickens swinging from their gloved hands.

Aidan forced himself not to look away. "I know. I appreciate all your help. Tell the men we'll have food for them at noon."

"You don't have to do that."

"Our women wouldn't have it any other way. You don't have people come to a workday and not feed them."

Joe nodded and tipped his hat. "You folks are decent. I've had farmers cuss me up one side and down the other over this thing. Kill the messenger and all."

"No sense in it."

"But it is human."

Aidan had never felt more human. He wanted to kick something. Yell. Throw something. Instead, he stood there, trying to look as stoic as his words sounded. If the man saw through his skin, he would see a man with a heart cut to ribbons. He grabbed his shovel and turned back to the trench. There would be more dead birds right behind these. Work had to be done.

TEN

Now or never. Aidan knocked the mud from his boots. He lifted his hat from his head and smoothed his hair. The hat went back on his head. Compared to this, dealing with the loss of his entire chicken population seemed less monumental. He could turn around and run back to the farm, where Timothy and the others continued to bury the birds under the constant vigilance of the state inspectors, or he could do this.

Timothy wanted to know where he was headed. His answer had been to check on a friend. Stinking bird carcasses seemed almost easier in this case. Nee. He was not a coward. In those last moments before Caleb succumbed in his arms, Aidan had promised him to keep an eye on his unborn child. Whether Caleb could hear him, Aidan couldn't say, but a promise remained a promise.

Shoulders back, head held high, he

stomped up the steps and rapped on Solomon's door. A few seconds later the sound of young girls' voices raised in good-natured shouts sounded. The door opened. He looked around and then down. Sarah stood at the door, both arms behind her, holding back older, plumper sister Rachel by the force of sheer willpower. "Hi, Aidan. I got to answer the door." She grinned as she tussled with Rachel, who squirmed and groaned. "Why are you here?"

Aidan leaned in and peered at the front room. Empty. "I heard you had a new arrival."

"Jah, the bopli is here. He's here!" Sarah danced a little jig and lost her grip on Rachel, who hurtled forward into Aidan. "Hey, I answered the door." Sarah tugged at Rachel's apron. "I got here first."

"You both answered the door. It's a tie." Aidan unwrapped Rachel's arms from his middle and set her on her feet. Her glasses, miniature versions of the ones worn by her mudder, Hazel, were cockeyed on her face. He straightened them with one finger. "Can I come in?"

"Jah, jah, jah." Sarah turned and ran across the front room, her kapp strings fluttering behind her. "It's Aidan. It's Aidan. He's here to see Joshua. He's here to see the bopli!"

Bess had named the baby Joshua. Caleb would've liked that. His grandfather's name. Aidan stepped into the front room. For the most part, it looked just like every other front room in their district. Two hickory rockers parked by the fireplace, a homemade braided scrap rug between them. A brown sofa sat along one wall with two straight-back pine chairs on either side. Gas-powered lamps dotted the room. A *Budget* newspaper and a seed catalog rested on the low table in front of the couch. The walls were bare except for a calendar.

It could be his front room. Yet it differed somehow. The aroma of roast beef lingered in the air, along with some kind of pie. He inhaled the scent of family and fraa so lacking in his own home. That was it. It smelled like home — the home he'd grown up in with his bruders and schweschders.

"Hush, kinner." Solomon trotted into the room, a pencil stuck behind one large ear. "No need to shout. We're not hard of hearing."

Truth be told, Solomon was a bit on the deaf side, but no one had the heart to tell him so. He pulled the pencil from behind his ear and pointed it at Aidan. "Freeman told me the news. The inspectors have already been here and took some samples. They say they'll be back tomorrow to tell us if we have to kill the birds. Would be a shame. We eat those eggs every day. You reckon we'll get the flu from our own birds? The kinner ate eggs for breakfast just yesterday."

"Nee. It's not something humans can catch. Leastways, that's what they tell me." Aidan slid his hat from his head and gripped it between both hands. "I didn't come about that —"

"Were you able to save any of yours?"

"Nee. All six thousand will be gone." Yesterday had taken on a nightmarish quality. As more and more carcasses were thrown into the long, narrow trenches and buried, the quiet had begun to build. It followed him into the house and kept him awake that night. The squawk gone from his life so suddenly he couldn't quite adjust. "I'll have to start over whenever they give me the go-ahead. I reckon it'll be a while."

"Gott will provide. There's a piece of blackberry pie in the kitchen, if you have a hankering." Solomon did an about-face. "*Kaffi*'s hot too."

Gott will provide. Aidan believed that. He prayed for it. *In the meantime, what do I do, Gott?*

He swallowed a lump the size of a boulder. "Nee, I just ate." A slab of ham plopped between two pieces of dry bread had been enough for him. He nearly choked on it. "I heard the happy news. I wanted to stop by and see how Bess and the bopli are doing."

"We're doing fine." Bess stood in the doorway, the baby cradled in her arms. "Better than you, I reckon. I didn't know about the chickens. No one tells me anything these days. Will you start over with new chickens?"

"I have to show that there is no trace of the flu on my farm before they'll let me begin again." If he could afford to do that. And if he wanted to do it. Hogs were looking mighty good to him right now. "It will take a while to sanitize the entire place. They'll require another six months of quarantine before I can even begin again. They even patrol by to make sure you don't jump the gun and start before they give permission. Just getting rid of all those dead birds is a chore like I never imagined."

Bess winced and shifted the bundle in her arms. The baby let out a bellow that made Sarah and Rachel, perched on the bottom step of the stairs that led to the second floor, giggle.

"You girls go finish washing the dishes and

sweep the kitchen floor." Bess cocked her head toward the door. "And don't forget to put away the dishes on the counter. Don't be shirking your duties because you want to finish your story before bed. Laura and Mary will be there tomorrow night."

She glanced at Aidan. "Rachel is reading *Little House on the Prairie* to Sarah before prayers every night. Sometimes they think they are Laura and Mary."

His sisters had spent some time with those books, if vague memory served. "Better to be reading than getting into some sort of trouble."

"Darning socks would be helpful."

"We like sewing too. Sarah sews while I read out loud." Rachel popped up from the seat and squeezed past Bess, Sarah right behind her like a shadow. "Can we take Joshua with us so you and Aidan can visit?"

"I reckon Aidan came to visit with him, not me." Despite her words, Bess looked tempted. "You just want to get out of your chores. Go on with you."

The girls scampered into the kitchen, leaving a trail of giggles and whispers behind them.

"You are a good mudder already, the way you handle those girls." Aidan took two steps toward her to get a closer look at the

111

baby. She took a step back. Why would she do that? He heaved a breath. "This boy of yours is smart too. He already knows how to get what he needs."

She didn't reply. Something in her face made Aidan want to take back his words, but he couldn't be sure why. What had he said? She made a wide berth around him and slipped over to the hickory rocker by the fireplace. As she settled in, Joshua began to fuss, his arms flailing.

Aidan searched for the right thing to say. Not knowing why she seemed so anxious made it impossible. "See what I mean. He's a loudmouth, this little one. Like his daed." There he'd said it. They couldn't have a conversation without acknowledging that Caleb was in the room. "He never knew when to close his mouth."

"I wouldn't mind hearing him natter on about the weather and the coyotes eating the cantaloupes and the fence that needs fixing about now." She smoothed Joshua's blanket with a shaky hand. "I miss the sound of his voice."

"How are you?" Aidan missed it too, but he could see no way past the pain except to tromp through it like a buck in the woods who knows he's being chased by a worthy hunter. "Feeling better than you did at church?"

"I'm fine." She hugged Joshua closer. "I was fine then too."

"You didn't seem so good. I wanted to make sure it wasn't something I said."

"You didn't say anything wrong."

Maybe not, but he should've said more. What did a friend say who had sent a woman's husband to his death? "I should've said I was sorry, I reckon."

"For what?" She studied Joshua's face as if she'd never seen it before. "You weren't driving that truck."

"If I'd gone for the part myself —"

"You wouldn't be here now."

"Joshua would have a daed."

"Caleb wouldn't want you to take his place. He'd want you to have your own fraa and bopli." Bess squirmed in the chair. Joshua fussed louder this time. She sighed. "Besides, it doesn't matter. Gott's plan is Gott's plan."

Did she know how much bitterness seeped into her words? "Either way, I'm sorry."

"Me too."

He eased into the chair across from her. "Can I hold him?"

To his surprise, she hesitated. Did she not trust him? Or didn't she want to let go of her baby? He hoped it was the latter. "I

113

won't hurt him."

"Of course you won't." She tucked the blanket around the baby's tiny body, but his arms immediately flailed, knocking the blanket away. "Truth be told, it would be nice to have a rest from him. He might spit up on you, though. He does that a lot."

Something that could only be described as rancor marred her response. A bitter taste in his mouth, Aidan took the tiny bundle, along with a cloth diaper as a spit-up rag, and settled him into his arms. Joshua weighed no more than a gnat and did, indeed, smell of spit-up. Aidan leaned back in the chair and rocked, just as he had done an untold number of times with nieces and nephews.

Never had a baby felt so light and so vulnerable in his arms. Caleb's son. His only child. The knot in Aidan's throat grew and tightened. He inhaled, but his lungs didn't seem to appreciate the effort.

"It's almost impossible, isn't it?"

He raised his head at the aching wonder in Bess's voice. "What's impossible?"

"To imagine that Caleb will never be here again. Ever."

"It's fairly impossible for me."

"I keep thinking he'll sneak into the kitchen while I'm fixing supper and tickle me from behind with those big hands." Her chuckle faded into thin air. "I always complained because his hands were dirty and he got my apron dirty. Now I . . ."

"You wouldn't mind a little extra laundry?"

"Nee."

Aidan continued to rock, letting a host of shared memories warm the space between them. Volleyball games, barn raisings, picnics on the last day of school. Rumspringa shenanigans that none of them would admit to now. The day of baptism the three of them had shared. Caleb and Bess sitting at their wedding *eck* after the ceremony eating, Caleb shouting that Aidan surely would wed next.

"Remember that day you fell out of the tree?"

Bess's chair rocked faster, the squeak punctuating the question. Maybe she didn't want to take that road. Maybe she wouldn't answer. It was too painful.

"How could I forget?" She swiped at her face with her sleeve. "Daed would've had my hide if it weren't for my broken nose. Mudder scolding me for being out there at all. I wasn't supposed to be with you boys. I never knew my place inside, doing girl chores."

"Your nose never did straighten out proper-like."

"My nose is fine." A faint smile appeared. Ever so faint. The lines around her mouth eased and the darkness in her eyes lifted.

Aidan tried out a smile in return. Hers faded and she ducked her head again, severing the connection.

"I will be here to help raise him." He blurted out the words. He'd said what he came to say. "Whatever he needs."

Surprise flittered across Bess's face. Her mouth opened, then closed. His statement should go without saying. He knew that. Bess knew it. Plain took care of Plain. They were all family. Faith, family, community. He'd heard it umpteen times in his life, during church services and from his father's and mother's mouths on a nearly daily basis. But somehow, he'd needed to say it. The burden weighing on his spirit demanded it.

"Hello there, little one." The lump was back. *Be gone with you.* "You don't know how easy you have it, eating and sleeping, no work, all play. Don't get used to it. Your day will come when I'll be putting you to work."

"No one knows what the future will bring." Her voice trembled and her eyes were wet with unshed tears.

Aidan swallowed hard against his own. "I will help you raise my good friend's son." He took a breath and steadied himself. "My good friends' son."

"If you're here."

"According to Gott's plan."

"Do you think this is Gott's plan?" She waved her hand toward him and the baby. "Caleb should be sitting in that chair, holding his son, you looking over his shoulder, making goo-goo faces and acting silly like you two always did."

He, too, could see that scene. So happy, so carefree. A gift given to others, but not them. He, too, found it hard to fathom. "We can't understand Gott's plan or His will. We can only live every day doing what Gott expects us to do. Including raising up the kinner He has entrusted to us."

Shadows had painted themselves under her eyes, dark against her pale skin. Despite having given birth only two days earlier, she looked gaunt. The baby weight had fled. "This is to be my lesson in *Gelassenheit,* then? Was loving my mann somehow so selfish that I had to be taught to yield to His will? Is our Gott that severe and peevish?"

Hurt and pain clothed in fiery, red anger. He understood this too. He had his own

117

lesson in Gelassenheit with the unnatural job of killing the chickens he'd nurtured and raised from chicklets in hopes of making a living from them. "We all have to learn those lessons."

"I'm too tired to try this hard."

"It'll get easier."

"How do you know? You've never even been married."

She had no way of knowing how her words hurt, like a flaming arrow piercing flesh and sinew. He stood and handed Joshua back to her. "I have work to do."

"I didn't mean it that way."

He couldn't blame her for not knowing about feelings he'd never dared to put into words. Still, he couldn't corral the anger that she would so simply dismiss his station in life at this moment. "If you need anything — if Joshua needs anything —"

"It's kind of you to offer, but Solomon and Mattie will provide. Hazel is here."

"Jah. They are a blessing."

He strode to the door without looking back. He'd done what he'd come to do. Time to get back to work and leave all this emotional falderal to the women.

"Aidan." Her voice held a note of pleading. "I appreciate you coming by. *Danki.*"

He couldn't look back. She'd see his face.

118

He shoved his hat down over his forehead and let the door slam behind him.

Eleven

Mary Katherine Ropp could be a mighty persuasive woman. Bess felt the urge to smile for the first time in forever. Her mother's best friend had a point. A person couldn't ignore the sunshine or the blue sky of a Missouri day in which the first hint of spring could be felt in the air. Both were so bright after a long, dark winter. She'd spent most of the last month sitting in a rocking chair, nursing Joshua or trying to get him to stop fussing and sleep. He was a little piglet who seemed to think day was night and night day.

She breathed the fresh air and allowed Mary Katherine to propel her through the double glass doors into the plant nursery. The air inside hung heavy and humid, wrapping her in an earthy, warm hug. The smell of mulch reminded her of her mother's garden on those long afternoons when she and her sisters had pulled weeds and giggled and told stories and wondered what the future would bring for each one of them. If only she'd known. "Tell me again what we're doing here?"

"Getting plants for your flower garden." Mary Katherine bustled around Bess, the rubber soles of her black sneakers squeaking on the damp cement floor. "I told you."

"Did Mudder put you up to this?" Her mother and Mary Katherine exchanged letters at least once a week. "It's not my garden. It's Mattie's. And Hazel's."

Their house. Their garden. She only lived there because of Caleb. She took care of the flower garden because it gave her pleasure to do so. Mattie and Hazel were far more interested in the vegetable garden. Which made perfect sense. Her love of flowers served a less practical purpose.

"Judith and I write about all sorts of things in our letters. It's not always about you." Mary Katherine's tone was tart, but her smile kind. "You always planted the flowers for Mattie. I've seen you out there weeding and pruning all the time. You're the gardener. Besides, Mattie hasn't been herself. Hazel has four kinner running to and fro."

Hazel and Isaac were blessed to have those kinner running to and fro. Mary Katherine's first words registered. *"Mattie hasn't been herself."* Neither had Bess. She had no idea who *herself* was anymore. Not a fraa, that was painfully evident every morning when she opened her eyes and the other side of the bed gaped empty and cold. Not a mudder. Not a good one anyway. Joshua cried and she simply longed to escape that high-pitched sound. The shape of his face, his eyes, everything about him reminded her of Caleb.

Guilt tightened around her chest until she couldn't breathe. She fought for composure. Mary Katherine couldn't know about this failing. No one could know. "We usually just buy seeds from the Burpee catalog."

"Takes too long." Mary Katherine dragged a flatbed cart from the wall and pulled it down the aisle, its wheels clacking. "You need flowers blooming ASAP."

ASAP. Mary Katherine spoke like that. She was the district scribe for *The Budget* newspaper. She wrote short stories and poems. She knew what everyone was doing in the district and why. If a person needed to know where someone was, he need only ask Mary Katherine. How she knew so much, Bess couldn't understand. "What's the hurry?"

"To lift Mattie's spirits, naturally." Mary

Katherine's tone suggested she had little patience for stating the obvious. "Focusing on another's needs helps us to forget about our own aches and pains."

A gentle chiding if Bess ever heard one. Mattie had lost a son. Bess lost a husband. Tragedy should've brought them together. Instead Mattie seemed to stare at her at the supper table as if trying to figure out who Bess was and why Hazel had invited her to eat with them. "I'm trying."

"I know you are." Mary Katherine tugged at her apron and smoothed her kapp. She always had something askew. "You would feel better if you got out more. Laura and Jennie have both invited you to our sewing frolics and you haven't come."

"I have the bopli to think of." If she thought it would be fair to leave Joshua with Hazel at the end of a long day, she would. Today she'd nearly flown from the house when her sister-in-law offered to watch him while she came with Mary Katherine. "It's not fair to dump him on Hazel."

"Simply bring him." Mary Katherine scratched her short, upturned nose that still featured a sprinkle of freckles, even at her age, which must be in the late fifties. "That's what mudders do. You'll get the hang of it."

Mary Katherine couldn't know Bess found

it impossible to breathe around Joshua. She felt smothered. Every time she looked at him, she saw Caleb in his dimpled cheeks and his dark eyes and his thin nose. "He's awake all night and fussy all day. He gulps his food like a little piglet, and then spits it all up, then cries because he's hungry. I can't see straight, let alone sew."

Mary Katherine selected a tray of marigolds, perused it, cocked her head, and returned it to the display table. "These are root bound. When Moses died four years ago, I thought I would lose my mind. Not that I ever told anyone how I felt. I had Angus, Barbara, and Beulah still at home. My older seven kinner had their families to worry about. They couldn't be taking care of their mudder. Stiff upper lip and all that nonsense. It's easy to say what we believe, but living what we believe, well, that's another pot of potatoes."

Mary Katherine and her sayings. Bess smiled for real this time. The stone entrenched in the spot where her heart once resided lightened. This woman understood. Not like the women at church who found it easy to mouth platitudes they themselves did not have to live. Maybe Mary Katherine was right. A garden might lift her spirits too.

Bess let her fingers brush over a row of pansies in fuchsia, purple, pink, and lilac colors. The petals were soft under her rough, dry fingertips. She'd neglected their upkeep. What did it matter? She touched no one except Joshua. She picked up a flat of purple, pink, and yellow pansies. These would brighten the garden beds in the front yard for sure.

"You have to get out of the house now and then. Come sew with us. Bring the bopli."

The knot in Bess's throat, her ever-present companion, swelled, daring her to try to respond. "I'll try."

"Try harder." Mary Katherine shook a plump finger at Bess, her blue eyes bright and hard as marbles. "Put your back into it."

"Everyone keeps saying that." She sounded like a whiny child who didn't want to take a nap. She knew it, but she couldn't seem to stop it. "My head knows what to do, but my heart refuses to do it."

The bald truth stood there, embarrassed, without a stitch of clothing, shivering in an early spring day.

"Because there's no going around this dark woods, you have to march through the gloom until you reach the light on the other side." Mary Katherine smiled, the severity gone in an instant. The gloom lifted for a second. "Don't worry. We'll help you."

"You have your own chores to do."

"Come sit with Jennie, Laura, and me. We'll help you find your way."

"I'd like that." Here in the bright, sunny light, it seemed possible. How she would feel in the dark of evening was another cup of tea. Or pot of potatoes as Mary Katherine was wont to say. "You're sweet."

"I'm a nosy old busybody." Mary Katherine clapped her hands, looking as pleased as a midwife delivering twins. Her kapp slid back. Hair of silver, white, and gray strands made an appearance. She tugged the kapp back into place — crooked. "I'll make extra lemonade. Now on to business. I want some tomato plants, some peppers, and some onions for my garden. I want to make hot sauce. When the boys and their fraas come over for supper, they like my taco casserole with hot sauce." She pushed the cart toward Bess. "You pick the flowers you like. I'll get my own cart and check out the vegetable section. I'll be back to help you."

"Wait." Bess didn't want to be left alone out here in the world. Even if this small world smelled like her mudder's garden. She turned, the flat in her arms. "I thought we were doing this together."

A man weighted down with three enormous bags of plant fertilizer loomed in front of her. The pansies knocked against him and tottered. She crushed them to her chest to keep them from hurtling to the floor.

"Ahoy there, who is it?" A voice so melodious and deep it might have belonged to the radio announcer she heard talking over the speakers in Jamesport stores wafted from behind the bags. "Did I step on someone?"

"I didn't see you. I was talking to Mary Katherine and she must've walked away."

The man peered over his load, his strawberry-blond eyebrows high over black-rimmed glasses smudged with fingerprints. "My fault, my fault!"

He lowered the bags until Bess could see the rest of his red face. He had a long nose and a thick beard that couldn't decide whether to be blond or strawberry red like his hair. His eyes were that faded-blue color she often saw in redheads. A floppy sweat-stained canvas hat kept her from seeing if he fit that bill.

"I have to say I've never been mistaken for a woman named Mary Katherine before. Lucy, once, but that's because my buddy lost his glasses when they fell in Stockton Lake."

"Sorry, what I meant to say was —"

"I know what you meant to say. I was just giving you a hard time. I didn't see you there. Didn't see anyone." The melodious voice had a distinct southern twang to it the faster he talked. "I should've done this one at a time like Mr. Spencer told me, but I thought it would be more efficient to move them quickly. That's me, always in a hurry."

"No harm done." She backed away, the pansies still clutched in her arms. "I'll get out of your way."

"Those *Viola x wittrockiana* look past their prime." The man dumped the sacks on an end cap and turned, dusting off hands the size of stew pots. "We just got in the *Petunia hybrida.* They're as colorful and they grow well in full sun. We have *grandiflora, multiflora,* and double types in a wide array of colors."

He sounded like a catalog brought to life.

"These will do fine." She edged toward the aisle. Mary Katherine had brought her here, only to abandon her to a strange man in khaki shorts and a tan shirt with *Woodson Nursery* embroidered in red on the pocket. "I have what I need."

"I don't mean to show off."

She tucked the tray on the cart. Mary Katherine shouldn't have left her like this. "Show off?"

"I'm working on a masters in environmental science at Missouri State. Leastways I plan to be, if I can get enough money together for my tuition. Had to drop out this semester, not enough money to stay in St. Louis." He wiped his hands on the muddied khaki shorts that sported pockets on the thighs. His bulged with an assortment of tools. He held out his hand. "I'm Dusty Lake. Short for Dustin. Today's my first day working here."

She gave the hand a quick shake so as not to be unfriendly. Plain folks weren't much for standing on ceremony, and Amish women weren't much for touching men who weren't their manns — Amish or Englisch. "Congratulations on your new job."

"I'm new to Jamesport too." If he felt it odd she hadn't shared her name, he didn't show it. He was a stranger, after all. He followed along after her when she started down the aisle, hoping to find Mary Katherine. His scarred, muddy hiking boots bound with multicolored laces squelched when he walked. "My parents decided to retire here. Usually, when people retire, they move to Florida and play golf, not my parents."

"People do strange things."

"Don't they, though?"

He chuckled, a deep-throated sound so infectious she caught herself about to laugh as well. Laughing and smiling all in one day. *I'm sorry, Caleb. I'm sorry.*

"I have to find my friend." She grabbed the cart handle and turned away. "Welcome to Jamesport."

"Are you planting a garden?"

What else would she be doing with the pansies. "Yes."

"May I suggest a few options. I know my stuff, I promise, and I really need to practice." His tone bordered on begging. "Mr. Spencer only hired me because I know plants, and he wants me to push sales up by helping customers find the best buys. If sales don't increase, I'm out on my keister. That's what he says. He didn't really need another salesperson, but I talked him into it with my silver tongue."

What could she say to that? He was trying so hard. She straightened and nodded. She would hear him out and go on her merry way as quickly as she could without being rude.

"What's your name?"

"My name?"

"It would be easier if I knew your name. Most people here are neighbors and everyone knows each other's names. So when customers come in, Mr. Spencer calls them by name." He hunched his shoulders. "If I'm going to have regular customers, I need to know their names. So when you come in, I can say, 'Hey.' " He pointed to her.

"Bess."

"Hey, Bess, what's up? What can I help you with today?"

"I don't come in often."

"You will now that you know I'm here to help. Right? Right!" He did a clumsy two-step and threw his hands up like a performer she'd seen at the county fair one year. His comical grin made her smile. What a clown. He was made for a sales job, no matter what he said. "If you really want to stand out, start with *Phlox divaricata.*" Until he opened his mouth.

"A what?"

"Sorry." He shoved his glasses up his nose with one finger. He had dirt under his ragged nails. "I've been practicing for school and I forget, this is a different audience. Blue phlox. Lavender flowers. Plant them now and they'll bloom through June."

"That sounds nice."

131

His face lit up as if she'd offered him a prize. He rubbed his hands together. "I'm just getting warmed up. Then there's *Polemonium reptans,* also known as Jacob's Ladder."

A pain so sharp it might be caused by a piece of broken glass pierced the spot where her heart, now scattered across a cemetery, once lived. Jacob's Ladder grew wild along the dirt roads of Missouri. Blue and lavender. Caleb used to point it out to her when they courted. He said Jacob's Ladder matched the color of her eyes. Blue when she wore blue and lavender when she wore the dark-purple dress she made, sitting up late into the night under the gas lamp to finish it, just for their drives.

"I don't think so."

"I know it grows wild around here, but this is especially bred for gardens. It's beautiful and it attracts bees, butterflies, and moths to your yard. Flies, too, but we won't hold that against it." He held up a pot heavy with the clusters of bill-shaped flowers tumbling over the sides as if searching for solid ground. " 'And [Jacob] dreamed, and behold, there was a ladder set up on the earth, and the top of it reached to heaven.' Genesis 28:12."

The pain dissipated. He looked so intent

and so happy in his knowledge. That this man not only knew and loved his flowers, but also his Scripture, caused a tiny, warm flame to flicker where only solid ice had been a few seconds earlier. How could a person not like a flower that reminded them all of the nearness of heaven? Where Caleb surely waited for her.

"Maybe I will."

A grin split his face as he hoisted the pot onto her cart. "Good choice. What about Oxeye sunflower?"

"Why would I choose a false sunflower when the real ones grow everywhere in Missouri?"

"You know your sunflowers!" He sounded like a teacher praising a good scholar. "*Helianthus annuus.* There are sixteen species of Helianthus in Missouri. They are grown worldwide for seeds and oil as well as ornamental uses. At one time Missouri was a leader in the production of sunflowers."

"You might want to think about how much people want to know about the flowers they buy."

"Why?" Now he sounded hurt. His big eyes reminded her of Aidan's hund, Ram, when he was begging for table scraps. "You don't think it's interesting?"

"I do." She really did, a fact that surprised

her. "But I doubt everyone feels the same way. They want to buy their flowers and get home to plant their gardens."

"The fun is in the learning about the plants." He pulled a bedraggled book from his back pocket and held it up. The paperback's cover was torn and the pages yellowed. "*The Sunflower* by Charles B. Heiser. He knows everything there is to know about sunflowers, and he put it all in this book."

"And you have it memorized?"

"Pretty much." His cheerful grin invited her to smile back. "Nothing much else to do in Jamesport, Missouri."

True enough. "I have to find my friend."

"Take these." He shoved a tray of golden yellow marigolds along with another of pink impatiens onto the cart. "Oh and these. You'll need these to balance out the colors."

Zinnias in pinks, yellows, and fuchsia. A cornucopia of color. Somehow she felt better already, and not a single flower had graced Mattie's garden. "Thank you."

He leaned closer, his grin infectious. She couldn't help but smile back. She'd smiled more today than any day since that day. Dusty touched her arm with a meaty paw, his touch surprisingly delicate for such a big man. "You're Amish, right?"

"Yes." She drew back. Such a feely, touchy

person, this strange man, who was nothing if not observant. "All my life."

"Hello, Bess."

She turned at the familiar voice. Sophie and Ruth. Caleb's sisters had matching sour looks on their faces. Although a few years apart, they might have been twins with matching personalities so like Mattie's. Bess forced a smile. "How funny. We all had the same idea today."

"I don't think we had the same idea you did." Sophie's stare went from Bess to Dusty and back as if to make sure Bess received her message. "We're buying seeds and such for our vegetable gardens. What are you doing?"

As if it weren't obvious. "I came with Mary Katherine. I'm to plant the flowers, and she's looking for vegetables."

As if she had to explain herself to her sisters-in-law. She was a grown woman.

"Bess was just making a little joke." Dusty smiled at the sisters. "She said she's been Amish all her life. I'd wager you two ladies have been Amish all your lives as well."

"You're not really Amish until you're baptized." Ruth brushed at her apron as if removing dust invisible to the rest of them. "Once you're baptized you're committed to your faith."

Her emphasis on *committed* and *faith* was not lost on Bess. "I just need to pay for these and then find Mary Katherine."

"We'll see you tonight. Mudder invited us for supper." Ruth's eyebrows did a little dance over her brown eyes. "See you at the house shortly then." Her gaze went to Dusty. "Mudder will be anxious for the garden to be planted. You could even do it today if you hurry."

With that Ruth marched away, Sophie trotting after her.

Whatever went through their minds, it wasn't good. And they would run right home and tell Mattie. Of that Bess was certain.

She turned to Dusty. "I need to go."

"This is my first day on the job, and I met an Amish woman and it's not even over yet. My parents think they're going to make big bucks because of all the people who come to Jamesport to see the Amish."

He was truly oblivious to the undercurrents. Bess nodded, still watching Sophie and Ruth. The latter glanced back, her eyes narrowed. Bess ducked her head and tried to block out the thought that her sisters-in-law were judging her and finding her wanting. Her first time in town since Caleb's death and they thought she was doing something untoward with an Englisch man.

"Do you think they will? Make a lot of money?"

"It's possible. It's not always fun to have them peeking in our windows, taking our pictures, driving on our land, and stopping in at the school in the middle of lessons, but we try to make the best of it. Tourists help everyone here to make a living."

The number of tourists flowing through the small town seemed to grow every year. She wouldn't complain. The money they made from their jams, jellies, and other canned goods, as well as the quilts at the festivals, market days, and craft fairs helped pay for the necessities they couldn't grow or make.

Dusty looked thrilled at the idea. He pumped his fist as if the money poured in already. "I'll ring you up."

"Ring me up?"

He waved his bucket-size hand toward parts unseen. "You know, at the cash register."

"Oh. Yes. Yes, but I have to find my friend Mary Katherine."

"Here I am." Mary Katherine tottered toward them, tugging a second cart behind her. "That late snow took out my tomatoes, my green peas, everything. So I got the tomatoes, the peppers, the onions, green beans, peas. Cucumbers. I'm ready to plant." She perused Bess's cart. "Oh, you did good. Very good."

"I helped." Dusty waved with both hands. "I'm new here, but I have all the poop on the plants."

"Poop on the plants." Mary Katherine chuckled. "I'll have to remember that. Do you have that Mexican parsley? I think it's called coriander or cilantro. I want to try making hot sauce fresh from my garden. I found serrano peppers and jalapeños."

"Yep, I'm sure we do." He lumbered off in the opposite direction, leaving Bess with her flowers. "I'll be right back to ring you up, Bess."

Bess? Mary Katherine mouthed the word, her eyebrows lifted as she brushed past Bess.

"He was just teaching me about flowers."

"Teaching you to learn new things." Mary Katherine kept moving. "To think about something new. That's gut. Gut, gut."

For a few seconds it had felt good. Bess would take it, no matter what her sisters-in-law thought or said.

Aidan shoved the box filled with bottles of bleach and a jumble of other cleansers in the back of the wagon, the smell clean and fresh, yet it reminded him of the stench of death, the stench of hundreds of dead and dying chickens. Ram leaped up next to it and flopped down. At least he smelled alive, like a dog who liked to roll in the dirt and any nasty stuff he could find in the yard.

"Fine, you'd rather sit back here and let me chauffeur you around like a taxi driver? So be it." Talking to the dog like he was a person, that's what his life had come to. Hunds made better company than most folks. "Get comfortable, then."

He strode to the front of the wagon, intent on getting back to the farm. After a month of sanitizing and resanitizing every inch of the sheds and all the equipment and all his boots and clothing, he could see a tiny sliver of light at the end of the tunnel. At least that's what he told himself when he fell into bed at night physically exhausted. A man should sleep well under those circumstances. His mind didn't seem to be getting the message.

He untied the reins from the hitching post Merle Walker had installed in front of his hardware store in deference to his many Plain customers. The sound of high voices and a familiar laugh made him turn. Bess stood on the sidewalk in front of Woodson Nursery, talking to a man Aidan had never seen before. She picked up a flat of flowers. The man tugged at them. She tugged back, all the while smiling.

Aidan hadn't seen her since that day after his livelihood came under fire and she had become a new mother. So much for his promise to help raise Joshua. How could he when she so obviously didn't want his company? He'd made a promise. He took a breath and let it out. Ram whined. "I know I said we're going. You stay here and take a nap. I'll be right back.

Ram's head flopped back on his paws. Too bad Aidan didn't talk to people as well as he did animals. He strode across the street, dodging a puddle of water and a gray car that decided to shoot past him rather than waiting. The driver tooted his horn and shook his finger as he whizzed by.

Bess turned. The smile on her face dimmed, then disappeared completely. "Aidan." She glanced at the man who towered over both of them. His smile stretched across his face revealing big, even teeth. He seemed too happy for words. "I'm buying flowers." She said it as if the statement made perfect sense. "This is Dusty. He knows about flowers."

She knew the man's first name. She let go of the flat to point at the man as if there might be another one about with that name. Her cheeks flamed red. The flat started to go down. Dusty made a grab for it just as Bess did. Their heads collided. She slipped on the curb. Dusty grabbed her arm. It all happened so fast. Flowers on the sidewalk. Dusty with his hands on Bess.

"I don't think they'll grow on cement." Aidan said the first words that came into his head. The first words he dared say, stupid as they were. She shouldn't allow the man to touch her. Though, he'd saved her from falling. More than Aidan had done. He hadn't saved her from anything. He squatted and began to set the flowers upright in the flat. The dirt smelled clean, a juxtaposition that always puzzled him. "They're bruised, but they'll be all right."

"No, no. It's my fault." Dusty hunkered down next to Aidan. He smelled of sweat and man's deodorant. "I meant to catch them. You don't want the roots messed up like that. I'll take them back in and replace them."

"No, your boss won't like that." Bess rubbed her head and then her arm. This man named Dusty had hurt her. Still, she smiled at him. "I don't want you to get into trouble on your first day."

How did she know so much about this

man? His name, his first day. What else did she know? "She's right. She should take them and get on home to plant them."

"Nope. Customer service first. That's what Mr. Spencer says." Dusty hoisted himself up, the damaged flat with him. "I'll be right back." He disappeared into the store, whistling.

Aidan stood. "How do you know him?"

"I don't."

"You know his first name."

"He told me."

"What are you doing here by yourself?"

"I'm not by myself." Her tone suggested it was none of his business and no rule existed that said a Plain woman couldn't go to the nursery by herself. Maybe such a rule was needed. "Mary Katherine is with me."

"I don't see her." Why did he say that? Like she would lie about such a thing. What had gotten into him? "I mean —"

"She's still paying." Bess crossed her arms, looking the spitting image of her mudder when they'd stolen cookies from the kitchen counter an hour before supper time. "How's Iris?"

What did Iris have to do with anything? He did not understand women's thought processes. They zigzagged all over the place instead of making a sensible straight line

142

like men did.

He hadn't talked to Iris much since the flu outbreak. He stared at his boots. She would understand. He had a disaster on his hands at the farm. Tempting him to lose faith in hard times. Nee, he would step up. He would believe. He would walk by faith. It was expected. But all this meant he didn't have time for courting.

Pretty Iris with her blonde hair and blue eyes and sweet disposition. Iris who left a casserole on his kitchen table with a note that read *"Hope you're okay. We're praying for you. Gott will provide. Take care."* In that sweet, swirly handwriting she'd perfected as she sat across the room from him at school all those years. Always smiling, always the first with a kind word and a laugh. She had the best laugh, not high and annoying like so many of the girls at school who wanted the boys to notice them.

Iris, who never complained and never chatted with a strange Englisch man on the street in broad daylight in what constituted downtown Jamesport. "She's just fine. As far as I know." Courting was private. What did Bess know about Iris and him? "She was fine at church on Sunday."

"She and her mother came by the house earlier this week." Bess's tone had a touch

143

of wonder in it. As if she couldn't believe how good folks were. "They brought some hand-me-down baby clothes and a nice Dutch apple pie."

"Nice of them."

"Jah. Nice. She's nice."

Iris was nice. He cleared his throat. "How's the bopli?"

"He cries." Her mouth closed. The pain in her eyes made his fists clench. She sniffed. "Boplin do that, I reckon."

"Did you ever plant the flower seeds I brought you?" He drew a breath. He shouldn't have asked. He should've let it alone. "Never mind."

"Nee." Her tone turned wooden. "I didn't. I couldn't."

"That's all right."

"I haven't been back to the cemetery."

"He's not there, anyway."

"Nee."

"I don't know what I was thinking."

"It was a hard time."

"Jah."

The silence stretched. The rumble of car engines filled it followed by a young couple who walked by, holding hands, their entwined fingers swinging between them, laughing, arguing, talking, as if life hadn't come to an abrupt halt. Bess watched them

144

go, her expression unfathomable. "Are you getting more chickens then?"

"Nee. Not yet. The inspector won't sign off on it for at least six months."

"What will you do?"

"Clean and disinfect some more. Work for Timothy. Expand my passel of hogs so I can earn money to restock the chickens when the time comes." He forced his gaze to the wagon across the street. Ram stood, his big snout sniffing the air. "I should get back. We're having another workday. We ran out of supplies."

The glass double doors of the nursery swung open. Mary Katherine trundled out pulling a cart behind her, its wheels clacking on the sidewalk. She held a pot of pink geraniums in her arm. "Spent all my jam money, but I couldn't resist a pot of flowers for the front porch." She smiled at Aidan. "Dusty said someone was out here. How is the big cleanup coming? Shall I bring a casserole tonight?"

"We're making progress." He moved back to let her through. Dusty lumbered behind her, a new flat of flowers in his arms. Aidan took another step back. "I still have the enchilada casserole you brought by Sunday. Laura brought me a stuffed-pepper casserole. Now I'm the one who is stuffed."

"We take care of our own." Mary Katherine handed him the pot. "Put that up for me. Dusty will do the rest."

Why did it bother him that Dusty seemed to have taken a place that should've been his? The man was simply doing his job. No more, no less. Aidan slid the pot into the back of the buggy. "I better get going."

He brushed past Bess. She didn't look up from the flowers. "Tell Hazel we finished off the chicken and dumplings."

"She brought you chicken and dumplings?"

"Solomon and Isaac brought it when they came to help out last week." It seemed strange that she didn't know they'd come. How could she not know? "Anyway. I best get going."

"I would've made something. I didn't know." She twisted her fingers together in a tight grip that left her knuckles white. "I mean, I knew, but I was . . ."

"We're getting fat, we're eating so much." An urgent need to wipe that anguished look from her face filled Aidan. "We don't need any more to eat. We won't be able to get any work done. We'll have to roll ourselves out to the pullet sheds in wheelbarrows."

"It wouldn't hurt to put some meat on your bones." Mary Katherine giggled. For some reason it didn't sound silly coming from a woman of her age. "I have a hankering for shoofly pie. Haven't made it in a while. Maybe I'll make two and bring you one."

His favorite. His mudder had made the best shoofly pie around. "I reckon I wouldn't turn you down." Aidan looked back. Dusty was still standing there. He should go back inside. Go back to work. "Don't you need to help other customers?"

"I feel like making cookies. Snickerdoodles." Bess's chin came up. She looked just as she had in school when she didn't want to read in front of the class. "You've been so helpful, I'll bring you some."

Dusty grinned. "You don't have to do that, but if you want to do it, that would be great. Mr. Spencer likes snickerdoodles."

"I'll make an extra big batch then."

Aidan walked away. He liked snickerdoodles too, but he hadn't been helpful. Not at all. Bess was doing fine. She was getting on with her life. He should do the same.

TWELVE

Running into Aidan in front of the nursery hadn't bothered Bess. Not one whit. Corralling irritation she couldn't understand, she tugged on the reins and came to a stop in front of Jennie Troyer's house. Her husband's best friend went around with a hangdog look that only reminded her of what she wanted to forget. That day in January when the bottom fell out of her life.

She stared at Jennie's house as if she'd never seen it before. The same two-story, white wooden building as Solomon and Mattie's home. Except it could use a new coat of paint and the hitching post leaned precariously as if it might fall over. In fact, the whole place looked like a garden that needed tending.

Here was a woman who would understand. Jennie tried to take care of the house, the garden, the fields, and the livestock — plus seven children she raised all on her own. Bess couldn't remember their ages, but the oldest couldn't be more than thirteen and the youngest was three, born right before his daed passed away. Jennie's brothers farmed her property, and she supplied produce, jams, jellies, and canned goods to more than one store in town. The girls sewed baby quilts and clothes to sell. The boys hired themselves out to mow yards and muck stalls, whatever they could find. They were good kinner.

Would Joshua turn out as well? A twinge of guilt resonated through Bess. She'd left him with Hazel. Her sister-in-law didn't mind and Joshua didn't seem to mind either. He cried when Bess held him, quieted when his aenti took him in her arms.

Bess needed a little break, that's all. A little break from the fussing that kept her awake all hours of the night. It wasn't the crying, really, but the way she saw Caleb's eyes every time she looked at Joshua's small, round face. He couldn't be blamed for the fact that he looked like his daed. He was a sweet, innocent little one who would never know his daed. He had no fault. Her own shortcomings sent her to the buggy this cool, clear evening.

"Are you coming in?" Jennie's middle girl, Celia, stuck her head out the doorway, her face a miniature of her mudder's. "It's too cold to be sitting out there. That's what Mudder says."

Bess shivered, but it wasn't from the cold. "I'm coming in." She hopped from the buggy and wrapped the reins around the hitching post. "I was just . . . thinking."

"I like to do my thinking inside where it's warm." Celia disappeared, leaving the door standing open. At that rate, it wouldn't be warm long.

Bess slipped in and shut the door behind her. The sound of laughter drew her toward the back of the house and the kitchen. Jennie stood at the stove, a teakettle in one hand. Mary Katherine sat at the table, Jennie's youngest, Francis, in her lap, a wooden horse in his chubby hands.

Laura looked up from slicing a loaf of what looked like banana bread. "You're here. Just in time. We're having a cup of tea and some bread before we start on the quilt for Leah and James's bopli."

"Where's Joshua?" Jennie peered past Bess as if the baby could be somewhere behind her, trotting in on his own. "We were looking forward to spoiling him."

"I left him with Hazel. He's been so fussy. He spits up a lot." Careful not to look at the other women, she slid into a chair across

150

from Mary Katherine. "Plus Levi and Gracie have had colds and now he has a cough. He doesn't sleep more than a few hours at a time."

"Maybe he's colicky." Jennie poured steaming water into a chipped brown cup and handed it to Bess. "Honey's on the table."

"How does a person know?" Bess inhaled the scent of chamomile and softened her tone. Not his fault. "It seems like all he does is cry."

"Have you thought about taking him to see Dr. Lowe?" Laura's gentle voice reminded Bess of that day when Joshua was born and the woman kissed her forehead as she laid him in Bess's arms. "An upset tummy and a cough is a lot for a little one. And his mudder."

"Maybe I just don't know how to be a good mudder." The catch in her voice shamed Bess. She swallowed the tears before they could betray her. "Hazel's so good with him. She knows just what to do."

"I remember how hard it was after Atlee passed." Jennie squeezed into the chair next to Bess. She sipped her tea, swallowed, and set the mug on the table. "Francis was a newborn. He must've felt my distress because he didn't eat good or sleep good for a long stretch. With time I settled down. So did he. You have Mattie and Hazel to help. You'll be fine." Her expression gave her away.

"Are you fine?" Bess set her cup on the table. "I'm so selfish. Is there something I can help you with?"

Jennie shook her head. She picked up her cup and tea sloshed over the edge, dripping on the table. "Micah was up during the night two nights in a row heaving and running a fever. Now Elizabeth has it. They pass cold and flu bugs around like ring-around-the-rosy."

Mary Katherine reached over and patted the other woman's hand. "That's why we're here. To help. I'll fix a casserole for tomorrow. Laura and Bess can help the girls straighten up the house."

"Nee. You're here to work on the quilt."

"Nee, not really. That was just an excuse to get our wily behinds in the front door. The quilt will wait. That bopli isn't coming for another six months." Laura shook a gnarled finger at Jennie. "We won't sit on our behinds when there's work to be done. I'll be back tomorrow to help with laundry."

Bess hopped to her feet. A sense of purpose, like an old friend who'd been away forever, joined her. She hustled over to the

152

sink and filled a bucket with soapy water. "I'll mop."

"Mop instead of mope." Laura's gentle tone held no judgment. "That's what we women do when times get rough. Work is salve for the soul. A person mends faster when she keeps her hands and her mind busy."

No doubt.

Time passed quickly as dishes were washed, floors mopped, and furniture dusted. Jennie's girls seemed pleased to have help. They sang and chatted and drilled Bess with questions about Joshua. Two hours later she realized she hadn't thought of Caleb all evening. She slipped into the kitchen where the aroma of potato-and-sausage casserole made her mouth water. Laura set the pan on the pot holders and smiled at her. "Smells good enough to eat, doesn't it?"

Bess hadn't had an appetite in a while, but Laura was right. "Did you plan this all along?"

"Plan what?" Laura picked up a washrag and scrubbed the counter. "We're just making ourselves useful."

"We always help out folks when they lose a loved one." Bess pondered a fact she'd always taken for granted. "But after a while, everyone goes back to their work at home and their families. Everything goes on. At least it does for everyone else. The person left behind might still be feeling blue."

"Jah, not everyone is on the same schedule. It behooves us to remember that and check up on folks once in a while. We're all guilty of moving on with our lives without thought for those left behind."

"I feel like I should hurry up and be all better. It's expected."

"It is expected, but you have to walk in your shoes. No one knows what that's like but you."

"How long did it take you to get over Eli passing?"

"I'll let you know when it happens." Laura stopped scrubbing. "It's not so much getting over it, it's learning to go on. You will learn to go on. You'll even marry again, most likely."

"Never." Bess snorted. Why would anyone want to take the chance of going through such an ordeal again? "I loved Caleb all my life."

"I was married to Eli longer than you've been alive." Laura laid the washrag on the washtub and turned to face Bess. The kerosene lamp's light softened the lines around her mouth and eyes. She looked younger than her years and pretty — if Bess could be the judge of such a worldly attribute. "You're young and just starting out. Gott will decide what the future holds for you."

Like He'd decided to take Caleb home after only a fraction of a second of married bliss. That same sinking sensation that sucked the strength from her body blew through Bess. She swallowed against the bitter, metallic taste in the back of her throat.

"He took my Caleb. Why would He do that?" The question bolted from Bess's heart. She could no more corral it than she could a wild, fearful stallion. "I know that sounds prideful, but I don't understand. I cannot understand. I know how I'm supposed to feel. I just can't find a way to get there."

She sank into the closest chair. Laura slipped over to her side and put her hand on Bess's shoulder. "Don't try to understand. Pray for acceptance. Pray for peace. Pray for joy. Pray for your bopli. Pray that you learn to submit to Gott's will. Once you do, peace and joy will follow."

Bess bowed her head and closed her eyes. Laura's hand tightened on her shoulder. The silence crackled with unspoken words. *Thy will be done, Gott. Peace. Joy.*

She would settle for peace. Joy was too much to ask for.

THIRTEEN

A man could only eat so much peach pie and ice cream. At first, it tasted like heaven. After the second piece, it tasted a little more earthly. Aidan cut into his third piece. He wasn't sure how that happened. He might be postponing the inevitable walk with Iris by saying yes when he really meant no.

She sat on the other side of the pine table, watching him eat with such a look of pleasure on her pretty face, he didn't want to disappoint her. He had disappointed her by waiting so long to make an appearance. The sow's farrowing. The bird flu. His second thoughts. Third thoughts, maybe. He couldn't keep her waiting much longer.

Seeing Bess with the *Englischer* outside the nursery had been a kick in the behind for him. Bess was getting on with her life. He needed to do the same. Caleb would want that. Aidan wanted what was best for his best friend's wife. Happiness did not involve an overgrown Englisch man with a wild beard and stained clothes. She was only buying plants. Nothing more.

Aidan took another bite. The pie tasted like sawdust now. Iris was a good woman, good fraa material. A decent cook, a fact to which the pie gave testimony, faithful, she had a strong back. She liked to work. What more did he require?

The feeling that he could spend the rest of his life with her at his side? He suppressed a groan. When had he become so fanciful?

The house was quiet. Her father and mother long asleep, same with her younger brothers and sisters. He should say something. Make conversation. They hadn't seen each other since Sunday service two weeks earlier. Nothing came to mind.

Aidan took another bite, chewed, and swallowed. He nearly choked. He laid the fork on the plate and pushed it back.

Iris shook her head, her face worried. "You didn't finish. Didn't you like it?"

"I ate three pieces. Doesn't that speak for itself?"

"Two and a half." She grinned. "Are you sure the crust wasn't a little tough? Mudder's is better. I can never cut the shortening and flour just right so it's tender like hers."

"It's gut, very gut."

"I'm not fishing for compliments." She tapped her fingers on the table. "I just want you to like my cooking, I guess."

"I do like your cooking."

"Gut. That's gut." She stood and picked up his plate. "More tea?"

He'd float away if he drank any more tea, and more tea would lead to more dead space that must be filled with conversation. "Nee."

"We could sit a spell on the porch."

"Or take a walk." Walking would be better than sitting. "Just a short one. I'm pretty tuckered out."

"I'd like a walk, but if you're too tired we can do it another night." She set the dirty dish in the tub in the sink and turned to face him. Her expression begged him not to back out now. "I'll wash this later. A breath of fresh air will do us good."

Like they were sick or not feeling well. Iris knew these things, it seemed. Aidan followed her out the back door and down the porch steps. Relief filtered through him. Outdoors he could think of something to say. They would walk and less talk would be required.

"What are you thinking about?" She skipped a little to keep up. Groaning inwardly, he slowed his pace. Iris tucked her hand in the crook of his arm. Her fingers were warm. "You're so quiet this evening. We haven't seen each other in forever, and you don't have anything to tell me?"

A mockingbird trilled in the branches of the elm tree overhead. He cast about for an answer that wouldn't hurt her feelings. "It's not you. I'm thinking about what to do next as far as the farm goes. Wait until the state gives me the go-ahead for a new flock, or find a new livelihood? It's a big decision."

"What other sort of livelihood?"

"I was thinking hogs. I already have three sows and one just had a litter, another will have one at the end of the month. They're a good cash crop."

"That's a good idea." Her enthusiasm brimmed over. "What about other animals? Sheep? Goats? You could diversify."

Diversify was a big word for a Plain woman. "Your daed talked about that at the supper table?"

"He was talking to Mr. Booker at the feed store the other day. I listen when they talk. Mr. Booker says having different animals is good for the land and good for the animals. He also said it's better to pasture-raise the

160

chickens than keep them all cooped up in a building. It's not natural, he says. They should run around and get sun and eat bugs instead of standing in their own poo."

Stan Booker was one of those free-range guys who liked to buy the overpriced chicken at the supermarket. It was expensive to raise pasture chickens because it took longer for them to get up to size. The expense inevitably was passed to the folks who simply wanted fried chicken on their table for supper. "My chickens don't stand in their own poo."

"I know that. I'm just telling you what he said." Iris smiled. "I try to pay attention so I can understand what you are dealing with. I think a good fraa helps her husband by knowing about these things and being able to put her two cents' worth in when decisions have to be made." She stopped talking and drew her hand away from his arm.

A response didn't come as readily as it should. She'd been thinking about how to be a good fraa to a chicken farmer. Her meaning was as plain as the snout on Ram's face.

"I can't believe I said that." The words came in a stuttered rush, so unlike the unflappable Iris he'd known since they started school. "I didn't mean to put you

161

on the spot. Forget I said all that. Erase it. Pretend we're just starting our walk. How long do the inspectors say it will be before you can start a new flock?"

"Six months minimum." He shouldn't ignore her earlier statement, much as she might say she wanted him to do it. She really didn't. She wanted him to rescue her. It was cruel not to do it. "I think a mann and a fraa should talk about problems and find answers together. It makes for a good marriage."

"Me too. Me too." Her hand returned to his arm. "My daed and mudder discuss, even though Daed has the final word."

"My daed wasn't much of a talker, but my mudder made up for it with her chatter."

"I remember your daed. He always looked so stern. Was he stern?"

"Sometimes. Though I always knew when he was disappointed in me, just by the way he looked."

Which seemed to be most of the time.

"He died young."

"His heart was bad. He just didn't know it." Gone at forty-six. Mudder had followed three years later. Cancer had taken longer, been crueler. "Gott's plan, I reckon."

By mutual, if unspoken agreement, they

turned and began the trek back to the house.

"If he were here, he'd say you're doing fine, taking care of the farm." Iris's voice was so soft, so caring. "So would your mudder."

"I hope so." He had been the logical one to take over the farm. Timothy had his own property already. Everyone knew Paul walked to his own beat, a beat no one else seemed to hear. He had his own little house on an acre of land on the edge of Jamesport. He showed up for church each Sunday, but seemed far removed from the community in every other way. His sisters had married and followed their manns to other Missouri communities. "They worked hard to bring all of us up right."

A few more seconds and they were at the front porch steps. Iris paused, her hands clasped in front of her as if ready to pray. She bit her lower lip, her eyes shiny in the full moon. Light bounced off her white cap and apron. "Everyone's asleep. It's so quiet. It's like we have the place to ourselves, isn't it?"

Sort of. Except her daed slept somewhere on the second floor. Soundly, Aidan hoped. "A little."

"We could go back inside or we could sit

163

on the porch. I could fetch us some more tea."

"I'm really tired."

Disappointment dashed across her face and disappeared. "I understand. It's getting late. You have a lot to think about." She took a tiny step in his direction and craned her head toward him. "And it's laundry day. I'll have plenty to do."

Another tiny step his direction. She had such fine features. High cheekbones, a long thin nose, full lips, beautiful blue eyes.

Full, soft-looking lips.

And yet. He slid his hat from his head and turned it in circles in his hands. "A lot to do too. A lot."

She nodded. "A lot." Her lips parted.

Aidan could hear her breathing, light and quick. Her hands fluttered, then stilled. She smelled of flowers.

He took a step back. He couldn't do it. Gott knew why. He simply couldn't. It wouldn't be right. He slapped the hat on his head. "I better get going, then."

She sighed and ducked her head. "Of course. Come back anytime."

"I will. It won't be so long next time."

"I'll hold you to that." She wrapped her arms around her middle, her smile waning. "Come for supper one night. You know

he smacked it with the hammer.

Caleb singing "Das Loblied" at the top of his lungs while she laid out his favorite PBJ sandwiches and barbecue chips on Sheetrock balanced between two sawhorses.

Stop it. Stop it. Stop it.

Here she stood, enveloped in the past so soon after her prayers in Jennie's kitchen. She prayed for acceptance. She prayed for renewed peace and joy. She prayed she found the strength to accept God's will for her. Yet here she stood in the house her dead husband had been building for her.

"I'm sorry, Gott."

She was losing her mind. Talking aloud to Gott as if He couldn't hear her every thought before she uttered it. "Truly, I am."

This long, rectangular space would've been the front room. She closed her eyes and inhaled the scent of wood and Sheetrock. The house already smelled musty. Unoccupied. Never occupied. Bereft and filled with should-have-beens and might-have-beens. Joshua's first steps. His first words. The birth of a brother or sister. Christmas holidays and family prayers. Weddings and church services. Welcoming of grandbabies. Two people growing old together.

Empty of life.

Solomon would decide soon what to do with it. Likely it would be finished by Caleb's brother Elijah. He hadn't said anything, but it was apparent to a person with eyes in her head that he and Clara Miller would marry in the fall.

She opened her eyes and slipped through the doorway into the kitchen. No woodstove graced the room. No prep table. Counters had been installed and a sink. She cocked her head and pictured the pine table her daed planned to make for her. With four chairs. A window over the sink would allow her to watch the purple martins when they arrived in the spring and took up homemaking in the little apartment complex Caleb had built on the evenings and weekends — as if he didn't get enough carpentry during the day. She breathed, smelling the aroma of baking bread.

She jerked her eyes open. Nee. Baking bread made her think of that day. The day Caleb died. She left the bread baking to Hazel these days and stayed out of the kitchen whenever her sister-in-law popped the pans into the wood-burning stove.

The heavenly scent was spoiled for her forever.

Freeman would say there was a thin line between heaven and hell. A person didn't want to step over that line.

She turned and fled back through the doorway into the front room and down the hallway. The bedrooms were mere shells. Skeletons. Bare walls and cement floors. One, two, three, four, five, six. Three on each side. A one-story house because Caleb said that would be easier for her. Running clean laundry up and down stairs or carrying babies would be easier this way. Not that Plain folks looked for easy, but Caleb thought of her comfort. He was like that. "Ach, Caleb."

The words reverberated in the cold, empty space.

She rushed on, until only the last bedroom remained. A little bigger than the others. Their bedroom. Caleb's toolbox sat in the corner. She should give that to Luke or Elijah. They would appreciate having their older brother's tools. Silly to leave them sitting here, unused. A beat-up red coffee can overflowing with nails sat next to it. A hammer lay across the metal box. She picked it up. It felt heavy and solid in her hand. Like Caleb. She could almost feel the warmth of his hand on it. His stubby, callused fingers with jagged fingernails, always needing a good scrubbing to get the hard work out from under them, had gripped this hammer. A sob burned her throat.

Nee. *Peace, Lord. I beg of You. Give me peace. Help me to bend to Your will. Return my joy. I can't bear this.*

You must bear it. You're called to bear the hard times as well as the times of joy.

The words brushed against her cheeks as surely as if the wings of a bird in flight had touched them.

"Gott?"

She was losing her mind, to be sure.

"Gott, is it You?"

"What are you doing here in the dark?"

She shrieked and whirled. The hammer flew from her hand. It somersaulted across the room, pinged against the bare cement floor, and skidded to a stop with a painful thump against Aidan's work boot.

"Why would you sneak up on a person like that?"

"I didn't sneak. I saw the buggy and a light so I stopped." Aggravation made his voice rough. "I called out at the door. No one answered. Who were you talking to?"

"No one. You must've whispered then."

"I heard your voice. I didn't whisper." His expression hidden in the shadows, he picked up the hammer. "I yelled. You were deep in thought or conversation."

"Nee. I mean, thought, jah, but not conversation. It's only me."

He didn't look convinced. He slipped the hammer end over end in his hands, like a baton. "What are you doing out here?"

Mooning over what couldn't be helped. "What are *you* doing here?"

"Like I said, I was driving by and I saw the buggy and the light —"

"Driving by? At this time of night?" She stopped. Courting, of course. Heat burned a trail across her neck and cheeks. "Never mind. None of my business."

He moved closer. She took a step back. He stopped. "Are you all right?"

"I'm fine."

"Why are you here then?"

They were standing, just the two of them, in the room that would have been Caleb's and her bedroom. Ridiculous as it seemed, it didn't feel right. Giving wide berth to Aidan, she moved toward the door. "I wanted to see it."

"Why?"

She turned her back on him and slipped through the door. Footsteps told her he followed.

"Bess."

She picked up the skirt on her dress and strode faster and faster until she burst through the space that represented the front door. Outside, she imagined for one brief second, Caleb had finished the porch. There would be hickory rocking chairs. They would've planted honeysuckle. Maybe even roses. Yellow roses. She could smell them. And tulips. She loved tulips, in many colors.

She and Aidan could sit on the porch and talk. No one would give it a second thought or whisper behind their backs. In the old days. Now?

"Bess."

His voice floated through the doorway, husky, as if he might be catching a cold.

"I don't know what I'm doing here."

Caleb stomped through the door and halted at her side. No, not Caleb. Aidan. He smelled of soap and manly smells just as her dead mann had smelled. The thought made her throat ache. He stood for a moment without speaking. His breathing sounded labored. He cleared his throat, once, twice. "I come here sometimes too."

"You do?"

"We had good workdays here. Good conversations while we worked. He always had a joke to tell or a story."

Bess ducked her head. She didn't want to think of those times. Tree branches backlit by a half-moon dipped and danced. The sound of leaves rustling and frogs croaking in an impromptu concert reminded her of long evenings playing ollie ollie oxen free until it was too dark to see.

"The last time I talked to him was in the kitchen that morning after breakfast. I told him I would make stew for supper." Simple, ordinary conversations they'd had hundreds of times. Conversations now worth their weight in everything valuable and sacred. She hadn't told him she loved him. Nor he, her. It was a given. They were married. No need to dwell on it. *I love you, Caleb.* "He said to go easy on the cabbage. He was never a big fan of cabbage."

"I wasn't a fan of him eating cabbage either." A faint note of laughter tinged the words.

"Why?"

"Gave him gas."

She put her hand to her mouth, but the snort escaped. "I reckon I can understand that."

They were quiet. A mockingbird trilled, its plaintive song soft on the night breeze. She wanted to go on standing here next to her friend who understood in a way no one else could. "Remember that time in school when you let the garter snake loose behind Joanna's feet, and she hopped up and ran to the front of the room in front of everyone? Ruth and Sophie ran right up there with her."

"But not you. You just laughed." Aidan chuckled. "I knew it was wrong. But I wanted —"

"Wanted to play around instead of doing your multiplication tables?"

"Something like that." His tone turned pensive. His eyes were warm. Something in them made her own cheeks heat. "I wanted you to notice . . ."

"Notice what?"

He shook his head. "Nothing. It was a long time ago."

"Not that long." Suddenly his answer was important. Everything about the way he held his body said it was important to him. "You were always doing things like that. Playing pranks. Telling jokes. Then you stopped."

"You had eyes for Caleb only. Even then."

It was true. She had lived for her sixteenth birthday and the right to attend the singings. The very first one, Caleb drew her away early and took her for a ride. She never looked back. "I'm glad we didn't waste time seeking the company of others. As it is we had so little time together."

"I'm glad you were happy together."

They'd all been happy, hadn't they? "Why

did you stop with the pranks?"

"I reckon I grew up."

She had liked the fun-loving Aidan. It never occurred to her that he sought her attention. The grown-up Aidan had her attention now. She pushed the thought away. It could only bring pain. She didn't need more of that. "Our mudders might beg to differ if they saw us traipsing around out here in the dark instead of back home doing grown-up things."

"Grieving is a grown-up thing."

He had a point there. She swallowed against the pain. "Danki."

"For what?" His hand crept in her direction, then fell back to his side. "I haven't done anything."

Her fingers ached to be held. Her entire body ached. An ache that likely would go unappeased for the rest of her life. "You don't expect me to be done grieving like everyone else?"

His harsh laugh held no mirth. "Not when I haven't managed it myself."

"Do you think Gott is disappointed in us?" She tried to make herself care. Gott had done something cruel to her. She was disappointed in Him. Not words she dared utter aloud. "In me?"

"I think humans disappoint Him all the

time, but He never gives up on one of His children."

A thought to be held on to in the middle of the night. The grown-up Aidan had acquired wisdom the hard way with the loss of his own parents far too young. "I'll try to remember that."

"You should go home. You're tired."

"How do you know I'm tired?"

"You have a bopli. I reckon he gets you up at night. I reckon he's hungry about now too."

Aidan was right. Still, she lingered. "I feel close to Caleb here too. Closer to what we were going to be, but will never be."

"I'm sorry."

Bess opened her mouth. Fear that a sob would escape forced her to close it again.

"It's my fault." Aidan's words were a bare whisper she had to strain to hear. "I'm so sorry."

Nee, nobody's fault. Gott's will. Gott's fault? She shook her head. Saying those words aloud could never be taken back.

"I asked Caleb to go to town that day." Aidan shifted his feet. He crossed his arms over his chest as if cold. "I could've gone, but I wanted to finish what I was doing. He dickered with me about it, but I told him I'd get the next trip."

176

"He liked going into town. He liked chatting with Mr. Riker at the hardware store and stopping for a doughnut at Louella's Bakery." She wanted to erase the sadness and the guilt in Aidan's voice. He'd been waiting a while to say this to her, that was clear. He needn't worry. She didn't blame him. He simply reminded her of what she wanted to forget, but never could. "He probably had a few dozen in the buggy when he started back. Maple logs and elephant ears and jelly doughnuts too. He had such a sweet tooth. He'd bring them home and tease me with them, telling me I would be fat and happy married to him."

She had been. Not fat, but happy. A hundred doughnuts couldn't erase the bitter taste in her mouth. She longed for a draught of fresh, sweet well water.

"Strange you should say that." A tiny tremor shook Aidan's voice. He cleared his throat. "He did have doughnuts in the buggy. They were strewn across the road."

He stopped, but the image grew in Bess's mind as clear as any photograph she'd ever seen. Nothing would erase it. "I should go."

"Jah, you should. I'll follow you."

"No need."

"You shouldn't be out on the road alone so late."

177

"No one out there but the night critters."

"I don't worry about the four-legged ones."

Bess didn't worry about two-or four-legged creatures now. The worse thing that could happen to her had already happened. She handed him the lantern and climbed into her buggy. He returned it, his features clearly etched in its harsh glare. He looked tired and sad and older than she knew him to be. She wanted to relieve him of that burden. "You don't have to be sorry. Caleb's days were done. That's what Freeman says. That's what Scripture says. Gott took him home."

He shrugged. "I know, but it's also hard for those who are left behind."

"It is."

"So I'm sorry I couldn't save him for you. I'm sorry for your loss and your sadness." His voice cracked. He stepped back into the darkness. "I'm sorry I can't fix it for you."

He needed this. He needed to say the words, so Bess did the only thing she could. She accepted his apology. "It's okay. You look as tired as I feel."

"Tomorrow is another day."

"Tomorrow is another day."

Whether they liked it or not. She waited until he climbed into his buggy to start home. To her surprise, the harmonious *clip-clop* of his horse's hooves joined with hers gave her a bit of comfort. The night didn't seem so cold and empty.

Tomorrow would indeed bring a new day.

FIFTEEN

A croupy cough turned to fussing and then to all-out wailing. Bess stopped singing, laid the trowel on the ground, leaned back on her haunches, and wiped at her face. "Jesus Loves the Little Children" didn't seem to impress Joshua. The sound of her voice simply mingled with his cries. She tried so hard, but nothing seemed to help. If the pain of childbirth didn't make a woman reconsider having more children, a baby's continual fussing might. Not that having more was an option for Bess.

The midmorning sun warmed her. She usually loved the feel of the dirt in her hands and the richness of the purples, reds, pinks, and yellows against the dark, black earth. The smell of fresh dirt rising up around her usually calmed her spirit. Not today. Sleep had been slow to come after her encounter with Aidan at the house. Her mind kept picturing him standing on the slab outside the house, his fists clenched, his head down. His words kept running through her mind. *"I'm sorry. I'm sorry."*

And then to the fists themselves. To his hands. To his long fingers, so different from Caleb's. Why did she keep thinking of those hands and the way they reached toward her and then fell away, leaving that ache for human touch to multiply until her entire body hurt?

Stop it. Stop it. The words were a refrain in her head that had built to a crescendo during the night and turned into a headache that no pill would assuage.

"I'm sorry. I'm sorry."

No one's fault. She forced away the thought that accompanied her day and night. Gott's fault.

Thy will be done.

Gott would know her true feelings. He saw into every nook and cranny of her heart.

I'm sorry, Gott.

The morning hadn't improved with time. She'd hoped laying the baby on a blanket under the elm tree next to the flower beds would calm him, but Joshua continued to fuss. She'd changed his diaper and fed him. Two minutes later, he spat up half of it down the front of her apron. She hadn't eaten onion or anything spicy that might upset his tummy. The cough seemed to hang around, but he had no other symptoms of a cold. No fever. No runny nose. Just the same cough Levi and Gracie had after their colds. What else did a baby his age have to cry about? Even the sound of her voice lifted in song didn't help.

Gott, I can't do this. I'm tired. It's not that I don't love him. I'm tired. I'm so tired.

That had to be it. It couldn't be that she held him, looked into his face, and felt despair. A despair so deep it made her bones ache.

"What are you doing? Why is the baby crying?"

Bess forced herself to turn at the sound of Mattie's querulous voice. Her mother-in-law stood on the bottom step in her bare feet. Her kapp hung around her neck, leaving her disheveled bun exposed. Bess rose to her feet. "I'm planting the flowers I bought at the nursery. Remember, I told you I was going to do that today."

"Caleb is crying." Aggravation mixed with uncertainty in Mattie's high-pitched voice. She cocked her head. "Don't you hear him? Surely, you hear him."

"It's Joshua crying." Bess swallowed against ever-threatening tears. She softened her tone. "Not Caleb. You know it's not Caleb."

Mattie blinked. "Joshua? Who's Joshua?"

"Caleb's son." Bess tried to keep concern from her voice. Mattie wandered about disconsolate, but she still cooked and cleaned and sewed. Sometimes she sang hymns from the Sunday service as she pumped the pedal on the treadle sewing machine. If she remembered those words, why couldn't she remember Joshua? "He was born on February twelfth. Remember?"

She stopped short of reminding Bess that Caleb had died on January tenth. A mere two month earlier and yet it seemed like a hundred years. Mattie wavered. She put her hand on the wooden railing for a second and then padded across the grass toward Joshua. She scooped him up. "There, there, bopli, there, there." She shook her head, her forehead wrinkled. "You're wrong. This is Caleb. What are you doing with my bopli?"

Bess fought the urge to snatch him back from his groossmammi. Mattie raised six kinner, she could hold one bopli. "He's your grandson. Joshua."

"Nee, nee. Look, he has brown eyes and his cheeks and his nose and even his hair is the same color." Mattie snuggled him closer to her chest. Joshua hiccupped a sob. "Why

183

do you let him cry like this? Why didn't you tell me? I would've changed his diaper and fed him. I'm a mudder. A very good mudder."

"I know you are. I married your son and he was a very good son." Along with the rest of the kinner Solomon and Mattie had raised. Not a troublemaker in the bunch. They wouldn't dare under Mattie's eagle eyes. Bess stepped around the flowers she'd planted and went to Mattie. She took her arm. "Why don't you sit on the step and I'll fix your hair."

"My hair?" A horrified expression spreading across her face, Mattie shifted Joshua to one arm and patted her head. "How did that happen?"

"It doesn't matter. Sit and I'll fix it."

"Fine, but I keep the bopli."

"You can keep him for now."

She led Mattie to the steps and waited for her to settle in. Then she loosened the bun and went to work. Mattie began to hum in a singsong, tuneless sort of way that reminded Bess of her own mother. Joshua's sobs quieted. Mattie continued to hum, the sound mingling with the buzz of bees drawn to the new flowers and crickets conversing in the yard. Bess let the sounds wash over her. The knot between her shoulders eased.

"There you go. You're all fixed up."

"So are you." Mattie cocked her head toward the baby. Joshua's eyes fluttered and closed. He slept. Finally. "He just needed a little help nodding off. I'm surprised you didn't realize that."

Stung by her accusing tone, Bess stepped back. "I sang to him. That usually helps."

"He wanted to be held." Mattie tottered up the steps past Bess. "I'll put him in the cradle and watch him."

Her tone left no doubt she thought Bess incapable of doing it herself.

Sixteen

A woman who'd raised six children knew a thing or two about babies. Bess watched as Mattie trotted into the house, still humming. Her mother-in-law knew about babies, but she was confused about this baby. She believed the baby in her arms belonged to her and as such, she would take charge of him. Had Caleb's death brought this on Mattie, or was it an illness long in the making? The thought only served to make Bess's heart hurt more. Mattie had an illness, but she still knew how to comfort a baby. Bess couldn't comfort Joshua. She couldn't calm him because she had no peace and joy to give. Swaying, she grabbed the railing and held on.

Hazel shoved through the screen door. She glanced back toward the dark interior, then let the door close. "Let Mudder watch him. It gives her comfort."

Bess sank onto the step. Hazel plopped

down next to her. The silence held for several seconds. Bess replayed Mattie's words in her head. *"What are you doing with my bopli?"* How to broach the subject without making Hazel feel worse. There didn't seem to be a way. "She's getting worse."

"No doubt." Hazel's tone was crisp. "But she was right."

Not the response Bess expected. "Right? About what?"

"We could hear him crying from the kitchen. You didn't pick him up."

"I brought him out here to try to calm him." As a last resort. She'd done everything she could, hadn't she? "I sang to him."

"It didn't work. He has a cough. Being outside probably doesn't help it." Hazel picked at a hangnail. "Why didn't you bring him back inside?"

Why indeed? She was exhausted from arising every two hours during the night to feed him. Something a new mother should expect and accept. "I needed to plant the flowers. I thought the sunshine and fresh air would soothe him. And me."

"If it's too much for you, I can watch him." Hazel put an arm around Bess's shoulders and squeezed. "All you have to do is ask. If you need help or don't know what to do, ask."

"It's not too much." Bess drew away from her touch. Hazel might be years older, but she'd always been a friend, long before becoming a sister-in-law. She meant well. She was kind to offer. "I'm able to take care of my bopli. Besides, you have your own four."

"What's one more?"

"I'm capable."

"I'm not saying you aren't." Hazel's eyes were full of sympathy behind her round glasses. "I think you might not want to do it right now — because of everything that's happened."

"You think I don't want to take care of Joshua because Caleb's gone? That makes no sense." Except it was true. "I should love him more. I do love him more."

"There's no right way to feel about all this. Only how you feel." Hazel leaned forward, head down, as if staring at her bare toes wiggling on the step. "You might have that sickness women sometimes get after they have a baby. It's not your fault."

"I'm not sick. Just sad."

"That's part of the sickness. I've read about it."

"I'm fine." Bess rose and did an about-face toward the house. Joshua was her baby and she loved him. All new mothers had to learn how to cope. "Nothing a little uninterrupted sleep wouldn't cure."

"Then let me keep an eye on him for you tonight while you sleep. We can move him into the bedroom with the kinner. He's old enough. You won't hear him every time he fusses, and he'll learn to put himself back to sleep."

"You have your own kinner to worry about."

"I'll move the cradle for you."

Hazel had a determined streak that reminded Bess of Caleb. They were cut from Mattie's cloth in that respect. Bess let the screen door close behind her, careful not to let it slam. None of this was Hazel's fault and she was only trying to help. As she had done many times before. Advice for courting Caleb. Advice about baptism. Advice for the wedding and the wedding night. And married life. Hazel had been willing to share every nugget of experience as Bess needed it.

So Bess would count to ten forward and backward and give her friend the benefit of the doubt. She counted a second time. It didn't help. She stomped into the kitchen and washed her hands, then rubbed them on the towel harder than necessary. Maybe a batch of oatmeal-raisin cookies would help. Cooking soothed her. Instead, she sank onto the chair at the table and laid her head down. Just for a second. Only a second.

Gott, is it supposed to be this hard?

She wanted a different life. Not this one. Gott would strike her dead for being so ungrateful. She had a healthy baby. She had Caleb's family. She could go to Haven and live with her own family.

Bess sat up. Was that what she wanted? An ache so intense her chest hurt filled her. Mudder and Daed had joined Christopher and Jasper in Haven a few years earlier, taking Mercy and Grace with them. If it hadn't been for Caleb, Bess would've gone too. It wasn't that far, but on days like today it seemed a world away. Taking Joshua away from Solomon and Mattie seemed cruel. They had their other grandchildren. But not Caleb's son. The only grandchild he would give them.

Nee, she couldn't do that to Mattie, much as she longed for familiar faces in a fresh, new place. A starting over. The poor woman had suffered enough. Bess couldn't be that selfish.

She rubbed her eyes and straightened her kapp. Time to stop feeling sorry for herself.

She studied the kitchen, searching for something to do. Hazel had washed the breakfast dishes and put a pot of beans on the stove to simmer for the noonday meal. A fresh batch of bread dough rested under a pale-blue dish towel on the counter. Even the floor looked freshly mopped. They didn't need her, not really. She was another mouth to feed.

"Gott helps those who help themselves." The words echoed in her mind in Freeman's sonorous Sunday-service voice. He had said once these words didn't appear anywhere in Scripture. But that didn't make them un-true, according to Freeman.

How? How, Gott? How can I help myself. Give me a hint.

Did she just give Gott an order? Tell Him what to do? *Nee, Gott, nee.*

Shaking her head at her own inability to talk sense even to Gott, Bess grabbed the Jamesport *Tri-County Weekly* newspaper and shook out the pages so they laid flat on the wooden surface. The scent of ink and newsprint wafted from it. Black smudged her white fingers. A recipe for chicken pot pie. They didn't need that, Hazel made a scrumptious pot pie. An article about teenagers arrested for underage drinking behind the bar and grill Saturday night.

191

Nothing new there.

She turned the page. Classified ads. She desired something with a desperation that scared her. Her heart's desire could not be found in the want ads of a small-town newspaper. She longed for her one true love. How could Gott be so cruel to tear him away from her after so short a time? A time that passed as quickly as a single breath?

She closed her eyes. *Gott, give me the strength to keep breathing.*

She forced herself to open them once again. Nothing had changed. The bright colors that painted the days before Caleb's death were still gone, replaced by drab grays.

She placed her index finger on the first ad, the way Caleb used to do when he read. He'd never been much of a student and reading came hard to him. He said the letters looked jumbled up, all catawampus. It didn't matter. He didn't need to read to farm and when he did need something read, she did it for him. The first ad offered a litter of Chihuahuas to anyone who would take them. Six puppies ready for good homes. Nee, puppies they did not need.

Ads for garage sales, a 2004 green Ford pickup truck with a hundred-thousand miles on it and four new tires available for best offer. Not something she needed. She bent closer, willing herself to think of nothing else.

A sewing machine for sale. They had three of those in the house. More than plenty. A table and six chairs and a water bed. How did one sleep on a bed that sloshed when you turned over? *Don't think. Don't think.*

HELP WANTED.

Yes, she wanted help too.

A maid willing to work hard cleaning house and bedrooms, helping in the kitchen and miscellaneous other duties at the newly reopened Heartland Bed-and-Breakfast. Under new ownership. Must be willing to work hard and be nice to guests. Decent wages. Apply in person. Amish Girls welcome. Scalawags, lazy bums, and scam artists need not come by. You know who you are and so do we.

The words made her smile. She read the ad a second and a third time. Someone with attitude had written this ad. Someone who had gumption like she used to have. Amish girls. That was her. She was willing to work hard and be nice. The ache in her chest that had been her closest friend for months eased a fraction. She recognized the address. Nelly and Ted Robertson had owned the Heartland B and B for years, until they retired in November and moved to Florida for beaches and warmer weather.

The FOR SALE sign had been up for a few months. She'd been too preoccupied to notice if it had been removed. She smoothed the paper. Her job experience was limited to the family produce stand frequented by Jamesport residents in the spring and tourists in the summer. She could make change better than her sisters, and she wasn't too shy to chat with strangers who bought their cucumbers and tomatoes.

In fact, it had been her idea to expand their inventory to canned goods, jams, jellies, and baked goods during the peak months and after they had less produce to offer.

A door opened in Bess's mind's eye. More like an escape hatch. The chains fell away. The padlock hurled to the floor with a clang. The door swung wider and light pierced the gloomy recesses.

Solomon and Mattie might not like it. The bishop might not like it. How could they not? Money was tight. Their farms weren't big enough to produce the kind of cash crops needed to support their families in these days of megafarms. Big businesses,

194

Caleb had called them. Family farms were a thing of the past her daed said. She only half listened as she baked biscuits and chopped vegetables, but she recognized her husband's frown as he poured over the spreadsheets in his accounting books. The same look appeared on Isaac's and Solomon's faces these days as they sat huddled over the kitchen table, the propane lamp spotlighting the bald spot on the back of her brother-in-law's head. She could help. She could pay her own way. Joshua's and hers.

Joshua. How could she work with a bopli so small, so dependent on her? She had to feed him.

Hazel had offered to care for him. She wanted to care for him. They had a manual pump. She'd used it for the trip to the store and her visit with Jennie Troyer. Joshua didn't mind, as long as he received nourishment.

The longing to escape seeped into Bess's marrow.

"What are you doing?"

At the sound of Hazel's voice, Bess jumped and slapped the newspaper shut. The offending want ad disappeared from sight. Feeling like a child who'd opened her birthday present early, she studied the ink on her hands. "Nothing."

"Your nose is red."

"It is?"

"Are you coming down with something?" Hazel passed by, a stack of dish towels in her hands. "Or have you been crying?"

"Neither."

Hazel shifted the towels so she carried them under one arm. Her free hand went to her belly. She grimaced. "Ach."

"What is it?"

"Nothing. Just a bit of a tummy ache."

Bess studied her sister-in-law. Hazel's face had turned white. She heaved a breath. Her hands cupped her stomach. Her round belly. "You're expecting." Jealousy, sharp as barbed wire, wound itself around Bess's neck, a painful, tight noose. "You're having another bopli."

Hazel's chest heaved. After a few seconds, she wiped at her face with the back of her sleeve. She sighed. "I'm so sorry."

"Sorry?" Bess stood and went to her. She swallowed hard, willing the pain to subside. "This is joyful news."

"For me and Isaac, jah, but I know how it must hurt you to think of us with yet another bopli when you can't . . . won't . . . It grieves me to cause you more hurt."

Bess swallowed against the pain in her

196

throat. "It's not your fault and you should never be sad over the gift of another child. I would give so much . . ."

"That's what I mean." Hazel swiped at her face again. "It breaks my heart to think that Caleb won't know this child. It breaks my heart that he doesn't know his own child."

"Mine too." Bess rubbed Hazel's shoulder, hoping she wouldn't notice how her hands shook. She would be stuck here in this house watching her sister-in-law's figure swell with each passing day until another baby cried in the night and suckled at his mother's chest. "It's not your fault. I'll be fine."

She trudged back to the desk. The newspaper caught her gaze. "I was thinking. I wondered what you might think of an idea I had. A way that I might feel better."

Hazel tottered after her and plopped down on a straight-back chair on the other side. Her eyes were bright with tears behind glasses that had slid down her nose, her dark eyes darker against fair skin from which all color had seeped. Her freckles stood out in stark relief. "What is it? I want to help."

Bess swiveled the newspaper so the ad faced the other woman. "I was thinking of getting a job."

Hazel's thick eyebrows, so like Solomon's, popped up. Her mouth dropped open. Her gaze dropped to the newspaper. She settled the towels in her lap and let her finger trace the lines, just the way her brother's always had. "You want to hire out as a farmhand?"

"Nee, nee, silly, the maid at the B and B."

Hazel's frown grew. Her thick eyebrows became one across her forehead. "I don't know. What would Mudder and Daed say? What would Isaac say? What would Freeman say?"

"I'm a grown woman. A widow with a bopli. I should do my part. I know times are hard."

Many of the young women in the district worked in the restaurants and stores owned by their families, which the church had approved at the meeting of the *Gmay* a few years ago. Farming wasn't enough anymore. For the first time in her life, Bess answered to no man. Not her daed. Not her mann. It made her sad to think it. A woman should have a mann as the head of the house. "Isaac is your mann, not mine. It's not his place to provide for me. Your parents are not mine."

"I know." Hazel smoothed the paper. "But you have a bopli. We don't leave our boplin for jobs."

"Fraas who have manns don't."

Hazel chewed her lower lip. "It isn't right to use that argument."

"It's true. You said you would take care of Joshua for me if I ever needed it."

"I meant at night so you could sleep or if you needed to take a walk."

"I need this."

Hazel rubbed her eyes. She delivered a quivering smile. "You know, I used to wonder if you were my friend because you wanted to get close to Caleb or because you really wanted to be friends."

"What are you talking about? You let me be your friend. You let me follow you around when the other girls told me to run along and play."

"I'm seven years older than you are. No one expected us to be friends."

"We had things in common."

"Like we loved Caleb."

"Jah, and we liked to play outside when we were supposed to be inside learning to sew."

"And build snowmen and throw snowballs at the boys instead of baking rhubarb pie." Hazel lifted her apron to her face and gave it a good swipe. "For Caleb, I'll do this. And for Joshua. I will care for him as if he was my own. Mudder will help. It will give her comfort to do it."

"Danki."

"Don't thank me. You still have to face the bishop and Mudder and Daed."

"First I have to get the job." Bess stood. The open door beckoned. "There's no point in asking if they already gave the job to someone else or they don't want me."

"Amish girls are hard workers and they don't ask for as much pay. They'll want you."

"I've never worked for Englischers." She paused, surprised at the sudden feeling of a burden lifting from her shoulders. "I don't know how to use the appliances. Maybe I'm not the person they should hire."

"You can learn to use a vacuum and a dishwasher. I reckon they'll have one of those too. They'll show you how to use it. You are a hard worker with a good head on your shoulders. They'll see that."

Hazel's kind words did little to assuage the nerves leaping and somersaulting in Bess's stomach. She patted her kapp. She studied her hands. No dirt under the finger-nails. She glanced down. Her apron, on the other hand, was covered with dirt and splotches of spit-up. "I need to change."

"You'll go now?"

"Now, before they give the job to someone else."

"What about feeding Joshua?"

"I have the manual pump. I can pump enough to tide Joshua over. I won't be gone long."

"I'll pray that Gott's plan for you will reveal itself so you will be happy and content again." Hazel's voice cracked. She ducked her head. "You made Caleb happy. I want happy for you."

Gott's plan seemed to involve misery and despair, but Bess clamped her mouth shut. She would not complain. She would simply see where this path took her. She scurried to the kitchen door and up the stairs.

She was headed in the right direction. She wouldn't think of Caleb. Joshua would be fine with Hazel. Better than with his own mudder. She couldn't look back, only forward to the open door that led someplace else, anyplace else.

SEVENTEEN

The B and B could use a coat of paint. The long, white columns had chipped paint that left gaping wounds in the wood. The grass needed mowing. Weeds huddled together in otherwise barren flower beds that wrapped around the porch. Her stomach roiling, Bess hopped from the buggy and tied the reins to the hitching post. She paused on the cracked sidewalk in front of the two-story white house and shielded her eyes with her hand. An old buggy sat in the front yard. Its leather seats were cracked and faded. Weeds grew up around the wooden wheels. Why did they have a buggy as a yard ornament?

All the way into town, she'd rehearsed her lines. *I'm here to apply for the job. No, I've never had a job before, but I've cooked and cleaned every day since I was a little girl. No, I don't have a husband who needs me at home. I can work anytime you need me.*

What else would they want to know?

How sore her heart was? How angry her soul was?

It seemed unlikely either would be on a job application.

"You — who, who are you?"

A high voice floated over her head. Bess looked up and squinted against the sun.

A woman sat in a rocker on the second-story porch. She waved. Bess waved back. "I'm Bess."

The woman arose and went to the railing. She leaned over too far for Bess's liking. "Good afternoon, Bess."

"Afternoon."

"Are you here about the job?" She had an accent that spoke of sweet tea and *bless your heart, child.* "Tell me you're here about the job."

How did she know? "Yes."

"Come on up."

Come on up? Bess hesitated at the steps and looked up again.

The woman flapped both hands. "Just follow the stairs."

The screen door creaked even more than the wooden steps did. Bess slipped inside and gave her eyes a chance to adjust to the darker interior. The stairs were to her right. To her left, the house opened up into a living room filled with dark, overstuffed chairs loaded with embroidered pillows arranged around a big, fancy-looking piano. Bookshelves filled with rows upon rows of hardback books took up one whole wall. A chandelier of dangly glass hung from the ceiling. Lots of dusting here. The floor featured a thick carpet with pink and pale-blue flowers on a royal-blue background so that meant the use of a vacuum cleaner. That was okay. Her friends who worked in Englisch homes were allowed to use electrical appliances.

She put a hand on the slick banister with its dark varnished wood and trotted up the winding staircase that took her to the second floor where she found a hallway with four doors, all open. She couldn't help herself. She peeked. Blue. The room on her left was very blue. Blue curtains. A blue-and-white quilt on a canopy bed that she would need a step stool to change the sheets. Paintings of girls in gingham dresses and white aprons hung on the wall. No TV. No radio.

She found herself tiptoeing for some reason as she slipped to the next room. Pink. If the other room was blue, this was the pink room. Again with the big canopy bed and tons of pillows. How did they sleep with so many pillows on the bed?

On her right was a much bigger room. Outside hung a sign that read Veranda Room. She slipped in. A huge bed with a Broken Dishes quilt filled one side of the room. On the other they'd placed two overstuffed chairs facing a fireplace. The painting over the mantel featured some Plain children fishing in a stream. They looked so happy. On the table between the chair were two Plain dolls. She knew they were Plain not only by the clothes but the fact that they had no faces. She couldn't understand the fascination of Englischers with Plain folks. They had their own dolls and toys and many choices in clothes. Many choices in places to go and people to see. Why come to little Jamesport, population five hundred something, for that one or two weeks they had of vacation in a year? They could go to Mexico or Spain or China. She thought it would be nice to go to the beach. She and Caleb had talked about taking the bus to Texas to the Gulf Coast.

But they never had.

"Are you there? Come on out. Come through the Veranda Room." The lady's voice carried. She sounded as if she were used to folks doing her bidding. "Don't worry. We're not open for business yet, so you won't find anyone in the rooms."

Bess followed the sound of her voice. "I'm here."

"Who exactly are you, dear?" The woman plopped a glass of tea onto a table next to her rocking chair. Despite the lines around her blue eyes and her thin red-painted lips, she had dark auburn hair without one gray strand. "Have a seat, tell me about yourself."

Bess perched on the edge of the rocker. Her hands felt sweaty despite the cool breeze wafting across the porch. Her heart seemed to have acquired a new, ragged rhythm. A litter of kittens played hide-and-seek in her stomach. "I came about the job. I've never had a job before, but I've done plenty of cleaning. I wash dishes and do laundry and mop floors at home. I figure this can't be any different."

Rambling on like that surely wouldn't help. The woman would think she'd lost her mind.

"I retired from teaching two years ago. Until then I had someone come out and clean my house." The woman sniffed. "Then I figured I could do it myself, being I was at home all day. Of course that reminded me how much I didn't like it."

So she bought a B and B?

"I'm Minerva. You're Bess. You're Amish." Minerva picked up a pair of reading glasses from the table and peered through them without actually putting them on her long nose. "Plain is what they call it when you talk among yourself, right?"

"Yes, I'm Amish."

"I hear you're hard workers." Minerva laid the glasses down and tapped a long, manicured nail painted red to match her lipstick on the glass tabletop. "You don't mind turning on a light switch, do you? Or starting up a vacuum? I know your kind don't use electricity."

"We don't mind working and we use electrical things when we work, if need be."

"What about answering the phone when customers call and we're not around?"

Talking to strangers on the phone would be a tall order. "I've answered the phone in our phone shack a few times." She sat up straighter. "I even made a call once, when my father-in-law had a fainting spell and we thought he'd had a heart attack. Turned out it was low blood sugar."

Why had she volunteered all that information?

"Marvelous." Minerva beamed. "When can you start?"

"When do you need someone?"

"Honey, did you see that kitchen?' Minerva leaned forward and patted Bess's hand. Her skin was dry and soft like parchment paper. "You have your work cut out for you."

"I didn't see the kitchen." Not that it mattered. She would get it in shape, just like the one at home. "I can start whenever you need me."

Joshua would be in good hands with Hazel. Better, more capable, experienced hands. Hazel with her four children and another one on the way. Hazel, whose body would swell and swell until another baby came into this world to be shared by his mudder and his very much living father.

"Of course you didn't. I need to give you the tour."

"Does that mean I'm hired?"

"It does."

So that was how job interviews were done. Her stomach quieted. Her heart resumed its usual routine. The shaking in her hands subsided. She stood. "What do you want me to do first?"

"Let's just go to the kitchen and get you a glass of sweet tea. Then we'll get down to specifics."

Minerva unfolded from her chair in one long, fluid motion. She towered over Bess even though her green sandals were flat. She wore a pale-green dress belted with a skinny strip of green at the waist and a wide skirt that rustled when she moved. She stretched her slim arms over her head and yawned. "My husband and I just moved here. We don't know a soul except my son and he's gone all the time. My husband went to hire painters. We have to get this place whipped into shape. Our first guests are arriving Saturday."

Two days from today. "Do you have everyone else hired?"

"Everyone else? Honey, so far it's you, me, and my hubby. My son has a job so he isn't around as much as I'd thought he would be. Has his nose stuck in a book when he is here." Minerva didn't seem to need to take a breath. She strung sentences together in a leisurely fashion that said she had all the time in the world to breathe and everyone else to listen. "I will hire a cook — soon I hope, but one thing at a time. I can handle it for now."

Minerva padded down the stairs ahead of Bess, her skirt rustling all the while. She paused at the bottom of the stairs. "I hope you're good with a dust rag. This place seems to attract every particle of dust from the road out there."

"Whatever you need." Bess followed, trying to keep up with the older lady's brisk pace. "Dusting is second nature for me."

"I have paperwork somewhere that you need to fill out. Do you have a social security number?'

She did, although she'd never used it for anything.

A door slammed somewhere below. Minerva strode ahead. "I imagine that's Gavin, my hubby. Come on, I want him to meet you. Then we'll get you that tea, and we'll settle on your salary and hours and such. I hope you don't expect an arm and a leg for your services. We're just getting started and the expenses have been astronomical. We might be able to get you a raise once we get a few customers through the door. Oh, here he is now."

Bess didn't try to respond to the steady stream of chatter. She hadn't given any thought to what she would be paid. She had no idea what would be considered a fair wage. Minerva would surely know. Or Gavin. Anxious to meet her new boss, Bess followed the woman into the kitchen. The scent of roses wafted over her. Minerva must've bathed in her perfume. "Do you have a gas stove or electric?"

"Gas. I abhor cooking on an electric stove."

"Good. I . . ."

There stood Dusty. Dusty from Woodson Nursery. Dusty of the bruised flowers and Jacob's Ladder. Dusty, whom she owed snickerdoodles.

"What are you doing here?"

They asked the question simultaneously.

Minerva's penciled eyebrows rose so high, they disappeared under her carefully arranged bangs and then fell to a new low. "You know each other. Son, you work fast. You've only been here a week."

Dusty grinned. "Bess was my first, best customer at the nursery."

"Now's she's our first, best employee."

His grin widened. "I reckon I'll be spending more time at home then."

EIGHTEEN

Bess would think he was addled in the brain. Aidan pulled into Solomon's front yard and stopped short of the hitching post. Misgivings assailed him. He hadn't much time with boplin in the last few years. Not since his brother Henry's youngest was born and Matthew was three now. He tightened his grip on the reins. Now or never. Turn around or stay. His final words to Caleb echoed in his ears. He had promised to take care of his bopli. Promised a dying man. His best friend.

Aidan blew out air. His problems with the farm couldn't matter. His mixed-up feelings couldn't matter. He had to turn and face them. Face Bess. Peanuts pranced and tugged at the bit. "I know, I know."

The screen door opened and Hazel stuck her head out. "Aidan? What are you doing here in the middle of the day? Solomon and Isaac are in the fields."

"Figured as much." Working, as he should be. What had possessed him to get in the buggy and come to this place when the sun hung overhead? Heat burned his cheeks. He swiped at his mouth with the back of his hand. "Is Bess here?"

"Nee. She went into town."

To the nursery? The memory of the big, hulking man with the rust-colored beard floated in his mind's eye. The man had been nice. Nothing wrong with nice. Bright pink and purple flowers dotted the flower beds that ran along the front of the house. She'd planted them. She didn't need more. "In that case, I guess I'll —"

A baby's cry wafted through the open door. Hazel looked back. "I have to go in. Joshua has been fussing all afternoon. Poor bopli, I don't know what ails him."

"Joshua's here but Bess isn't?"

"Come in, have a glass of tea." Hazel disappeared. The door slammed behind her.

The baby's cry interspersed with a croupy cough propelled Aidan from the buggy and into the house. The cries grew in volume and pitch as he approached the kitchen. He seemed to be choking on his own cough. Joshua did, indeed, need someone and, for some reason, Aidan had been appointed to the job.

"There, there, you little munchkin, you're fine, you're fine." Hazel nattered on as she rocked the baby in one arm and manhandled a pitcher of tea with the other. "Sit, sit. I could use the company. The girls are at school. Mattie's at the dawdy haus doing something or other. My little one is down for a nap. Perfect time for tea."

Aidan had always liked Caleb's middle sister. She was kinder than the others, more like Solomon and less like her mother. "He sounds croupy when he coughs."

"He's getting over a cold, I reckon."

"And Bess went to town?"

Sadness flitted across Hazel's face and disappeared. "I have plenty of experience with colds and babies. He most likely got it from my Gracie. Bess is trying to get a job she saw advertised in the paper."

"A job?" Aidan shook his head. He must've heard wrong. Surely she was joking. "She has a new bopli. Isn't that enough work for her?"

A bopli with no father. A child who needed his mudder.

"She does, but she decided to get a job." Hazel plunked a glass of tea on the table in front of Aidan. Then she proceeded to plunk Joshua in his arms. "Hold him while I cut

214

us a piece of pie. I think we could both use pie."

Normally, he would agree, but at the moment, Aidan was more interested in the earlier statement. He jostled Joshua until he fit perfectly in the crook of his arm. His face pink with exertion from alternating coughs and cries, the baby stared up at him, eyes so like Caleb's. He smelled of spit-up and baby poop. "She always was a hard worker. She had more energy than three of us put together."

"She's still that way, but it's more that she needs to get her mind off her sorrow and onto helping others. Sitting around here feeling sorry for herself was not working well for her or this bopli."

She had been sad at the house, but then so had he. The connection had been strong. They'd both felt it. He was sure of it. He was not alone in his feelings. The fact that she might need him lifted his spirits. Or she might need anyone who could make her feel less alone. His spirits plummeted. "I saw her in town the other day buying flowers at the nursery." It seemed unlikely that Bess had shared her foray into the house that Caleb would never finish with anyone, even her sweet sister-in-law. "She looked pretty chipper to me."

"She tries, I'll give her that." Hazel plopped into the chair across from him. She sipped her tea, then settled her cup on the table. "I don't know what I would do in her shoes. Without my Isaac, I don't know what I'd do. It would be a hard row to hoe. But she seems lost. She's not finding comfort in Gott's plan or in her bopli."

"It hasn't been that long."

"That's what I said, but my daed says it's time to move along. 'Course he's got his own row to hoe."

"We all do, I reckon."

Her expression grim, Hazel nodded. Joshua gurgled. His tiny fists flailed and his bare feet kicked. He seemed to be in perpetual motion, just the way Aidan remembered Caleb. "What kind of job?"

"Cleaning house at the B and B."

"Did she ask Freeman about it first?"

"She thought she'd apply first, see if she got the job, then ask."

"Do it first, then ask forgiveness?"

"I don't reckon she thinks she needs to ask forgiveness. She's a grown woman, a widow with a bopli living with her in-laws. Other women in our Gmay work. She only wants to earn her keep."

The way Hazel defended Bess warmed his heart. In the home of her husband who no longer lived there. Bess had an ally in a place that must be difficult to live. Still, Hazel wasn't telling him the whole story. She mumbled and her gaze skittered off to one side as the words meandered away. He would talk to Bess himself. First chance he got, but right now he had another mission. "I'd like to take Joshua for a ride."

"A ride?" Hazel's eyes widened behind glasses that had slid down precariously close to the end of her upturned nose. Pursing her lips, she leaned forward as if to take the baby from him. Aidan leaned back. "I told Bess I would take care of him for her."

"So did I."

Hazel's dark eyebrows rose and fell. "Anything happens to him, she'd be lost forever."

"So would I. He's Caleb's only child."

The stark words hung between them. Hazel's eyes brightened with tears. "You ever changed a diaper?"

"I birthed a dozen piglets the other night, I reckon I can figure it out."

She sniffed, the disdainful sound of a woman who knew men could mend fences, chop wood, and build barns but couldn't be trusted to properly change a diaper. "Don't keep him out too long. It's nap time. And be sure to change his diaper. I don't want him getting a rash and being up half the night. Keep the blanket around him, the sun's shining, but the air still has a bit of a chill —"

"Jah, jah, he's a bopli. How hard could it be?"

Her expression darkened. "Spoken like a man who doesn't have any."

Not for lack of want. He stood and backed away from the table. She swept from the room, her shoulders stiff with indignation. She was so like her brother. So sure she was right.

Caleb had always been right about everything. From the best way to get a buck on the first day of hunting season to the surest way to get a girl to go for a buggy ride. Especially when that girl was Bess.

A few minutes later Aidan had the hefty woven basket holding Joshua swaddled in a blanket wedged onto the seat next to him in the buggy. A bag on the other side held diapers and a bottle that Hazel had explained held expressed milk. Her cheeks had turned bright red and he didn't dare ask what exactly that meant. She said Joshua wasn't picky and had decided a bottle was better than nothing when his mudder had failed to materialize with the usual method of feeding him.

Hazel stood on the porch and waved as if they were leaving on a long trip. Maybe they were. A journey of sorts. He tucked the baby quilt up under Joshua's fat arms. "Here we go, friend of mine."

Joshua cooed.

"I know. People will talk. A Plain man riding around the countryside with a baby not his own." A chuckle burbled up in his throat. "Talking to him like he understands."

He glanced at the road, then back at Joshua. "You understand me, don't you? Your daed always did."

Joshua opened his mouth wide and yawned.

"Don't you go to sleep on me, you hear. I have things to tell you. Stories about your daed. Stories about your mudder. We grew up together, you see. From the time we were knee high to your groossdaadi's britches."

Joshua sputtered, a bubble of spit forming on his lips.

"Your daed was as excited by my stories as you are." A sharp pain pierced Aidan's side and burrowed in his chest. "You look an awful lot like him. Same eyes, same nose. But you have your mudder's chin and her skin. Her hair."

Strange how kinner got a little of this and a little of that from their parents. One, then the other, like a patchwork quilt that looked all topsy-turvy at first, then beautiful when fully formed.

He guided Peanuts along the dirt road that took them beyond the Weaver farm, over the creek, and into the open fields of his land. The stories formed a line in his mind, jostling for position, all demanding to be first.

"There was this time when we decided we would go ice skating at the pond. Your mudder had a cold and your groossmammi said she couldn't go. Your mudder was fit to be tied so she did something I would never do and you should never do either. She sneaked out the back door and ran down to the pond. We were already on the ice when she showed up. Your daed was speechless. He told her to go on home before her daed took her to the woodshed for a switching. She said it would be worth it because she couldn't miss all the fun. She loved to ice skate. She wouldn't let no little cold keep her from all the fun.

" 'Course then her cold proceeded to get worse and she had to stay in bed for days and missed her own birthday. So that's what happens when you disobey your parents. You get your just desserts, whatever that means. It's a funny saying, isn't it?"

Joshua let out a loud squawk that surely startled the birds perched on the branches of the elm trees that lined the road. Aidan nodded. "I guess you agree."

That story was more about Bess than Caleb. "My earliest memories are of your daed and me on the back of my daed's wagon. We were bailing hay. Then I remember planting peas and green beans and cucumbers. Caleb — that's your daed — dug the holes and I followed behind and dropped in the seeds. We got sunburned and dirty, but as soon as we got done eating supper, we scooted off to the pond with my big brother, Timothy. He would be like an *onkel* to you, I guess, even though we're not related. It feels that way."

He stopped, the lump in his throat so tight, he couldn't swallow. He clucked at Peanuts and guided the buggy onto the dirt road that led to the cemetery. "Anyways, Timothy chucked us in the old canoe my daed gave him for his birthday and we went on the pond to fish. He had a pail of night crawlers and he showed us how to stick them on the hooks and toss them in the water. Caleb was a big talker. He wouldn't shut up, even though Timothy told him we wouldn't catch a thing if he didn't be quiet. He kept sticking the worms in my face and

221

trying to get me to eat one. I dared him to do it. So what did he do? He stood in the middle of the canoe and slapped one of those muddy, fat, wiggly worms in his mouth and swallows it whole. He's grinning like a coyote that just ate a chicken. Then he leaned over the side of the canoe and upchucked."

Aidan tugged on the reins and brought the buggy to a halt. He hadn't thought of that day in years. His chest ached. He cleared his throat. No sense in setting a bad example now. "Me and Timothy laughed so hard. Caleb started laughing too and pretended to eat another one. We dived for the pail like we would all share in the feast. We got so carried away we rocked the canoe so hard we tipped it over."

He couldn't help it. He laughed. And laughed. So hard, tears came to his eyes and streamed down his face. The sound, loud and raucous, echoed around him on the empty dirt road. Joshua's round face with Caleb's eyes staring up at him scrunched up in a frown. His nose wrinkled. Caleb's nose. Aidan snorted and hiccupped. The laughter of a crazy person. Thankfully, the only people in the cemetery slumbered peacefully, unconcerned by his inability to control himself.

He breathed in and out, willing himself to calm. "We decided swimming was more fun than fishing, anyway. When we told your mudder about it the next day, she said she reckoned we were crazy, but I could tell she was jealous she'd missed out. As she got older, she missed out on more stuff because it wasn't right for her to hang around boys. Your groossdaadi saw to that."

Aidan hopped from the buggy and pulled Joshua from the basket. He sniffed. No telltale smell that a diaper needed changing. *Danki, Lord.* "I reckon your mudder hasn't been out here since the funeral. Which makes sense. Your daed isn't here. I reckon he's with Gott. I mean, I don't pretend to know what Gott decided about him, but he was a man who was humble and obedient and relied on Gott in all things. He believed. So I reckon his chances were good, you know?"

He settled the baby into the crook of his arm. Joshua stared up at him, his fists tight against his chubby cheeks, his eyelids heavy as if he might drift off to sleep at any moment. "Hang in there, little one. Don't go to sleep on me now."

Aidan wound his way through the rows of simple, white headstones, each identical. Some were whiter because they were newer, but otherwise they were indistinguishable. Caleb's was the newest, stark white against the still-barren earth that marked the length and width of his coffin. "Here we are. This here is where your daed rests. His remains rest. Caleb, this here's your suh, Joshua. I know they'll all think I'm crazy standing out here talking to a headstone, but I don't know how else to do this."

He shifted Joshua to his other arm and shoved his hat back on his head. He inhaled the sweet scent of dirt and fresh green grass. The air hung heavy in an afternoon sun that caressed his shoulders. The warmth felt good. He lifted his face to the sun's rays. *Gott, I'm here. I don't know where else to go. Or what else to do. I don't have any words.*

Obedience. Humility. Patience. Waiting on Gott's plan. All these things he understood. It used to be easier. When order reigned. Everything and everyone in their places. Now Caleb was gone, the farm gone, Bess gone. Nothing filled these cold, empty voids. His heart should be crowded with obedience, certainty, and comfort in knowing that God had a plan for him. Instead a chilly draft swept through the emptiness where his heart should be.

"Shame on you." He said the words aloud. "Shame on you."

Joshua squawked.

"Not you. Me. I should have more faith. That's what Freeman would say. Freeman is the bishop. You need to be a very good boy around him. Well, all the time, but especially around Freeman. That's what your daed would say if he were here."

Caleb would shove his hat back on his head, remove the piece of straw he liked to chew on, and drawl, "Stop thinking on it and get back to work. Work is the best medicine."

And he would be right.

Aidan loaded his baby cargo back into the buggy and headed toward Solomon's place. Nothing had changed, but somehow he felt more at peace than he had since Caleb's death. He still had to figure out what to do about the farm, and his heart still hurt every time he thought about Bess, but he would get over it. He would work hard and wait upon the Lord.

No matter how long it took.

Girded by the thought, he hummed a few notes from his favorite hymn. A buggy rounded the bend, headed toward his. He strained to see who might share the road with him on this spring afternoon. He had no desire to exchange pleasantries with another soul. Not right now.

Freeman.

Aidan closed his eyes and took a breath. The bishop would find it more than odd that Aidan gallivanted across the countryside with a baby as his sidekick.

Freeman pulled abreast of Aidan's buggy and halted. Aidan did the same.

"Afternoon." Freeman managed to layer those three syllables with a mixture of question and faint criticism. His straw hat hid his eyes, but the pinch of his thin lips gave a hint as to his state of mind. "I stopped by your house." So did his tone.

"I wasn't there." Aidan cringed inwardly. Something about the other man always turned him into a simpleton. "I mean to say I'm sorry you wasted your time."

"No waste. I've found you now."

"Why were you looking for me?"

"Cyrus, Solomon, and I discussed the situation this morning. After much prayer, we agreed that no payment shall be accepted from the government for the birds." The word *government* was tinged with a bitter flavor. Freeman pulled at his gray beard with one pudgy hand. He cleared his throat. "Yours is not the only farm affected by this flu. Donald and Louis also are losing their flocks. Our emergency funds will go a ways to helping all three of you. Not enough to

226

cover your costs, I reckon, but a start."

Aidan's gut twisted with doubt. Donald and Louis were both married. Donald had five kinner and another on the way. Louis was a newlywed, just starting out. They needed help more than he did. The fund was meant to help families with medical needs, a child with cancer, a family whose home burned to the ground. His situation didn't measure up on the dire scale compared to the other men or the other families in the Gmay with need. "It's kind of you to consider me, but I'll be fine. Help Donald and Louis. They need it more."

"It's not for you to decide. We must keep our farms strong. Our Gmay strong. If community funds are needed to sustain farms in situations such as this, so be it. Yours is to be ready when they decide to let you start again. Figure out how to supplement what you'll receive from the Gmay."

Joshua fussed in a pay-attention-to-me-I'm-tired-and-hungry tone. Freeman frowned. "A bopli?"

The incredulity in his voice caused Aidan to stiffen. He might not have a fraa, but he had experience with boplin. "Jah." Pure stubbornness kept him from offering an explanation.

"Whose?"

Freeman *was* the bishop. "Bess's . . . Caleb's."

The other man leaned back in his seat, the reins wrapped around his hands resting on his knees. He sighed, a sound of sweetly strangled sorrow that pierced Aidan's heart. Freeman felt this loss too, somehow. A man of Gott he might be, but he felt as keenly as the next. The silence stretched and reverberated between them.

Freeman cleared his throat. "Would you like to talk about it?" He sounded as if he'd rather chop his foot off with an ax and reattach it himself.

Aidan shook his head.

The gusty sigh could only be one of relief. "Life isn't always easy to understand."

"Nee."

"Don't forget about Gelassenheit? A person who fully yields to Gott accepts suffering without complaining."

He hadn't forgotten. Nor had he complained. Not aloud, leastways. Shame burned his cheeks as surely as if Freeman held a candle to his skin. "I have not forgotten."

Freeman's gaze found his way back to Joshua. "Some questions aren't meant to be answered. Gott's providence is all we need."

"Jah."

Freeman cocked his head toward Joshua. "He should be with his mudder, his family."

"I know, but I always felt that I was part of Caleb's family too."

"A person shouldn't meddle where it isn't needed."

"Bess —"

"Bess has Solomon and Mattie looking after her. She needs to look forward now, not backward."

"I reckon she knows what she needs to do." Aidan studied Joshua's face. He had Caleb's eyes and Bess's mouth. "She's gone to get herself a job. I thought I'd take him for a ride in the meantime. Nothing more."

"First I've heard of it." Freeman's expression darkened. "She should've spoken with me first."

Aidan tasted something sour in this mouth, surely toe jam. Another thing for which Bess would need to forgive him. "Other women have jobs with Englischers. The *Ordnung* permits it."

"Not when they have new boplin." Freeman's thick, dark eyebrows popped up, then down. "You say with Englischers? She should've talked to me."

"I'm sure she wanted to help earn her keep."

"Do you?"

"Want to earn my keep?" What a question. He'd been doing that since he finished school at eighth grade. "I do."

"I wouldn't think a man with his livelihood in jeopardy would gallivant about the countryside in the heart of the workday with a bopli not his own."

Joshua's squall filled the air, giving Aidan a reprieve. He bent over the basket, letting his hat hide his expression. Freeman was right. What ailed him?

"I was headed back to Solomon's." He cradled Joshua against his chest and patted his back. The baby burped, a loud, satisfying sound. Freeman's dour expression didn't change. "I have seed money from my last sale. I'll make it work."

"The Gmay needs every farm to sustain itself."

"Mine will."

"Keep your mind and your heart on Gott and everything else will fall into place."

"I will."

"If you need guidance, let us know."

"I will."

Freeman pursed his lips as if tempted to say more. He snapped the reins and the buggy jolted forward.

Aidan buried the urge to glance back. Like

Freeman said, look forward now, not backward.

Joshua wiggled in his arms. His thumb landed in his mouth, the sucking sound a *thwamp, thwamp.*

"Suh, you are the future, not the past." Aidan tucked him in the basket. Joshua's eyes were huge and the thumb came out, followed by a burp. The baby spit up all over Aidan's hand. He wiped it on his pants and dabbed at Joshua's clothes with the burp rag. "I bet that felt good. Don't worry. No harm done. I might not be your father, but I can be your onkel by choice. Onkels don't mind a little spit-up."

He urged Peanuts forward. "No harm in that, no harm at all."

The bishop made it clear he thought differently.

Obedience.

Gelassenheit. Gott, I would yield to Thy will if I knew what it was.

NINETEEN

Finally. Bess rose from the steps and planted her bare feet on the dirt path that led from the front porch to the barn. She'd been sitting here waiting since returning from her strange, rather wondrous job interview for more than thirty minutes, her joy at the job draining away with each passing second. Was this Gott's way of saying she shouldn't leave the bopli to go into town every day? Should she be here making sure he wasn't traveling the countryside with a bachelor whose knowledge of boplin surely fit on the head of a straight pin?

The thud of the horse's hooves beat in time to the pulse in her temple. Why would Aidan take Joshua for a ride in the middle of the afternoon? He must be sick. The baby was just getting over a cold. He didn't need Aidan's germs. She shaded her eyes with one hand. Aidan waved as if it wasn't the strangest event in the world, him pulling up to the house with her baby in his buggy on a perfectly good workday.

"See I told you he'd be fine." Hazel shoved open the screen door and stuck her head out. Despite her words she surely stood inside watching for the buggy as well. Feeling responsible. "Aidan may be a bachelor, but he's an onkel and he grew up with younger brothers and sisters. He knows what to do with a bopli."

She sounded as if she were justifying her actions to herself. Bess swiveled to look back at her sister-in-law. "You're right. I was just surprised."

"Let him say his piece before you start jawing at him."

As if she would jaw at a man. She knew better. "I'll hold my tongue."

A smile spread over Hazel's face. "If you do, I'll be forced to take your temperature and figure out what ails you."

"I'm not that bad." Bess managed a return smile. "I know my place."

"Since when?" Hazel let the screen door slam behind her.

Bess turned to see Aidan hop from the buggy and stride around the front. He tugged Joshua from the basket. The baby's head lolled back. He slumbered, loose limbed and at peace. Not a care in the world. No coughing. No fussing. "Where have you been?"

"I figured it was time for Joshua and me to get to know each other." He held the baby out. She took him. Joshua looked none the worse for wear, but Aidan still looked as guilty as the day he'd broken the wooden swing on a rope in her backyard all those years ago. "Besides, you were off getting yourself a job."

He sounded surprised at the idea. Why? "Is it wrong to want to help out?"

"Nee, but did you think about your family? Solomon will have to talk to Freeman about it. Makes it a bit awkward for him that you didn't ask first."

"I didn't think they'd offer me the job just like that, on the spot. It all happened so fast. But it'll work out. Hazel has agreed to watch the bopli."

"Joshua, you mean?"

"What?"

"The bopli has a name. Joshua."

"I know my bopli's name." Joshua began to fuss. "Now you've gone and woke him."

Aidan stuck his hands on hips, his shoulders hunched. "I thought I'd get to know Caleb's suh. I thought he might need some company from a man who could start to teach him what he needs to know."

Something about his eyes made Bess's heart constrict in a painful, ragged beat that had no discernible rhythm. She studied her dusty feet. Her toes curled into the dirt. "I suppose there's no harm in that."

"Gut. I'll go then."

Inexplicably, she didn't want him to go. Nee, she did know why. He understood. He, of all the people in her life, knew. They were connected by the terrible hole in their lives that gaped and overlapped. "You don't want to come in for a glass of water? You must be parched."

"I best get back. I might not have chickens anymore, but I still have livestock that needs tending." Aidan heaved himself into the buggy. "It'll be dark soon."

"You never said where you took him."

He picked up the reins and wrapped them around his fists. "Here and there. Stopped at the cemetery."

The last word burned her ears like a blustery, cold winter wind. "Nothing much to learn there."

"We talked. I told him stories about things I used to do with his daed."

He couldn't say Caleb's name aloud. Like she failed to call her baby by his name. Nee, it was different. Bess wanted to say her mann's name over and over again as if it would bring him back. Not saying it sent him farther and farther into the past. "You talked? Did he talk back?"

"He blabbered a little."

Bess managed a smile. "When he's old enough to understand, you'll have to tell him again."

Aidan shot back a lopsided smile. "I want him to recognize my voice and my face."

"That would be good."

"It's gut that you think so. You might not when you know . . ." His hands dropped into his lap. "I saw Freeman on the road. We stopped and talked."

Nothing unusual about that. Yet Aidan looked powerfully uncomfortable. "Strange he wasn't in the fields working himself."

"He'd gone up to my place to tell me they wanted to help me out from the emergency fund, along with Donald and Louis. They have the flu in their flocks too."

Aidan looked as if he'd been held responsible for this latest travesty.

"That's a good thing, isn't it?" Bess studied his face. He looked like he did when he had a burr stuck in the sole of his big foot. "You'll be able to restock more quickly and get back on your feet."

"The fund was meant for real emergencies like families with sickness that costs a lot of money in hospitals and such."

"They wouldn't offer if they didn't think it was best. The Gmay needs every farm and family to be in good shape."

"True." He swatted at an overly friendly horsefly, looking more irritated than the action warranted. "I might also have told him you went looking for a job."

"Why would you do that?"

"He wanted to know why I had Joshua."

"You had Joshua because you came and got him."

"I know, I know, but one thing led to another. He looked none too pleased. I reckon he'll come talk to you himself."

Aidan had never been one to stick his nose where it didn't belong. Everything had changed when Caleb died. This apparently was one more of those things. "I don't mind talking to him. He's a fair-minded man."

Which made him a good bishop.

"Gut."

"Jah, gut." Any lingering warmth from their encounter at the house only a few nights earlier dissipated in the unspoken words that bounced between them. "Other women have jobs."

"That's what I told him. He pointed out they don't usually have small boplin." Aidan tightened the reins in his hands. The horse jolted forward as if tugged from sleep. "Where are you working, then?"

"At the B and B."

"Cleaning?"

The litany of questions aggravated her. Not that he was interested, but that he seemed to think he had some right to know. He wasn't her mann. She had no mann. Maybe that's why he cared. For Caleb's sake. She tried to hang on to that thought as kinder. "Why are you so interested?"

"I thought you were . . . are a friend."

Jah, kinder. He cared. It hurt to swallow yet again. Every day, moments came when the simple act of swallowing became almost impossible. "Your best friend's wife."

"Jah, but my friend too. Since those days when you sneaked out to go ice skating or fell out of a tree and broke your wrist or decided to go to a concert in St. Louis during your rumspringa."

The memories played across Aidan's face like the movie screen at the dollar theater where she'd seen a showing of *Gone with the Wind* during that same rumspringa.

If men and women — especially Plain — could be friends, she would count Aidan as one. He was present in almost every memory she had with Caleb growing up and many, many more during their brief marriage. To rebuff him now would be wrong and cruel and no one had so many friends she could afford to do such a thing. "Jah, we're friends."

"Still friends?"

She nodded. "Always."

"Gut."

They had said that several times already and yet it bore repeating. "It is gut."

He ducked his head. "Then I can come back sometime?"

"Anytime."

In the past he hadn't needed an invitation. He came and went like one of the family.

Another thing that had changed. She wanted change to stop. She wanted him to come and go as he pleased. Often. This train of thought would lead her off the tracks into some strange new place. She tried to find her way back. "How's Iris?"

She wanted the question back before the words spread on the late-afternoon breeze.

Pain flitted across his face and disappeared as quickly as it had appeared. An odd, neutral look spread in its place. "I don't know."

What had possessed her to ask such a question? Courting was private. "She spends a lot of time with your sister-in-law. That's why I —"

"Iris will always be fine. She is gut that way. I reckon she'll tell you that herself."

The heat that burned her cheeks had nothing to do with the sun. "I better help Hazel with supper."

He tugged his straw hat down over his ears, pulled away, and headed down the road. Despite her words, Bess couldn't move. Something had happened here in this spot. She couldn't be sure what, but it felt strange and worth hanging on to for a few more seconds.

Joshua's face wrinkled and he half-squawked, half-coughed.

If riding around in Aidan's buggy all afternoon had caused his cough to worsen again, she would have a word — a severe word — with Aidan. If it kept him up during the night and thereby kept her up, she'd be knocking on Aidan's door. Let him walk the floor with his "nephew" half the night.

Her cheeks burned. Thinking of knocking on Aidan's door in the middle of the night. *Gott, forgive me, I don't know what is wrong with me. Please forgive my waywardness. Thy will be done about the job and about my life.*

Thy will be done.

Joshua squawked again, this time more

240

loudly. But no cough, thank the Lord, no cough.

Maybe he, too, felt keenly the absence of their new, old friend.

She trudged into the house, intent on helping Hazel with the cooking. She couldn't let a job get in the way of her responsibilities here. She would carry her weight and keep herself busy. Idle hands and idle minds. She rounded the corner, headed to the kitchen. Solomon stood in the doorway, arms crossed, his expression dour on a face sweaty and smudged with dirt.

"You're back early." Her words sounded critical in her ears. If her father-in-law finished the day's work before sunset, it was for him to decide whether to come in from the fields. "I mean —"

"Hazel says you went into town to see about a job."

"I did."

"You don't have enough work here?"

He had never spoken to her in that tone before. In fact, he rarely spoke to her at all before Caleb's death, and less since then. "It's not that. I want to help out. With Caleb gone —"

"We don't give you a roof over your head and food to eat?"

241

"You do —"

"You married my son. You live in my son-in-law's house." Solomon wiped at his face with a blue bandana. His hands were as dirty as his face. "What you do reflects on me and mine."

"Plenty of women have jobs with the Englischers. The Gmay has allowed it for many years."

"Not married women with kinner. Their job is to care for kinner and take care of the house."

He didn't mean to be cruel. Surely he didn't. "I'm not married, not anymore." She swallowed against the never-ending ache in her throat. "And it's not my house."

"Do you feel unwelcome here? You are our daughter by marriage." Solomon's Adam's apple bobbed. He cleared his throat. "You have a bopli. Leaving him to go off and work for Englischers, it doesn't sit well."

A drop of sweat tickled her temple. Her hands felt damp against Joshua's back. "Are you saying I can't keep the job?" *Please don't say that, please don't say that.* He was the head of this household. If he said no, then no it was. "I accepted their offer, but I didn't actually start working. They want me to start tomorrow."

"I'm saying you should've asked first." He

lifted his straw hat and ran his hand through iron-gray curls. "I'm saying I'll talk to Freeman. Better I do it before he finds out another way."

Too late. "Aidan told him."

Solomon flopped his hat back on his head. "Why would he stick his nose in our business?"

"It wasn't intentional, I reckon." Bess explained the circumstances. "He had Joshua with him. Freeman wanted to know why."

"Aidan is another one floundering about since Caleb died. A person is expected to bear the cross of Christ without complaining." Solomon's voice fractured. "This here's a mighty fine example of why you shouldn't be in town instead of here with the bopli."

Aidan hadn't complained. Not once. She did her complaining silently, but then, it wasn't silent to Gott. He heard every word and He knew how recalcitrant His daughter was. Solomon had no way of knowing, other than an unerring ability to read her face. She did live in his son-in-law's house. He did have a say. She should have talked to him first. "Don't blame Aidan. I'm sorry I put you in this predicament."

"I'm not blind to how this is for you. Liv-

243

ing here without your mann." His voice dropped to a hoarse whisper. "Gott's will is Gott's will. With time the wound will heal. It will get easier to submit."

The words might have been said more for him than for her. Joshua gurgled and whined. She shushed him. "I will try not to make it harder for you and Mattie."

"Mattie's fine."

The force with which he uttered the words said she was not fine. "I know. I only meant —"

"Freeman hired a van to take him and his fraa to La Plata to see his new grand-daughter first thing tomorrow morning. I'll talk to him when he returns."

"In the meantime, I can keep the job?"

"For now."

"The pay is nine dollars an hour. It'll help."

"The money is not the point. We made do before; we always make do."

"I know."

"Caleb is gone. We are still here. You best find a way to make peace with that."

If anyone knew how hard it was, Solomon did. Her heart hurt for him. "I'm trying. I'll do better."

"Don't forget, you can always go to your

parents in Haven. A fresh start might be good."

Did he want her gone? She served as a living reminder of Caleb's life. Would it be easier not to have to look at her and at Joshua every day? She hadn't walked a mile in his boots. Maybe it was selfish of her to stay. But going home to her parents — as much as she missed her mudder and daed — didn't constitute a fresh start. Living in her parents' home would mean going back to where she'd been before she married Caleb. "Wouldn't you miss Joshua?"

"Mattie would."

Somedays Mattie didn't know who he was. "Do you want me to go?"

"Nee, but you must do what is right. For everyone, including the bopli."

"How do I know what that is?"

"Pray and submit to Gott's will for you." Solomon moved from the doorway, his steps heavier, his back more bent than it had been only a few minutes earlier. "I reckon Hazel could use your help with supper."

He disappeared into the front room, leaving her to trek into the kitchen, his words ringing in her ears. *Pray and submit. If all else fails, work.* That's what Solomon did. That's what she wanted to do. The anguish in Solomon's voice reverberated in the air around her. He knew how she felt, but he wanted to do the right thing.

So did she. If she couldn't work at the B and B, maybe she should go to Haven.

Where no trace existed of her life with Caleb. Could she leave the pain and heartache behind? Joshua had fallen asleep in her arms. He would go with her and in his presence, so would Caleb. A bittersweet remembrance she could never leave behind.

His face was so sweet in repose. She didn't want to leave him behind. He needed her. With time, the bitter would fade, leaving behind the sweet. She had God's promise of that. *Gott, give me the patience to wait on the good You promise.*

"Can you open a jar of pickled beets?"

Hazel stood at the stove, frying pork chops.

Gott helped those who helped themselves. She went to work.

TWENTY

Scrubbing dishes so they could be stacked in a machine and washed simply made no sense. Bess rubbed the itch on her nose with the back of her hand. The clean, bleachy smell of the dish soap wafted around her. She marched the long-handled brush around the china plate to remove congealed egg yolk and slipped it into the bottom rack. Dishwashers were supposed to make life easier for the Englisch folks, but she couldn't see the advantage.

She'd offered to wash them by hand as she'd been doing all her life. In a jiffy. But Minerva wouldn't have any of that. Dishwashers were a convenience, she insisted. In Bess's way of thinking, washing dishes to wash dishes only took more time. Time that could be spent with the mounds of sheets and towels that littered the back room Minerva daintily referred to as the utility closet. Then Bess needed to dust and vacuum and remake beds in all the rooms. She had her day cut out for her.

A surprisingly warm contentment enveloped her at the thought. She had her place here at the B and B, a place respected and valued by Minerva and Gavin, who sought her out three and four times a day this first week on the job to add to the list of tasks they would "love" for her to do before she rushed home to help Hazel with supper.

The fact that Freeman might return from La Plata any day and decide she shouldn't be doing this only made time more precious. She knew what to do here and no one looked at her with that half-pitying, half-judging look that said she needed to buck up and get on with her life. This job was her way of getting on with it. Here, she was far too busy to think about Caleb.

At night she fell into bed exhausted, too exhausted to moon over the patch of tangled sheets and blankets next to her. She needed this job as much as Minerva needed her. Joshua was cooperating too, worn out from days of being lugged around and "playing" with Hazel's little ones. Feeding times had stretched to every three hours.

Six guests — three couples — now occupied the B and B rooms. The older man and woman, Mr. and Mrs. Dunlap, had the

Veranda Room. They were from Joplin and had lots of luggage. They left their dirty clothes all over the bed and the floor, making it hard for Bess to change the sheets and tidy up the room. Bill and Lydia from Kansas City were younger. They insisted everyone call them by their first names, and they raved about how cute the Blue Room was. Lydia employed the word *cute* for everything, even the biscuits and molasses served for breakfast. Lastly, Mr. and Mrs. Waters occupied the Pink Room, which Minerva insisted was the Salmon Room. They were from Denver and they kept to themselves. Why they stayed in a bed-and-breakfast when they grabbed breakfast after the others left and barely said a word to anyone, Bess couldn't say. An impersonal hotel might more suit their needs.

She dumped in the machine soap and then studied the buttons on the dishwasher. *Pots & Pans.* Nee. Those at least she was allowed to scrub with the usual tools of hands supplemented with a liberal dollop of elbow grease. *High Temp. SaniRinse. Heated Dry.* Not only did the machine wash the dishes, it dried them. There was something to be said for that. She jabbed buttons and stood back. A pleasant hum filled the air.

"That's that." She dried her hands on her

apron. "We'll see who does a better job washing, you or me."

"Talking to dishwashers now?"

She swiveled. Dusty stood in the doorway, a sack of potting soil under his arm. Heat bloomed on her neck and cheeks. "No, I mean, well, a little. I was just studying the settings —"

"It's okay. As long as it doesn't answer you back, you're not crazy."

His silly grin made her smile. She tried to see some hint that he and Minerva were cut from the same cloth but couldn't. His mother was all fancy and elegant with her dresses that rustled when she walked and her painted nails. Dusty's pants were baggy, the knees dirty and threadbare, his shirt stained with whatever he ate for breakfast, and his shaggy beard looked like a bird's nest. Only his fair skin tone and strawberry-blond hair suggested they were related. "Aren't you working today?"

"Nope. I'm off since I have to work Saturday. So I thought I'd tackle the front yard. Want to help me?"

The thought of being outdoors in the spring sunshine this fine morning called her name. So did the laundry and the dusting and the unmade beds. "Nee, I have chores to do." Many chores. "I'm still cleaning up from breakfast."

"This is important B and B business. My mom will want you to help."

"Your nose will grow if you fib."

"I'm serious. We need to spruce up the front yard so the place looks picturesque when the new guests arrive. It looks like no one has taken care of it in years. The whole place looks abandoned. If we don't do something quick, they might turn around and skedaddle down the road to that other B and B." He waggled his bushy, reddish-blond eyebrows. "If we don't have guests, we don't need a maid. Besides, you like to garden and you're good at it. I diagrammed the placement of each kind of plant and flower for us, based on available light, temperature, and soil types."

He surely had his arguments lined up. Sounded as if he'd been planning them for a while. Why it was so important to him, Bess couldn't fathom, but his enthusiasm tickled her for some reason she didn't want to examine too closely. "I mostly just dig a hole and stick the plants in the ground. How would you know if I do it well?"

"You bought flowers from me, remember? A very nice selection. You have an eye for plants."

She did remember that day, especially the

251

part where Aidan showed up and seemed peeved that she was there. Aidan, who had told the bishop about her new job and who thought she wasn't a very good mudder, so poor in fact, that she had to have others care for her bopli. "Mary Katherine picked out those flowers. Besides, I can't."

"Yes you can. I actually asked my mom and she agreed. I'll mow, weed-eat, trim the trees, edge, all the manly stuff." He flexed his free arm. He did have quite a muscle mound from carrying all those big bags of seed at the nursery. "In the meantime, you can be planting. A couple of hours, max, then you can finish up your chores inside. I have everything laid out. Come on, come."

He turned and motioned toward the door, the look on his face matching his comically pleading tone.

Bess looked around the kitchen. The pots, pans, and skillets were washed and drying in the racks. The floor had been swept and mopped. The table cleaned and the salt and pepper shakers shaped like roosters and hens returned to their spots at either end. One room done, at least eight to go. "I don't know."

"Mom left me in charge while she went to the store for supplies." His voice floated behind him. "Don't make me pull the boss card and call it an order."

Technically Minerva's absence meant Gavin was in charge, but Dusty's dad disappeared into his study every morning "to do the books," as he called it. The doors closed behind him and didn't reopen until Minerva called him for lunch. Afternoons, he "fixed" things around the house, tinkering with this and that, hammering, sometimes singing, sometimes whistling, but almost always cussing a blue streak. Bess heard an entire litany of words she'd never heard before on her very first day and had added to the collection every day since.

"Fine." She marched from the kitchen, through the living room, and out to the front porch. Dusty squatted next to the sidewalk, an array of flats spread across the grass. Reds, blues, lavenders, yellows, pinks — a riot of colors surrounded him. He smiled up at her. "What do you think?"

She padded down the steps, hand to her forehead to shade her eyes from the sun. "Beautiful."

His smile widened. "The *Caladium X hortalanum* and the *Coleus hybridus* are for the beds along the foundation of the house. They do nicely in the shade. Then we'll add the *Impatiens walleriana* to add color." He pointed to several flats closest to the house.

"See, red, pink, blue, and lavender. They love the shade. They'll go wild."

"You're doing it again."

He smacked his hand to his forehead. "Oops, sorry. Caladium, coleus, impatiens. You know what I mean."

Not really, but when it came to flowers it didn't matter. They were Gott's way of adding beauty to His world. The variety of shades and sizes and colors of the petals and leaves enchanted Bess. She knelt next to him and traced the violet petals of a pansy. "What is the scientific name of a pansy?"

"Viola x wittrockiana." Dusty's smile faded. His big, meaty fingers touched the pansy next to hers. "These are tender. We'll plant them around the buggy in the middle of the yard. I already took a spade to the soil so it's loose and aerated. We'll do the *Tagetes erecta* there as well — that's African marigolds to you — and some *Phlox drummondii*. I know you love sunflowers. We'll do those at the corners. Folks will want to sit in the rockers on the front porch and just absorb the beauty."

Bess had never heard a man talk like that. Not even Caleb with his flights of fancy. Dusty's way with words painted pictures in her mind, captivating her with what could be long before it became real. "What about these?" She inhaled the sweet scent of peat moss and soil as she pointed to lavender and blue flowers. "I love morning glories."

"It's hard to be in a bad mood, isn't it, when you look out and see God's creation blooming in living color right outside your window?" Dusty nodded so hard, a shower of toast crumbs fell from his beard to his knees. "*Ipomoea tricolor.* We'll plant those at the base of the trellis along the porch. They grow fast but they need the support."

She grabbed a trowel and stood. She wanted to sit on the porch and drink in those Gott-made colors. "Where shall I start?"

Knees creaking, he stood as well, a flat of pansies in his hands. "Being Amish and all, you should start with the buggy." He handed her the flat. His fingers brushed hers. His face reddened. "Happy planting."

She did feel happy. Content, at the very least. Her flowers clutched in her arms, she trotted out to the remnants of a buggy. Pots filled with dirt and the remains of long-dead plants sat on the scratched, faded seat. One of the wheels teetered at an odd angle. Dusty had missed some of the weeds that covered the back axle. She would have to do some work on the buggy itself, but first these flowers needed the nourishment of real soil and water. She knelt and tucked her skirt around her.

The *clip-clop* of horses' hooves on asphalt sounded in her ears. Probably one of her friends on the way to the grocery store or the fabric store. She lifted her hand to wave. Freeman waved back. Freeman and Solomon.

The bishop had returned. He had come to the B and B, and he surely wasn't there for the Veranda Room.

TWENTY-ONE

Bess dropped the trowel and wiped her shaking hands on her apron, waiting for the buggy that held the bishop to come to a complete stop. Along with everything else in her life. *"Guder mariye."*

"Guder mariye." Freeman shoved his hat back. He wasn't smiling. "We'd like a word."

Bess studied his expression. It would not be a word to her liking. "Here, or would you like to go inside?"

Freeman stared at Dusty, who had stopped the mower and stood watching with undisguised interest. "Who is this?"

"Dusty is the son of Minerva and Gavin Lake, the new owners of the B and B."

"You work with him, then." He nodded at the flowers. "Out here."

"Nee, I clean in the house mostly, but he said I was good at this and he just wanted help." The words came out in a stuttered mess she couldn't seem to corral. They ran about willy-nilly. "We're only gardening, that's all."

"Hello, hello."

She turned to see Gavin barge through the screen door. He wore his usual long-sleeved white shirt, crisp and starched looking, punctuated by a red bow tie and suspenders that held up his baggy beige linen pants. His bald pate glistened in the sun as he clattered down the steps, his red-and-white wing-tipped shoes beating a brisk rhythm on the wood. He smiled broadly and ran his chubby fingers over his head, making the sparse tufts of auburn hair that decorated the space above his ears stand straight up. He looked like the ringmaster she'd seen at the circus that came to the Daviess County Fairgrounds many years ago.

"I'm Gavin Lake. You must be friends of Bess's." He trotted past her, in a beeline to Freeman, hand held out, fingers stretched as if he absolutely could not wait to greet this guest in his home. "I must tell you we have been so blessed to have her here, working with us as we start this new endeavor. We couldn't do it without her."

After a week and a half? Freeman frowned on exaggeration, as did her father-in-law. Bess glanced at Dusty. He shrugged and winked. She could hardly wink back, with Solomon and the bishop standing there, but she managed a tiny jerk of a nod.

"We came by to talk with Bess." Freeman extricated his hand from Gavin's. "It's a private matter."

"I understand, I understand." Gavin held his ground. "I simply wanted to take the opportunity to let you know what a stellar worker she is. We understand that you don't take lightly having your young folks — especially young women — working in English establishments. Just to put your minds at rest, she's never alone with our customers. She is supervised at all times. My wife works with her when the rooms are cleaned. We're very strict about these things."

Bess hadn't given it a thought, but she found herself nodding. She worked in the kitchen until the customers left for the day and then Minerva was always nearby when she worked upstairs. Now she knew why.

"This is between her and us."

"Understood, but I do pay her wages and she is on the clock, so to speak."

Freeman's long nose wrinkled. His thin lips turned down. He sniffed as he crossed his arms over his rotund frame. "Did you know she has a baby only six weeks old?"

A dull thud made Bess look over her shoulder. Dusty had dropped the Weed Eater. "Sorry, sorry," he muttered as he picked it up. "Sweaty hands make for a slick handle."

"I didn't know. It's common for our womenfolk to go back to work after six weeks, but I imagine that's a different cup of tea for all y'all." Gavin snapped his suspenders, a pained look on his chubby face. "The father, what does he say about his wife working outside the home, leaving a little whippersnapper behind?"

"He's gone. He passed."

Freeman said the words as if commenting on the weather. *It's warm for spring, isn't it?*

"I'm so sorry." Gavin's face suffused with a compassion that made Bess want to cry. "It'll be Mrs. Weaver, then."

"Nee, no, it's only Bess." She gripped her apron to still the shaking of her hands. "I'm only Bess."

"Well, only Bess, I reckon it's up to you whether you stay on here, if these gentlemen give you leave." Gavin held out his hand to Freeman a second time. The bishop took it as if it might blow up in his face. "She's welcome to bring the little fellow to work anytime. My wife is gaga over babies. We were only able to have the one. She

260

turns into a big feather pillow every time she sees one. Your wives that way?"

Freeman and Solomon nodded in unison, looking ever so much like two Chihuahua dogs she'd seen in the window at the pet store in St. Louis the last time they traveled to the city.

"Come, come, you must come in for a cup of coffee." Gavin motioned with an expansive wave. "Let me extend a little southern hospitality your way."

Solomon moved forward as if caught in the currents of that wave. "We really —"

"Do you do carpentry? Or maybe you know someone who does?" Gavin kept moving, propelling the other two men forward as if by sheer will. "I also need a grandfather clock. I'll show you the spot in the living room next to the baby grand. You must know someone around here . . ." His voice faded into the distance as he whisked the men into the house and out of sight.

After a second Bess remembered to close her mouth. "I can't believe they went inside with him."

Dusty slapped his gardening gloves against his thigh, a pensive look on his red, sweaty face. "That is the powerful charm of Gavin Lake in action. The man could sell sand to the Saudis. He could charm a snake. He could get you to buy oceanfront property in Arizona. The man should've been a used-car salesman. He was a college professor before he retired. Physics."

Physics? Bess wasn't at all sure what physics was, something like arithmetic, if memory served. She stared at the now-closed front door with its bronze knocker and evergreen fir and pinecone wreath. Freeman would not speak the language of an educated college man. Neither would Solomon. He would still want to talk. Later, at home, when the outside world couldn't interfere.

"And he decided owning a hotel would be better?"

"No, Minerva decided and when Minerva decides something, you might as well give in at once, because there's no going back and talking her out of it."

"Why do you call your mother Minerva?"

"Because that's who she is. She was never a mother like other mothers. She fed me salmon pâte for breakfast as a baby. She taught me to fence — which I'm very bad at, by the way — because she says all gentlemen should know how to fence. She knows five languages and I never know when she's going to test my fluency in any one of them. Spanish and Italian are fairly easy, but Russian and Japanese are enough to give me a migraine."

"A different way to grow up." That could be described as an understatement. Bess knew three languages, with the high German used in their services, but she didn't really speak it or read it. Canning, sewing, gardening, cooking, cleaning, mothering — those were the important skills her mother taught her. "I guess there must be some use for Russian somewhere along the way."

"I liked it when she paid attention to me, even if it was to learn useless things." He wielded the Weed Eater as if he jousted with an unseen opponent for two quick swipes. "And both my parents would say all learning is worthwhile, all information useful. They believe in learning for learning's sake. A person can't know too much."

Her parents believed in working for working's sake. A person could never work too much. "You liked it because it meant spending time with her."

"My dad only had time for his students and his research and trying to get published. He worked all the time. My mom taught classes, but only part-time. Guess who I spent the most time with?"

"Seems like you turned out okay."

A furious red blush blossomed on his already-dark face. "You really think so?"

"I do."

He moved closer, his big boots making footprints in the mud where he'd watered the newly planted flowers around the trellis. "That means a lot coming from you."

His tone made the hair on her arms prickle. It plucked a string somewhere deep in her memories. Caleb talked like that when they courted, as if she were the only woman he could see in a room crowded with women. She took a tiny step back, the mud making a squishing sound under her sneakers. "Why would you care what I think?"

She truly wanted to know. No one cared what she thought about anything now that Caleb was gone.

"Are you kidding?" Dusty snorted. "From the day we met at the nursery, I've thought you're the sweetest, nicest, prettiest woman I've ever met. I don't know anyone like you."

If his face turned any redder, he would burst into flames.

He endowed her with qualities she had never possessed. "No, I'm not. I'm just a regular girl."

"You're special." He studied Freeman's horse as if it was the most interesting animal he'd ever seen. "I could see that the first time I saw you, looking so sweet and so sad.

Why didn't you tell us you had a baby?"

Maybe she was afraid they wouldn't give her the job. Maybe she didn't want to think about whether Solomon and Freeman were right. Maybe she didn't want to think about how she abandoned her crying, fussy bopli with Hazel each day to come here. "It's neither here nor there when it comes to being a hard worker and getting hired for this job."

Not a real answer.

"I'm sorry about your husband. That really stinks that he died. You're so young to be a widow." Chewing at his lower lip, Dusty squatted and stuck a trowel in the wet earth. "What happened to him? What's your son's name?" He ducked his head. "I'm asking too many questions. Minerva says I take being curious a little too far sometimes, even though she's the one who taught me to be curious about everything."

Curiosity killed the cat. Bess knelt next to the old buggy and picked up a pot of pansies. Better to keep her distance with Freeman nearby. "It's okay that you ask. It's because you're kind. One of the kindest people *I* know."

Dusty looked up. Something sweet and light and airy fluttered between them. She hadn't felt that in a long time. A sort of contentment. Not like the fierce electric lightning that so often sizzled between Caleb and her. More like a breeze wafting between Dusty and her, felt by no one else. "My son's name is Joshua. My husband died in a truck-buggy accident in January."

"That was your husband? I read about that in the paper. It's strange how you see things and they really don't mean much to you. You think they're sad, but not as sad as if you know the person. Now I know you and that newspaper article has a whole new meaning. That wasn't so long ago, either. Yet here you are, making the best of it, working and making a life for yourself. You're very brave." Dusty heaved a breath as if he'd run out of steam. "I'm sorry for your loss."

No one else thought so. They thought she was daft in the head from grief. So daft, she'd taken a job and left others to care for her child. The hole in her heart shrank ever so slightly. "See, you are kind."

She looked away first, unable to bear the sweet light in his eyes as if he probed for something, sought something within her that he desperately needed.

Instead, she focused on turning the dirt, the trowel heavy in her hand, the sweet scent of pansies and morning glories and impatiens heady in the damp humidity of a spring day. Dusty began to hum a tune. Something she recognized from the radio station Minerva blared in the house all day long. K-LOVE. Call letters that spelled a nice word. She hummed along, trying to remember the words about a house, a very big house. Dusty broke into song with an abandon that made three boys passing by on their bikes look back and grin. Dusty waved and started the Weed Eater, ending their impromptu duet.

She almost forgot Freeman and Solomon were inside. Almost.

A good thirty minutes passed. They decided her fate without consulting her. Surely she would be required to return home. To Solomon's home, where she felt a guest with no clear-cut place to be, no role to play.

Where no one called her brave or pretty or nice. Where she wouldn't see Dusty every day.

The screen door opened. Freeman marched out, Solomon close behind. Gavin was nowhere in sight.

Dusty stood. They walked past him with a nod but nary a word. At the buggy Freeman paused so suddenly, Solomon nearly walked into him. The bishop did a two-step that made the horse toss his head and nicker.

"Solomon and I have discussed your situation with Mr. Lake. He understands your responsibilities at home. He's asked us to give this situation some time, in fairness to him as your employer. You took the job and it would be unfair to simply remove you without notice. So you'll stay, at least for now. You'll not shirk your duties at home."

The men had decided. She could live with that if it meant she kept the job. "I understand."

"I'll be watching. So will Solomon." Freeman tugged his hat down as if to shield his eyes from her offending face and turned away. "If you cannot handle both, the job will go. In the meantime I'll let your parents know what has happened. Your daed may have other thoughts on how this should be handled."

Solomon shook his head as if to say *tut-tut* and climbed into the buggy. Neither man said good-bye.

She still had her job. All she had to do was be a good mudder to her bopli. A good helper to her sister-in-law. A good employee at the B and B. She could do all that. Anything to keep from wallowing. She could strike a balance. She would do it.

A soft *whoop* behind her told Bess what Dusty thought of their decision. She turned.

He held up a flat of impatiens. "We should finish planting these. You'll need to get the house chores done so you can get home to Joshua."

He said Joshua's name as if the baby were a close, special friend. She swallowed the lump in her throat. "Thank you for understanding."

"We need you here." He laid the flowers at her feet. "Joshua needs you at home. How does that sound?"

It sounded as if she had made a new, much needed friend.

TWENTY-TWO

Getting on with his life meant stepping out in faith. Letting go of childish notions. Letting go of old feelings that would come to naught. Aidan knew that. As much as he cared for Joshua, as much as he inserted himself into Bess's life, she saw him as someone who meddled where he shouldn't. He'd told Freeman about her job. He'd expressed an opinion when none was requested. He had no clear place in her life now that Caleb was gone. She took a job in town working at the B and B. She'd moved on. So must he. He had no right to expect otherwise. If Gott had intended them to be together, surely it would've happened before she married Caleb, not after his death.

He would do what a man was expected to do. Marry. Have children. Work hard. Pray hard. Love hard. Accept Gott's plan for him, which surely did not include his best friend's widow. Time to accept that. Move on.

Iris had waited patiently. Their time had come. And nearly gone. He slowed the buggy and turned into the rutted dirt road that led to her parents' two-story, white, wood-frame house. The buggy snapped left, then right, jolting him from side to side, but not nearly as much as the turmoil that wracked him inside.

The cool night air brushed his face. He inhaled the scent of fir trees and wet earth. They smelled fresh and clean. How could mud smell clean? Anything would smell better after the gut-wrenching smell of chicken carcasses that clung to his nostrils even now that all the chickens were gone. Sometimes he awoke in the night sure the smell had seeped into the house, into the front room where he'd taken to sleeping on the couch with its scratchy covering.

How could he continue to court Iris when he didn't know what his future held? Was bird flu an excuse to postpone his future with her? If he kept her waiting much longer, she might decide to move on. Mahon Kurtz had made it clear he was ready to step in any time Iris gave him a by-your-leave. She'd never once looked Mahon's way. If she was willing to take a chance on a life with Aidan, who was he to tell her no? He would do the honorable thing. A fraa supported her mann in times like this. Together, they would build a life. He would learn to love her. They wouldn't be the first couple to gradually come to love each other after being bound by their vows.

It was the right thing to do.

He parked the buggy and hopped out, anxious to take this next step before he lost his nerve. He would move past Caleb's death and his feelings for Bess. They were wrong. They'd always been wrong. The window to the room Iris shared with her two younger sisters was dark. He flipped on the flashlight. The front door opened with a squeak. Iris peeked out. "I thought it was you."

"You're still up."

"I couldn't sleep." She slipped out and shut the door behind her. "I'm surprised to see you."

"I know. It's been a while."

"Almost two weeks since the last time I saw you at church." Iris smiled, but sadness marred the effect. Her head down, she smoothed her apron. "Longer since you've been out here. Since we took a walk."

Took a walk that hadn't ended with a kiss. "With the bird flu —"

"I know. I forgive you." She said the words, but faint accusation still managed to worm its way into them, spoken so softly he had to bend down to hear. She brushed past him and hoisted herself into the buggy without looking at him. "Can we take a ride?"

"That was the plan."

She settled into the seat, her hands folded in her lap. The silence stretched while he clamored into the buggy and grabbed the reins. "The spring air feels good, jah?"

She nodded.

Not even the weather then. Aidan snapped the reins and Peanuts took off at a brisk trot. The silence ballooned in the space between them until Aidan had the urge to grab the railing to keep from being squeezed overboard. "I thought we'd go down by the creek. Skip a few rocks."

She nodded again but didn't smile.

"I know you're mad at me, but wouldn't it be better to talk about it."

"It's not my place to be mad at you." She shook her head, exasperation creeping into her voice for the first time. In fact, Aidan didn't remember a time he'd ever heard Iris be angry with him. "Women wait for men. That's what we do. It's what we're taught. You know that."

"But a mann and a fraa —"

"Which we aren't."

"I know, but —"

"I know I shouldn't interrupt, but you must not feel as if you owe me an explanation for anything. I'm just someone you take for a ride now and again. You eat my pie, but that's all."

"You're more than that."

"Am I?"

This wasn't going well at all.

Aidan guided the buggy down the back road that led to a creek that cut across the Beachy property and meandered along the fence line that separated their land from the Gringerichs'. His face felt hot. Pain throbbed in his temples. "I'm sorry."

"I know, but you don't have to be." Iris smiled that sweet, sunny smile usually reserved for when he did something nice for her. "It's not your fault."

He pulled the buggy to a stop. The water lapped against the creek bed in a familiar, rhythmic sound that steadied him. He and Caleb and Iris's bruders, Joseph and Rueben, had fished in this stream many a summer evening. They stuck night crawlers on their hooks, wiped their hands on their pants, and set the lines sailing into the water. Between bites, they mulled the question of just how to get a girl to slip away from the singing for a buggy ride that ended in a kiss. What if they were no good at it? That was the real question none of them dared put into words.

Aidan still didn't know. He hadn't kissed Iris. Another failing on his part. By now, after three years, this omission was an enormous, elderly buffalo with gray on its snout, slumped in the backseat of the buggy every time they took a ride. Iris's curious look of expectancy as they approached her house after each ride had never faded, despite the disappointment she surely felt each time he rode away without holding her close the way a special friend should.

"It is my fault." He hopped from the buggy and stalked around to her side. "Let's take a walk."

She ignored his extended hand and jumped down on her own. "I thought we were going to skip rocks."

"You just like to do it because you know you're better at it than I am."

She snatched a rock that lay a few inches from his worn, dirty boot. "I am."

She proceeded to demonstrate her technique. The rock skimmed across the narrow creek and skidded to a stop on the other side. She dusted her hands, a satisfied look on her face. "What are we doing here?"

"Skipping rocks."

"Aidan Graber."

He scooped up a handful of rocks and did his best to match her effort. His first rock sank without ceremony. The second one managed a paltry two hops before disappearing into the depths.

"You're not doing it right."

He wasn't doing a lot of things right. "Show me."

Grinning she took two of his rocks from his outstretched hand with nimble fingers that didn't touch his. "It's all in the flick of the wrist. Watch."

He watched. Her, not the rock. She took pleasure in such a small thing. Her cheeks were rosy from the cool night air and exertion. She managed to look content, no matter that he had failed her miserably. "Iris, will you marry me?"

"What?" The second rock slipped from her fingers and tumbled into the slips of green grass just beginning to lift their heads through the dry winter straw. Her smile died. "What did you say?"

Aidan took a step closer and reached for her hand. She let him take it. Her skin felt soft and warm against his callused fingers. "I asked if you would marry me."

She tugged her hand free. Her arms went around her ribs. She whirled and trudged along the creek bank, her sneakers making a squelching sound in the mud.

"Iris?"

She stopped walking but didn't turn to face him. His heart hammering against his breast bone, he stalked forward until he could step in front of her. Tears ran down her face.

"Why are you crying?"

She shook her head and wiped at her face with her sleeve. "I'm not crying."

"You are too crying."

"Nee."

"I can see . . ." He brushed her tears away with his thumbs. "Why does me asking you this question make you cry? I thought that's what you wanted."

"Ach, men." She threw her hands up and marched forward, dodging him, her head down. "My mudder was right. They don't understand anything."

"What don't I understand? I don't like to make you cry." The throbbing at his temples reached a crescendo. He hated it when women cried. His sisters always cried when they were sad, when they were happy. How was a man to know the difference? He rubbed his forehead as he strode after her.

"I thought this would make you happy. Are those happy tears? I know women sometimes cry happy tears."

"Not happy. Nee. Not happy." She shook her head. "I've waited a long time for you to ask that question. It is what I wanted. But more than that, I wanted you to want it."

"And now I do, so those are happy tears."

She whirled and faced him so suddenly he plowed to a stop inches from her. "Not happy, because I can't marry you."

"Why not?" He threw his arms up, hands stretched toward her. "You aren't in *lieb* with me?"

The rose in her cheeks darkened. More tears flowed. She traced a line in the mud with the toe of her sneaker. "Why haven't you ever kissed me?"

Gott, if ever there were a time for a deep, deep hole to open up in the earth, this would be it. Or a whale to appear. He'd happily join Jonah in the belly of the fish. "I just never."

"That's no answer and you know it."

"The time never seemed right."

"The time was right over and over again." Her tart tone rose. She switched feet and dug the line deeper. "You never had a hankering, did you?"

278

"Of course I did, but I wanted to do it right." He waved his hands, sure his face was the color of radishes so fresh they still had dirt clinging to their roots. "A man wants to be certain of such a thing. A first kiss should be for the woman he'll marry."

"I'm in lieb with you."

"That's good." So what was the problem? Aidan knew a lot about chickens and pigs and horses and farming in general, but what he knew about women apparently fit in a thimble. A small thimble. Did thimbles only come in one size? He surely had a fever, such was his confusion. "Say jah and be done with it."

"Are you in lieb with me?" The ferocity with which she hurled the question at him left no doubt she believed she knew the answer to her question.

Aidan swallowed and breathed. "If you don't want to marry me because of the chickens dying, I understand. I may have to sell the farm, but I'll farm with Timothy if need be, until I can make my own way again. I'm thinking about expanding my pig operation —"

"This has nothing to do with chickens or pigs or farms." Her voice rose another decibel. "Answer the question."

"I wouldn't ask you to marry me if I

didn't have feelings for you."

"Feelings so deep you can't even say the words?"

"That's one way of putting it."

"You're a good man, Aidan Graber. You don't lie, so you want to avoid answering the question. You don't want to hurt my feelings."

"That's not it. I'm not good at this."

"You're not good at it because you're asking the wrong woman."

"I am not."

She slapped her hands on her hips. She looked just like her mother Josephina for a split second. "Now you *are* lying."

"I don't lie."

"You're not being truthful. That is called lying."

Aidan tugged her hands from her hips and squeezed them. Inches separated them. Her chin came up and her lips parted. He leaned closer, close enough to feel her breath on his check. She smelled of vanilla. "What if I kissed you now? Would that convince you?"

Her eyes widened. They were wet with tears. She jerked away. "That's called being a day late. I won't settle. When I marry, it will be to a man who loves me as much as I love him."

"You are a good woman." Aidan knew

what it was like to wait like that. He should never have involved Iris in his life. She deserved better. "I would be blessed to have you as my fraa."

"Jah, I am. And jah, you would." Her expression softened. Her voice trembled. "And I would be equally blessed to be your fraa, but I can't. Give it time and then go ask her."

"Ask who?"

"Bess."

Aidan closed his eyes. Frogs croaked. A mockingbird sang its sad song. Indeed, it mocked him. Bess's father had known. Now Iris. "I don't know what you're talking about."

Iris shook her head, her eyes full of a kindness that made Aidan want to look away. He didn't need her pity. "I saw the way you looked at her after church that day. Your heart is broken for her."

"My good friend died. Her mann. We share that grief. Nothing more."

"I wish that were true. I prayed to Gott that it would be true. Gott's plan is not clear to me, except for one thing." She squeezed his hand and let it drop as she walked on by. "I can never marry you."

He stared at the water. The reflection of tree branches shimmered in it. The moon's light revealed a turtle scurrying along a log sunk in the mud. Swarms of gnats billowed, like a living, tattered blanket shaken by unseen hands. "It'll be my loss."

"Nee. Marriage is for a lifetime. Being yoked with a fraa you don't love would make you unhappy. I can't bear the idea of being the one who makes you unhappy." Iris climbed into the buggy. "It's settled. Take me home."

"Why did you wait for me then?" He strode to the wagon and planted himself by her side. "Why keep trying all this time?"

"I kept praying. I tried to believe I would get the answer I wanted." She folded her hands in her lap and stared straight ahead. "But it's not Gott's will. I can see that now. So I must be obedient to His will and wait for His plan to unfold. I won't be waiting for you any longer, but for another."

Aidan climbed into the wagon and picked up the reins. He had no farm, no livelihood, and now no special friend. He had no clue what Gott's plan might be for him. The future stretched, an empty road that meandered out of sight. No road signs appeared to give him an inkling of his destination. Only darkness that surely held potholes and sharp drop-offs and dead ends. Peanuts started forward with no prodding. She seemed to know where they were going. If only she could talk. She could let Aidan in on the secret.

TWENTY-THREE

Burning the candle at both ends made for long days and nights. Her arms heavy with exhaustion, Bess laid Joshua on her shoulder and patted his back. Rocking him as she traipsed up and down the hallway outside the bedroom he shared with the other kinner hadn't helped. His wails brought back memories of chalk screeching on the teacher's chalkboard during long-gone school days.

"Shh, shh, shh," she shushed him, knowing it would do no good. He'd been like this off and on during the night, throughout breakfast, and through any effort on her part to help Hazel with Saturday chores. Inconsolable. He would wake Gracie and Levi from their naps if he didn't stop fussing.

"Do you want me to take him?' Hazel appeared at the top of the stairs and padded on bare feet down the hallway. She had a mop in one hand and a bucket of soapy water in the other. Her face featured that gray-green tinge it had every morning these days. "I know you didn't get much sleep last night."

"You have your own chores to do." Freeman's ferocious words *"Don't shirk your duties"* uttered outside the B and B echoed in Bess's ears louder than Joshua's insistent cries. "And you don't feel good. I can see it on your face."

"I ate some crackers and had a cup of chamomile tea." Hazel set the bucket on the floor. Her hand went to her throat, a look of panic on her face. The mop dropped and rolled up against the bucket. Water sloshed onto the wood floor. "I'll be right back." She fled down the stairs, surely headed for the bathroom.

"See, others have problems too." Bess trudged up and down the hallway, sure her legs would crumple under her. She fought the urge to lay her bundle, her burden, on the floor and walk away. "You have nothing to fuss about. You've been fed. Your diaper is dry. You've been burped. There's not a spot of diaper rash on your behind. Stop fighting it. Take a nap. You'll feel better. We both will."

Please, take a nap.

285

Instead, he opened his mouth and spit-up ran down the front of his nightgown and the front of her apron. Again. She held him out, legs dangling. "Ach! Again. No wonder we have so much laundry."

If her mudder could hear Bess right now, she would be so ashamed. How could taking care of one small bopli be that hard? Most Plain families had five, six, seven, ten, or more kinner.

Just one, only one. The only one she would ever have and she couldn't handle him. Her eyes burned with fatigue and unshed tears. *What is wrong with me, Gott?*

More wails greeted her whispered words. She halted, eyes closed. *Gott, help me. I can't take this anymore.*

The wails escalated and reached a crescendo.

A ride. Go for a ride.

A ride? Really, Gott?

A desperate, almost giddy hope filled her. She rushed to the barn with Joshua, still complaining at the top of his lungs, writhing in his basket. A few minutes later they were on the road.

To where? She'd give no thought to destination. Only to leaving behind her ugly feelings of inadequacy. She tugged on the reins. The horse nickered in complaint and stopped in the middle of the road. Mary Katherine had gone to visit kinner in Seymour for the day. Jennie had her own squalling kinner.

Laura's sweet entreaty to drop in anytime echoed in Bess's ears. It drowned out Joshua's sobs long enough for her to plot her course. "Giddyup."

The creak of the wheels and the steady *clip-clop* of the horse's hooves filled the air. Joshua's cries subsided. Blue jays chattered in the sycamore and elm trees that lined the road. Mourning doves cooed. Bess tried to loosen her grip on the reins. *Please be home, please be home.*

Laura was indeed home. She sat alone in a hickory rocking chair on the dawdy haus's small front porch, a closed book in her lap, her hands clasped on top of it. She looked as if she might be sleeping.

"Whoa." Bess hesitated. She didn't want to wake her. She might have delivered a baby overnight. One never knew with midwives. "Easy there, easy."

Easy. She might have spoken those words to herself instead of running over here to bother a tired, elderly woman.

"Well, are you getting out or what?" Laura's eyelids popped open. "I'm itching to hold that bopli of yours."

"You can have him." The words burst forth before Bess could contain them. "I mean —"

"Having a rough morning, are you?"

"A rough dozen mornings." Bess climbed down from the buggy and took Joshua, who glared — she was sure of it at her — to the older woman. "He cries and cries. He eats all the time and he never wants to sleep. I don't understand. I thought all women knew how to be mudders. I don't know how. I'm . . . defective."

Laura chuckled, a tiny burble at first, then bigger until the burble became a belly laugh.

"How can you laugh? I'm a horrible mudder."

"Nee. You're human and you sound so surprised and disgusted at that simple fact. I'm sorry. I shouldn't laugh." Laura laid the book, a German language Bible, on the table that separated her chair from a second one. "Sit, sit, before you fall down, my sweet girl."

Bess sank into the other chair, light-headed with relief. "I can't make him happy. In fact, he looks at me and throws up."

"I don't think looking at you makes him throw up." Laura began to rock, Joshua snuggled up against her ample chest. He nestled closer, eyes closed, breathing soft.

The silence had never sounded better. Laura smiled. "Sweet thing. I think he might have a food allergy. I've heard of that. Maybe you need to stop drinking milk. Maybe he's allergic to something you're eating."

"How do you do that?" Bess wanted to scream, but she didn't. That would only bring on more crying. She couldn't bear more crying. "Why does he do that for you and not me?"

"You're tense, my child. Your emotions drown him." Laura continued to rock and pat. "But it's not your fault. You have to understand that. You've been through something awful. You're still coming to terms with it. Joshua loves you. You're his mudder. You have a bond with him no one else will have. Ever. With time, you'll feel better and he'll feel that you feel better."

"It doesn't seem like I'll ever feel better."

"But you will. I promise." Laura eased from her chair, stood, and held out Joshua. "Take heart and take your bopli. Let his repose seep into you. He sleeps, putting his whole trust into you. Rest in that trust and that love."

"He'll wake up."

"Just breathe him in. You know what boplin smell like?" She leaned over and sniffed

289

Joshua's tiny curls as if to remind herself. Her face, wrinkled, skin weathered from sun, work, and laughter, was beautiful. "They smell like innocence and joy and peace because they've known no troubles yet. They're unaware. They simply know that they are cared for."

Bess did as she was told. She held her son close and inhaled. Joshua smelled of her. Of her milk. He also smelled like he might need a diaper change. She didn't dare or he would awaken, and she wanted nothing more than to sit in this chair and see in her mind's eye the picture painted by this woman who had raised nine kinner and helped with the birth of hundreds more. She sank back and let the sleeping weight of her child rest against her. "Why is this so hard? Is something wrong with me?"

Laura kissed Joshua's forehead, then Bess's. She straightened, knees cracking, and smiled. "You're handling what life has given you as best you can. Not every woman is filled with joy after birth. There are hormones involved. Add that to your terrible loss and I think you're doing remarkably well. You get up every day and put one foot in front of the other. You work at the B and B. You do chores. You do what other mudders do. You worry about your suh."

"Worrying is a sin."

"Worrying is human. Stop expecting to be perfect and start relying on Gott to see you through."

"Having said that, we'll have a visit with Doc Lowe. I'll go with you. She'll have a peek at little Joshua to see if something ails him and then at you."

"This hormone thing. It doesn't sound like something a Plain woman can have."

"Plain women are no different from other women. They get cancer. They have high cholesterol and high blood pressure. They get diabetes. Why wouldn't they get depression?"

"I can't have depression. Freeman says I have to carry my own weight at home or quit the job at the B and B."

"And you want the job."

"It keeps me from sitting in the room I shared with Caleb and trying to remember what his laugh sounded like and worrying that I won't be able to smell his smell there anymore. It keeps me from looking at his suh's face and seeing Caleb's and missing him more than I can bear."

She stopped, afraid tears would follow.

"Then we need to find a way for you to do both." Laura settled into her chair and picked up the Bible. "I'll pray on it and

Monday you'll go to work a little late so we can go see the doctor. Now close your eyes and rest. I'll keep an eye on you both."

Bess closed her eyes. The sun warmed her face. She breathed in the scent of Laura's roses and honeysuckle. "It's a beautiful day, isn't it?"

"It is." Laura's words mingled with the rustling of pages turning and leaves lifted from the branches of nearby trees by a soft breeze. "This is the day the Lord has made. Remember that. Many good days are to come."

Bess held on to the thought even as she held on to Joshua.

TWENTY-FOUR

Still time to escape. Only the memory of another sleepless night with Joshua ensconced in the bed next to her because she was too tired to tromp back and forth to his crib kept Bess's behind on the plush chair in Dr. Lowe's office, staring at the Winnie the Pooh prints adorning walls painted bright green and purple. The air was cool and smelled of a flowery air freshener. A child with a runny nose cried. A little boy slept, his mouth open, snoring on his mother's lap, while she read a *Highlights* magazine story to her daughter, who stuffed Cheerios into her mouth by the fistful. Twins fought over a fire truck, pulling on it until the siren went off — again and again. Bess should be at work, not here waiting to whine to the doctor about her lot in life as a new mother. Everyone experienced this. She needed to get some backbone and muddle through it.

She contemplated the distance to the front

door. If it weren't for abandoning Joshua, she could make a break for it. Knowing Jennie and Laura, they would race after her and drag her back. They had shown up on her doorstep with Mary Katherine just as she washed the last breakfast dish. Mary Katherine claimed she didn't want Laura driving the buggy with her painful, arthritic hands. Jennie insisted she wanted to pick up some ointment for Micah's pinkeye. Bess suspected the women simply wanted to make sure she didn't back out from Laura's plan to see the doctor. Bess might have, had it not been for Joshua's insistent, mournful cries. Of course, he now slumbered in Jennie's arms as if he hadn't a care in the world.

The thought made her wiggle in frustration and sigh. Laura looked up from her book. "Settle down, child. They'll work you in when they can. Waiting is expected when you show up without an appointment."

"I should be at work getting the dishes washed and the beds made up."

"Mary Katherine is letting the Lakes know where you are." Jennie tucked Joshua's blanket up around his chin. "Anybody who has had kinner will understand. You never know when you'll have to contend with an ear infection or strep throat or a broken wrist or a bean stuck in a nose."

294

"Or in an ear." Laura chuckled. "I think I counted twelve broken bones over the course of raising nine kinner. You?"

"Mine are younger. We're not done yet." Jennie commiserated. "The last one was Celia's collarbone when Matthew hit her with a bat at the end-of-year school picnic. The worst was Mark's broken leg when he fell off the trampoline. He had to have physical therapy to learn to walk right after that one."

They sounded so at ease with all those broken bones and emergencies. A club to which Bess didn't belong. Not yet, anyway. The thought made her stomach clench. "I don't know if I can —"

The door opened, letting in a stream of early morning sunlight. Mary Katherine bustled into the waiting room. "That Minerva is quite the interesting character." She plucked something that looked like oatmeal from her apron, then waved at the other ladies in the room. The boys dropped the fire truck and ran to greet her. She handed out hugs without missing a beat. "She said to take the whole day if you needed it. She'd have Dusty help out and her sister is in town visiting. Two peas in a pod, those two. She didn't seem the least bit perturbed."

She settled into the chair next to Bess.

"How are you doing, missy? Nothing to worry about here. This is what doctors are for."

So why did she feel so miserably ashamed of her own shortcomings? Bess swallowed tears that would only bring more shame. "I'm fine."

"Dusty asked about you." Mary Katherine's tone was mild. "He didn't take to your absence as easily as his mudder. And I didn't get the impression it was because he didn't want to help with the housework. He seemed downright worried."

"He's a nice man. He's been very nice to me since he learned I lost my mann and have a suh." Bess stumbled over the words. She searched for reasons why. She'd done nothing wrong. Dusty *was* a nice man. Very nice. "He's a friend."

Mary Katherine's eyebrows rocketed to spots near the crown of her head. "Friend? I —"

Before she could finish her objection, the door on the other side of the receptionist's counter opened. Nurse Tammy stuck her head out. "Bess Weaver." Her wide smile invited Bess into the inner sanctuary. "I have a room for you now. Let's get your vitals and get you settled."

All three of her companions stood. Nurse

Tammy shook her head. "Sorry, ladies, you know how small these rooms are." In unison, they sat, but not one of them looked happy.

The next few minutes passed in a flurry of weight and height and temperatures for both Bess and Joshua. The wonders of a small-town family doctor. Dr. Lowe saw all ages, shapes, and sizes, entire families. Then more waiting. By God's grace, Joshua continued to sleep. The doctor wouldn't believe he spent all his time crying at home. Bess closed her eyes, resting them for a few seconds. The *tick-tick* of the wall clock made her drowsy.

"What do we have here?" Dr. Lowe strode into the room. With her gray curls and ample figure, she looked like someone's grandma and not one of Jamesport's only homegrown doctors. Her white jacket's pocket bulged with suckers and stickers. Her sneakers squeaked on the polished tile floor. She plopped onto a stool on wheels and patted Bess's arm. "You look tired, sweetie. I got an earful from Laura in the waiting room. Tell me all about it, lovie."

Bess didn't know how to start. When she did, the words poured out. Dr. Lowe would never tell anyone. She could be trusted and Laura could be trusted when she said this was the best thing to do for Joshua. "He's tired. I'm tired. He throws up all the time. He cries all the time. I'm a failure." She whispered the words. Every second Joshua slept was golden. "What's wrong with me?"

"Honey, it's called the baby blues and it's more common than you imagine." Dr. Lowe took Joshua and laid him on the exam table. Her movements were crisp and economical. As she examined him she continued to talk. "It's not a character flaw or a weakness. You're not a failure as a mother. You're not worthless. That's hogwash. All women have crazy hormones — that's a medical term by the way — after giving birth. They're sleep deprived as well. You, on top of all that, have suffered a terrible loss. You're bound to experience depression."

"What do I do?"

Dr. Lowe listened to Joshua's heart, checked his ears and then his mouth. By now he gurgled at her with a sleepy grin. "I don't believe you need medical intervention, Mrs. Weaver. You have a tremendous support system in your community. Much more than a lot of the women I see in here from the non-Amish population. Those three ladies out there in the waiting room, take their help. Let them baby you. Let them care for Joshua while you take a nap. I want you to give yourself a break. In the meantime I'll order some blood work and make sure there's nothing physical we need to be concerned about. There are medications you can take, but you're breastfeeding so I'd rather not — at least not yet."

"If Joshua didn't cry so much, I wouldn't be as frazzled. I've never seen a baby cry this much. Or spit up so much."

"He's gaining weight and all his vitals are good." Dr. Lowe scooped him up and cuddled him close. "It's likely reflux."

She went on to explain how the stomach connected to something called an esophageal sphincter. Two words that meant nothing to Bess. The important point was that it was immature in a baby and food came back up with acid in it that irritated the baby's throat. "It hurts. Just like when you eat spicy food and get heartburn or acid indigestion."

"I don't eat spicy foods."

"He may also be allergic to milk or eggs. Try eliminating one and then the other from your diet and see if it helps." Dr. Lowe patted her small patient's back. Joshua cooed. Even a stranger had better rapport with him than Bess. Little traitor. "Smaller feedings. More burping during feedings and afterward keep him upright for twenty or thirty minutes. Most likely, he'll outgrow it."

"And if he doesn't?"

"Let's not borrow trouble. Most babies do. In the meantime I prescribe regular doses of Auntie Laura, Mary Katherine, and Jennie." Dr. Lowe tugged a handful of lollipops from her pocket and held them out. "They can help out and you can get some z's. Sleep is the best medicine for tired mommies."

Lollipops and friends were the best medicine. After the lab work, Bess trundled into the waiting room, Joshua wiggling in her arms.

"What did she say?" Laura hopped up, Mary Katherine and Jennie right behind her.

"She gave me a prescription."

"For what?" Jennie elbowed in front of Mary Katherine, angling for first dibs to hold Joshua. "For you or for Joshua?"

"You." Bess held out three of the lollipops Dr. Lowe had given her. "All of you."

Laura clapped. Jennie grabbed the red sucker. The other patients stared. "I told you she was a good doctor."

TWENTY-FIVE

A trip to the doctor's office and people thought she was dying. Bess grabbed a dish towel from the kitchen counter and sopped at the dishwater that soaked her dress, turning the pale lilac material to a darker purple. She tried to ignore Dusty's entreaty, but the sweet way he said her name made it impossible. His face looked worried. He'd been hanging around the kitchen offering to help her with her chores for two days. Now, he wanted her to go with him to the flower farm. It wasn't even fall. The mums weren't ready. They were barely planting the seedlings in the pots and plopping them down in the open field. Yet he insisted on making his case.

"Fresh air is good for you and flowers will cheer you up." He offered his reasoning with a diffident smile. "If you won't stay home until you feel better, then I think you should at least take it easy. A trip to the flower farm

301

will help."

"I feel fine. I'm being paid to work. Your mother already gave me a half day off on Monday. I don't want to take advantage of her kindness."

"Minerva actually suggested it. She's as concerned about you as I am. She feels bad for your loss as well. You never said a word when she hired you. She wants to do something nice for you. We'll only be gone an hour or two. I need to do research. Mass growing of *Chrysanthemum X morifolium* — of course, taxonomically there's been a lot of contention concerning the correct scientific name. Many prefer *Dendranthema X grandiflorum* — is something I'm considering doing when I get my own place."

"You're getting your own place?" If he moved into his own house, he wouldn't be here making the bed-and-breakfast a brighter, prettier place with beautiful flowers or encouraging her to dig in the dirt and feel the sun on her face as what he called therapy for her melancholy. "Does Minerva know that?"

"Not a house. I want to start my own business."

"I thought you wanted to go back to the university."

"I realized that what I want has changed."

He ducked his head and studied shoes the size of boats. "That happens sometimes. Priorities shift. Feelings change."

"But you'll do it here in Jamesport?" The thought of Dusty leaving Jamesport caused a prickle to run up Bess's arms. "I don't think this little town can support more than one."

"I wouldn't want to leave here, that's the whole point of not going to the university." A sudden smile creased his face. "You don't want me to go, either, do you?"

"I don't know. You're a friend. A new friend." Flustered at his surprisingly astute insight into something she hadn't realized herself, she bustled across the kitchen and grabbed the broom from its resting spot next to the pantry door. She employed a vigorous stroke that caused Dusty to hop back with a yelp. "I just don't want you to start a business that goes bust. You'll be back here at the B and B bothering me quicker than you can shake a stick at a dog."

"Why would anyone shake a stick at a dog? Never mind." He slapped a big hand on the broom, his pinky finger touching hers. "If you'll go with me, I promise to have you back by lunch and I won't bother you for the rest of the day."

"And you need me to go because?"

"Because you're Amish and they're Amish. You know them. You can introduce me and get me the behind-the-scenes tour. I don't want the tourist version. I want the whole kit and caboodle."

There wouldn't be much difference, if any. Growing mums had no secrets, whatsoever. Which led to the question of what Dusty really wanted with her time.

She had no choice, it seemed. "You're sure Minerva won't mind?"

"She gave her blessing. She said to bring her back some flowers for the centerpiece on the supper table. She wants to see some color on your cheeks and a smile on your face when you come back."

It was a beautiful spring day. Summer heat hadn't descended on Jamesport yet. The urge to be outdoors, the feel of the sun and breeze on her face, overpowered Bess. Two hours. Two hours outdoors talking about plants and flowers. It would buoy her up for the rest of the week and the weekend spent caring for a fussy baby. Dr. Lowe had prescribed rest. A ride would be restful.

A moment's respite.

The trip took longer than expected after they were stuck behind not one, but two of the tour buses that clogged the roads lead-ing to and from Jamesport now that tourism season was in full swing. Tourists stared out the windows of the black monsters with burgundy writing on them, straining for the first glimpses of what they'd paid to see — the Amish. What could be so interesting about a bunch of farmers? Bess contemplated that question as the old delivery truck Dusty had commandeered puttered along, complaining at every bump in the road. It needed new suspenders or whatever those things were called that protected riders from the potholes.

"You're awfully quiet." Dusty had been equally quiet once he maneuvered the truck out on to the road. "Are you regretting your decision to come along?"

"Just thinking."

"Don't think too hard, you'll give yourself a headache."

His funny little sayings made her think of Mary Katherine. She didn't want to think of Mary Katherine. If the woman saw them together, she'd have a sharp word to say. If Bess was worried about being seen with Dusty, she shouldn't be with him at all. "I really should be back at the B and B, working. I've changed my mind. This wasn't a good idea."

"I only thought it would make you feel better, less sad." He glanced her way, then back at the road. "I care about you — a lot. I know it's bad timing, but I can't help it. I think I may be developing feelings for you."

The words might have been in Japanese. Bess couldn't — didn't want — to comprehend them. "We should go back."

Before it was too late. They could rewind time and make those words unspoken.

In his anguish, Dusty must've hit the gas hard. The truck jolted forward. Bess's neck snapped. She grabbed the door handle. The engine snorted and belched. The passenger-side mirror gave her a clear view of the smoke billowing from behind them. "Slow down."

"Sorry. Sorry. I don't mean to make you uncomfortable. I might be falling in love with you. I've never been in love before so it's hard for me to know, but I'm almost sure of it. I want to spend more time with you and help your heart start to heal. There's no rush; you've been through so much. I just want you to know I'm here, whenever you're ready."

Finally, he ran down. The flow of words, so like a waterfall, died away.

The sound of air rushing around them filled the silence.

Out of the corner of her eye she could see him glancing her way. Waiting. Wanting.

Wanting her.

Bess hadn't heard many declarations of love in her lifetime. One, to be exact. Caleb had expressed no reservations. He had been certain, but he'd known her his entire life. The declaration was expected. Anticipated. When it came, there was no equivocating. She'd simply answered as she always knew she would. With her own declaration.

"Say something." He peered at her, his face as red as any tomato ever grown in a garden in these parts. "Anything. Please."

The truck veered toward the center lane and kept going. An oncoming tour bus loomed. A horn demanded he pay attention. "Dusty, the road! The road."

He jerked the wheel. They veered right. Tires squealed. The truck jerked left. The force sent Bess's head slamming against the passenger window. Dusty threw one arm out in front of her, trying to push her back in the seat. He swerved back into the proper lane. Bess's body righted itself. She clasped her hands to her forehead. "Ouch. Ouch!"

"Sorry. I'm so sorry." Dusty's arm withdrew. His hands gripped the wheel, his fingers white. "Are you all right? Are you hurt? I only want to help and look what I've done. I'm sorry."

The spot on her temple that had connected with the glass throbbed. She rubbed and breathed through tears that welled. She tried to suck in air. Nothing happened. Her lungs were flat. Her heart pounded in her ears in an erratic rhythm that left her light-headed. "It's okay. I'm not hurt. I'm fine."

"I should never have said anything. You're not ready. I thought I could help, but I said it all wrong."

He sounded so bereft. Her breathing caught up with itself. Her heart returned to the corral. "It's sweet of you to care. It really is, but we're very different. My community will take care of me. I'll get better. You can't be thinking that something will grow between us. It can't."

"It's not something a person chooses to do, like go to college or not go to college or be a vegetarian or not." He looked her way again, but this time his gaze returned to the road in a timely fashion. "You've been in love, so you know. Falling in love is like having ocean waves crash over you. There's no stopping them. It's too late to run. They envelop you, take your breath away, knock you off your feet, swallow you whole. The rest of the world disappears. Nothing else matters except being in that moment."

Bess had never seen the ocean, let alone been knocked off her feet by the waves.

308

Somehow his description made her ache to experience it. It didn't seem possible for a landlocked Missouri girl. "I'm Plain. You're not." Which had not one iota to do with feelings. "It won't work."

"I'm a man. You're a woman. We both love plants. We love gardening. We love being outdoors. We have plenty in common. Just tell me if you have feelings for me. You do, I know you do."

She opened her mouth to deny it. No words came out. Like Dusty, she couldn't be sure. If she wasn't sure, then it couldn't be love. With Caleb she'd known. No second thoughts. No regrets. No thoughts at all. Simply following her heart.

The flower farm came into view. Dusty pulled into the dirt plot that served as a parking lot and shoved the gear in park. He turned the key off and sighed. "I'm here for you. I just wanted you to know that. With time, you might see your way to care for me. If not, I'm still here for you. Whatever you need."

To bare his soul to her like that and then offer to step back was so like him. He hadn't a mean, selfish bone in his big body. "That's so kind of you."

"If you saw your way to love me back, you'd make me the happiest man in the world." He ducked his head. "I think I'd be a good daddy too. A little boy needs a man in his life."

Her throat tightened. She swallowed against tears that burned. "I know he does. It makes me so sad to think of Joshua growing up without his daed."

Dusty slid across the seat. His hand sought hers. He squeezed. "I'm sorry for your pain and your loss. I didn't mean to make you cry."

"You didn't." His grip on her fingers, his arm pressed against hers, everything about his nearness, should've made her uncomfortable. Instead, comfort wrapped itself around her. "Your offering is so sweet."

"You don't feel that way about me. I understand." He laid her hand in her lap with infinite care. His fingers brushed against her cheek. He slid back across the seat. "I'll keep praying that one day you do. You deserve to love again, even if it isn't me who is blessed enough to receive that gift."

To love again meant risking loss. She'd loved Caleb and look where that got her. Riding in a cargo truck with an Englisch man who professed to possibly loving her. He couldn't. A person had no guarantees when it came to love. Dusty was a special man with an enormous heart. He had good

310

intentions. He offered her the gift of a chance to start over, to start fresh, to get far away from the memories. She couldn't do that. If she did she would lose everything. Family and faith. Faith and family. They came first, before individual needs and wants.

And what about Joshua? He needed his family. He needed his groossmammi and groossdaadi.

He also needed a daed.

Dusty would never be a daed. He'd be a father. A daddy.

Bess swallowed against hot tears. "We have to look at mums."

"Right, mums." For the first time since Bess had known Dusty, he didn't sound the least bit interested in flowers or plants. "You're right. I said my piece and I promise you I won't say another word about it."

Dusty shoved open his door and hoisted himself from the truck so fast a person would think a bobcat or a rattlesnake pursued him.

Before Bess could open her door, he tugged it open and held it wide. She slid out. Beyond him stood Elizabeth Gringerich, married daughter of the flower farm owner Silas Eicher.

Talking to Iris.

TWENTY-SIX

Who are you when no one is looking? Bess apparently was someone who let an Englisch man hold her hand when no one was looking. The thought sent goose bumps scurrying up her arms where they nestled at the base of her neck like chills caused by a fever.

She trailed after Elizabeth and Iris, letting Dusty's bulky frame serve as a shield. They walked toward the fields where the Eichers grew the mums in long rows of dusty, black pots. Her attempt to hide didn't work. Iris popped back and slid into step next to her. Her long-legged stride slowed. Politeness forced Bess to slow as well. Dusty was far too engrossed in his conversation with Elizabeth regarding the finer points of growing mums to notice that they had dropped back a pace.

"It's been so long since I've seen you." Iris shielded her face from the sun with a hand already tanned from planting a spring garden. " 'Course, this is the last place I expected to see you."

And the last person with whom she expected to see Bess. "I heard you were working at the B and B."

"I am. Dusty is the son of the owners. He's interested in plants, and he asked me to introduce him to the Eichers." Offering an explanation for which none had been asked.

"I see." Iris's tone said she saw a lot more than Bess wanted to reveal. "He's an odd one, so excited over mums and plants."

Plain folks didn't get excited over plants. Plants were woven into their everyday existence. A fundamental building block for every farmer. "He works at the nursery in town. He wants to have his own nursery and plant farm one day."

"You seem to know a lot about him."

"I work at the B and B every day. He's there sometimes, when he's not working at the nursery." Time to change the subject. "Why are you here today? There's no mums to be had until fall."

"Elizabeth is expecting. Laura and I will deliver the bopli in a few months. She's been feeling poorly, barely able to stand some days. I came by to bring her some herbal supplements Laura wanted her to take."

In other words, she had a perfectly good reason for being at the flower farm while Bess did not. "You are a good midwife. You must be happy to do something so useful."

So joyful. To bring life into the world.

"In training. Laura is the real midwife. I'm learning so much from her." Smiling, Iris inclined her head, but her expression said she had no intention of allowing the change of subject. "I heard that Freeman and Solomon visited the B and B."

She heard a great deal. The grapevine doing its self-sworn duty.

"They did."

"Yet here you are."

Running around with the Englisch man as if planting flowers with him in front of the B and B hadn't resulted in enough trouble for Bess. Iris had a succinct way about her.

"It's only a trip to the flower farm." She didn't have to justify herself to Iris, yet she found herself seeking to do it anyway. "For his research. Because his parents are my employers."

Truth, but not the whole truth.

Which could only be called a lie.

"It's none of my business." Iris hesitated for the first time. Her gaze went to the man who tromped along, hands gesticulating, head bobbing, as he told Elizabeth all about some aspect of the mum-plant family known to him as *Compositae* or *Asteraceae*. Poor Elizabeth probably had no idea what the man meant with his strange scientific gobbledygook.

Iris ducked her head as if watching her bare feet to make sure she didn't step on a prickly burr. "It's just that there's Aidan."

Aidan. His fingers had come close to touching Bess's that evening in the shell of a house that Caleb would never finish building. He knew what a Plain man must do and in what order he must do it. He was a godly man. He had done nothing untoward. Yet Bess's face burned at the memory of how much she'd wanted him to entwine his fingers in hers. How much she wanted to be touched, to be comforted, to feel wanted. How could she want something so much when it would surely lead to devastating loss? She'd loved Caleb and lost. How could she dare to love again? With Aidan or with Dusty?

With anyone. Even Joshua. She had no guarantee she wouldn't one day lose her son. Guarantees didn't exist.

Gott, why? Why suffering? Why prayers unanswered?

She drew a breath and exhaled, trying to erase the sight of Aidan's pewter eyes searching her face, looking for something she couldn't identify, something she couldn't find the courage or the strength to offer again. Swallowing the bitter taste in the back of her throat, she managed a shrug. "What about Aidan?"

"Don't do that."

"Do what?"

"Pretend." Iris's cheeks turned a fierce red as if she'd suddenly acquired a sunburn. "It's not fair to me. You know my feelings. It seems the whole world knows."

"I may know your feelings, but I don't know of Aidan's. He's said nothing to me."

"He cares for you." Pain mingled with regret in the rush of her words. "He always has. You and Caleb were the only ones who didn't see it."

"He did not. He does not." Surprise pummeled Bess. Aside from Caleb, Aidan was her oldest friend. In so many ways, their friendship, as sturdy as a Plain home, had been the exception to all the rules. No one understood it, least of all Bess. "He was a good friend to Caleb."

And to me. Especially to me.

"So good he let him marry the woman he loved."

316

"Nee." Her voice sounded weak in her ears. "You don't know what you're talking about."

"I know I can never marry him because he loves another." Iris wiped at her face with her sleeve. Her voice quivered. "So don't waste his feelings for you. I want him to be happy. Someday, when you're ready, he can make you happy."

"I don't know what to say. I'm sorry your feelings are hurt."

"I just wanted to say my piece."

Iris dashed ahead without looking back, leaving Bess to catch up on her own. They joined Elizabeth and Dusty as they approached the field where the long flatbed trailer set, a beehive of activity. Elizabeth glanced back, her face full of curiosity, but she said nothing, instead pointing to the cluster of girls, including her six sisters, who were bent over piles of potting soil, scooping it up and filling pots. They looked like flowers themselves in pastel greens, lavenders, blues, and an occasional dark burgundy dresses, with long v's of material down the back like leaves and white prayer kapps like centers. They were barefoot, their faces flushed with exertion and good health. They looked as if they didn't have a care in the world. Bess longed to join them.

"We fill the pots first, then once they're in the field, we add the seedlings." Elizabeth scooped up a handful of soil and let it trickle between her fingers. The smell wafted around Bess, a heady scent of earth, rich and heavenly, better than any man-made aroma. "Everything is done by hand. That's why all the girls are here. The more hands, the faster it goes."

"Why do you plant them in pots?" Only Dusty could look so enthralled over plastic pots. "Why not in the ground?"

"Because we sell them at produce auction in the fall, and this way we don't have to dig them up and pot them for the auction." Elizabeth seemed totally at ease answering this towering giant's questions. She surely had plenty of experience with tourists who were equally curious. "It saves us a lot of work and they're better off not having to be transplanted."

"So what happens next?"

Elizabeth pointed at the open field where plastic had been laid down to keep the grass and weeds from growing up around the pots. "We'll set them out here in the sunshine. Then we add drip irrigation so they get plenty of water during the summer."

"Genius." Dusty nodded so hard Bess feared his head might fall off. His look of rapture was akin to what she'd seen on a Plain man who'd just bought a new horse or buggy. "No depending on nature to make sure they get enough hydration."

"When the fall produce auction comes around, we load them up on the flatbed trailer and away they go. We'll have purple, red, orange, maroon, yellow, all the fall colors. People come from all over to buy them along with the pumpkins and gourds. They love their fall decorations." Elizabeth dusted her hands as if the job were already complete. "We never have any to bring back. We sell them all."

"No doubt. No doubt."

"Any more questions?"

None that could be asked — or answered — here in the middle of a field of mum seedlings.

Dusty frowned as if sensing the tension in the air. "How many do you plant? How much is your initial investment in soil, pots, seedlings, and so on? What kind of profit margin are we talking about?"

So many questions as if bombarding her would sink the real questions. What was Bess doing out here with him? What would she do about his declaration of love in an old, beat-up truck?

Elizabeth's eyebrows rose and fell. She

raised her hand, fingers spread wide. Soil caked her nails. A bandage covered the tip of her middle finger. "These are questions for my daed. He's up at the house doing some paperwork."

"Let's go." Dusty turned on his heel, then looked back at Bess. "Come on, just a little longer."

"I can't. I have to get back." She didn't want to see Silas Eicher. Rather, she didn't want Silas Eicher to see her. "I have chores to do and Minerva will be fit to be tied if those beds don't get changed and the laundry done."

"Come back later." Elizabeth rescued her. "Daed likes to talk mums. He'll talk your ear off."

Come back alone. She didn't say those words, but Bess heard them loud and clear.

The question was, did Dusty?

TWENTY-SEVEN

The aroma of baked pork chops seasoned with hickory smoke salt, Worcestershire sauce, and lemon juice normally caused Aidan to pick up his fork and knife before the food hit his plate. The fact that he'd raised the hog that had provided this repast for the Weavers should give him a feeling of job-well-done. His efforts to diversify and overcome the loss of his flock were paying off. Little by little. Happy news. Instead, the sight of Bess rushing through the door, late for supper, her expression grim, squelched the hunger pains in his stomach quicker than the avian flu and sent his contentment packing.

He'd begun to think his efforts to talk to her would be in vain, that she would not make an appearance at this family supper. That in itself would cause her trouble with Mattie, who never lost an opportunity to scold her girls for not carrying their weight.

Bess would be no exception, especially now that Caleb wasn't here to serve as a buffer.

The tale of her working side by side with Dusty Lake in the front yard of the B and B, planting a garden, had winged its way to his ears faster than a speeding arrow. Bess might never know how Aidan felt about her, but she would know that he cared about her eternal salvation. Spending time with an Englisch man could only lead to disaster. She couldn't leave her faith — not for that man, not for any reason. He had to convince her to stay away from Dusty Lake. From the B and B. If that meant she had to move to Haven with her parents, so be it. He would learn to live with that.

"You're late." Her tone sharp, Mattie shook her head. Her nose wrinkled. "Hazel and the girls cooked supper. The least you can do is help serve it."

"Sorry. Sorry. I got behind on the bedrooms and the laundry still had to be done . . ." The words trailed away. Bright-red spots appeared on Bess's cheeks. "Anyway, I'll do the dishes after."

"Indeed you will."

Disheveled, her apron stained with what looked like grape jelly, her kapp askew, Bess had a strange expression on her face. Guilt, he would say if he didn't know better. Guilt over being late? Guilt over spending no time with Joshua? Guilt over spending the day in Dusty Lake's company at the B and B? Aidan had no chance of spending that kind of time with her. Was she late because she'd lost track of time with the Englischer?

His throat tightened. The pork chops no longer smelled enticing. His appetite disappeared.

She bustled from the kitchen, the platter of pork chops in her hands.

He gritted his teeth, forced a smile, and accepted her offering.

"So you've expanded your hog operation?" Apparently oblivious to the tension in the room, Isaac heaped mashed potatoes alongside a slab of cornbread the size of his massive fist. "No chance you'll get back to chickens, then?"

"Hogs give me a source of income now. I can't raise chickens until the state gives me leave. Eventually, I'd like to do both." Needed to do both if he was to be a mann and daed. Picking up his knife and fork, Aidan forced himself to focus on the question. Bess leaned forward and set the platter in the middle of the table. She smelled like dish soap. His thoughts trailed away into a fog that came out of nowhere. *Stop it.* Isaac would think he was daft. He cleared his throat. "It's a matter of having the money to replenish my stock. Selling hogs will allow me to do that."

"I sure miss fresh eggs in the morning." Solomon sighed, a mournful sound, as he slathered butter on his cornbread. "Our little flock wasn't much, but it kept us in good eats."

"The store-bought ones are fine," Mattie muttered. The woman had never been particularly round. Now she was a wisp of a figure, an outline of her former self. She coughed, sipped from a glass of water, and coughed again. "No sense in crying over spilt milk."

"No one's crying." Solomon's tone stopped just short of crabby. "Leastways far as I can see."

"We don't need another reason to go into town." Mattie's tone left no doubt as to what she thought of that. "Seems as if some of us do plenty of that."

Bess picked up the basket of rolls. She held it out to Aidan. His fingers brushed hers as he accepted. Warm. Soft. The frown on her face softened. The girl with the beautiful, open face untouched by grief and tragedy shone through for a few seconds. A tremulous smile appeared, then fled.

His breath fled with it.

She picked up the butter and held it out. The blue of her eyes held him like the blue of Stockton Lake at sunrise as he stared out over the water seeking Gott's face. Her cheeks were red from her headlong rush into the house. In the simple, every day, she was beautiful. A Plain man didn't put much stock in looks, but Aidan had never been able to get her image from his mind, no matter how many other women passed in front of him. She filled the space in his heart where he kept the hope of a woman who would be a fine fraa and mudder. And someone with whom he could spend the rest of his life. He seemed to have forgotten how to raise his hand to accept her offering. He swallowed and willed his heart to stop its jittery dance.

"It's only butter." She cocked her head toward the dish. "For your cornbread. It won't bite."

"I know. I just . . ."

Stop it. Through the fog came the realization that a bruise darkened her temple, half hidden by the hair that peeked from her kapp. He latched on to this new thought, shoving away the troublesome images that pursued him. "What happened to your head?"

She froze. The butter dish slipped from

her fingers. The dish shattered on the wood floor.

Silence prevailed for several seconds.

It was only a question.

Bess knelt and picked up the broken bits of china.

"Bess, Aidan asked you a question. How did you get that bruise?" Solomon dropped his fork on his plate and stared at his daughter-in-law, his expression mild. "You always were a bit of a *doplisch* girl."

Aidan opened his mouth to protest, then closed it. He should not have an opinion as to her clumsiness or lack thereof.

Bess looked up at him, her expression begging him to save her. How could he? He had no idea what she'd done. She sighed and stood, pieces of the shattered dish in her hand. "I hit my head on the truck door."

"What truck door?" Solomon's tone sharpened. "Whose truck were you in? Why were you in a truck?"

She ducked her head, then straightened, and lifted her gaze, letting it land squarely on Solomon. "The B and B truck. Dusty and I went to the flower farm today."

Gallivanting about the countryside with Dusty Lake. Not simply gardening in the front yard of the B and B. Going here and there with him in a truck. For all the world to see. Time spent together talking, getting to know one another, and doing who knows what else.

Aidan chewed on his lips, willing the words to stay in their places. He had no right to question her. Not about Dusty. Not about anything. Solomon and Mattie had to handle this in the absence of Bess's parents. In the meantime, they would likely speak to Freeman about it. And Jeb.

"That doesn't explain the bruise." He could ask about the bruise. Concern for her well-being was acceptable for a family friend. Had the man raised his hand to her? That seemed impossible. He might be a giant, but he exuded a sort of innocence usually only seen in children. "Did you have an accident? Are you hurt?"

"Nee." Her hand went to the spot, fresh purple and red, on her temple. "It's nothing."

Solomon shoved his plate away. "Not nothing. You were traveling the countryside with this man after our talk. You were to stay away from him, not spend time . . . alone in his truck."

"It was only to introduce him to the Eichers." Her words were a stuttered mess. "That's all. Elizabeth will tell you. Iris was there. We talked about mums, that's all."

"And you were hurt." Aidan couldn't get past that thought. "Surely that tells you something."

"It's not for you to worry about." Solomon picked up his knife and cut his pork chop. "It's time to call her parents. They'll decide what to do with her."

"Surely she won't be allowed to continue to work there in the meantime."

The flash of anger that lit up Bess's face could not be mistaken. "I made a commitment to Minerva and Gavin. I can't leave them in the lurch. It would be wrong."

"I'll discuss it with Freeman."

Solomon's tone brooked no argument.

A crimson blush raced across her cheeks. Her lips pressed together as if to keep sharp words from escaping, but her eyes glittered. He'd brought the bruise to their attention. He'd caused her this new problem. For her own good. It had done nothing to help his cause. Then again she knew nothing of his cause. Also his fault. "No one was hurt. That's the main thing. No harm done."

She pivoted and trudged from the room without looking at him.

Mattie's *harrumph* filled the silence. Sarah and Rachel went back to arguing over which book to read after supper.

Aidan contemplated the doorway to the

328

kitchen. She was out there. Mooning over Dusty Lake?

Or contemplating the error of her ways.

He needed to know.

Not now. Not with Solomon, Isaac, Hazel, and Mattie glancing his way, odd expressions on their faces.

"Who is Bess?" A puzzled look on her wrinkled face, Mattie speared another pork chop and plopped it on a plate that still held her first one, uneaten. "Is she one of those Planks that moved into the old Detweiler house last month?"

Pain pierced Solomon's face. He dropped his fork with a clatter on the table. He shook his finger at Hazel, who'd opened her mouth. "Rachel, Sarah, start clearing the table. Supper's over."

Mattie's furrowed brow said she was still waiting for an answer to her question.

So was Aidan.

TWENTY-EIGHT

Pounding on the door on a Sunday afternoon was an unusual occurrence. Folks who were visiting usually simply came on in. Bess wiped her dishwater-red hands on her apron. The kinner played out back on the trampoline. Their shrieks of laughter serenaded her as she washed dishes. Solomon and Isaac headed out to the pond to try a little fishing. The other women napped. *So did Joshua. Thank You, Lord.*

She was too restless for napping or reading or a puzzle or sewing. Or anything that involved sitting still. Dusty's declarations whirled in an endless ring-around-the-rosy in her head. *All fall down.* Followed by the fury in Aidan's face when he learned how she'd received the bruise on her temple. Why he cared so much confounded her.

Two men from two different worlds who wanted to tell her what to do. Oh, and there were more. Solomon, Freeman, Daed. Men ruled her world. She'd never cared before, but right now, it seemed they all had a say and she had none. Solomon had spoken to Freeman. Freeman called and left a message at the phone shack outside her brother's farm. Her daed had not returned the call yet. When he did, she knew what the answer would be. They would come. As soon as they finished planting, they would come and she would have to leave for Haven.

Only because she had made this commitment to the Lakes, would she be allowed to continue to work until her parents arrived. She would tell Minerva and Gavin of her impending departure so they could find someone to take her place before then. No sense letting others down over her foolishness.

Solomon's exact words. *"Her foolishness."*

She trotted to the door, hoping Mary Katherine, Jennie, or Laura had stopped by to check on her. They could take Joshua for a walk. She'd followed the doctor's advice and he seemed to spit up less. Still, he didn't sleep more. Or cry less. She tugged open the door.

Aidan stood there, his straw hat in his hands, a red band imprinted on his skin under damp bangs.

331

"Oh, it's you."

His tentative smile fled. "It's me." He took a step back. "I know you don't want to see me. I know you're mad at me for pointing out the bruise. It's my fault you'll have to quit working at the B and B, but I just thought you might want to know. The purple martins are here."

Truth be told, Aidan wasn't to blame. She could only blame herself for her actions. She'd known better than to get in the truck with Dusty, but she allowed herself to ignore her misgivings. Which resulted in earnest declarations that had no place in her world. "Forgive me?"

Confusion blanketed his face. "Me? Forgive you?"

"For putting you in such an awkward position. It was my fault. I did something I shouldn't have and then I blamed you."

"If you need forgiveness, I'll give it." His smile returned and the man she'd known before tragedy and grief appeared. A handsome face with a grin that stretched from Kansas City to St. Louis. "Did you hear what I said? The purple martins are here."

For a fleeting second, the dark pain of regret and grief and loss that had engulfed her for months dissipated. Life did, indeed, go on. They could still count on some things to happen every year, year after year. "That's wonderful news." Her voice choked up. She swallowed. "Danki for letting me know."

"They've discovered the houses Caleb put up yonder where your . . . where you . . ."

The younger, innocent man disappeared. Aidan ducked his head and stared at the hat in his hands as if it suddenly appeared from the wild blue yonder like a bird who decided to nest in his palms.

"You can say it. Where Caleb and me were going to live." She closed the door behind her and went to stand on the porch so she wouldn't have to look at the raw pain in his face. "Caleb said if we did it right, they would take the little houses over and turn them into homes in a jiffy. He said they're always looking for new hidey-holes because the Englischers are building up so much of the property around here."

"Maybe you could see fit to go out there with me." His tentative tone said he wasn't at all sure she would say yes.

"Are you sure you want to be seen with me? I went in the cargo truck. I went to the flower farm with Dusty even though I knew then it was a mistake."

"Why *did* you do it, then?"

"Because a friend asked me to go with him as a favor."

"He's just a friend? An Englisch man friend?"

"I guess so. I don't know what else you call it. I know it's odd for a Plain woman and an Englisch man." She stopped, teetering on the precipice. This wasn't something a Plain woman discussed with a Plain man, either. "He's been kind to me."

Suddenly, she wanted to be anywhere but standing on this porch with another endless Sunday night in front of her. She wanted to live. Aidan would have to take yes for an answer. "What about the baby?"

The shift in topic only threw Aidan for a second or two. He grinned. "Bring him, of course."

To see the house he would never live in. She forced her brightest smile. "The fresh air will do him good. He'll sleep well — better, at least — tonight."

She rubbed her eyes, slipped past Aidan, catching the scent of his man sweat and soap so like Caleb's. So many sweet memories tied the two of them together with knots made of love and companionship and laughter and friendship.

Time to make new memories.

She made quick work of fetching Joshua, changing his diaper, tucking him in a new nightgown, and carrying him out to the buggy before she lost her nerve.

Grinning as if she'd brought him a new puppy, Aidan held Joshua while she climbed into the buggy. He tickled the baby's cheek with a long finger and babbled something she couldn't understand. Baby talk from this grown man of twenty-two years and change?

Joshua giggled and cooed.

"He smiled." Aidan's grin grew wider. "Look at that, he smiled at me."

"He did not. He doesn't smile. Not yet anyway." She peered at her son's face. A smile. A perfect, toothless smile formed dimples on his chubby, fair cheeks. Could it be possible that he remembered Aidan and their sojourn to the cemetery? Surely not. "It's that you have such a comical face, I'm sure."

"Ha, ha." Aidan tickled Joshua's cheek again, this time adding what surely sounded like *ku-che-ku* to the mix.

Joshua's arms flailed and he laughed. Aloud. Babies his age did not laugh.

Unless confronted with such a comical face as that which belonged to Aidan Graber.

"He likes his onkel Aidan, that's what it is. He knows I'm his friend." Aidan landed a kiss on the baby's forehead and handed him over. He rushed around the buggy, head down, as if to hide his face from Bess. He grabbed the reins. "Unlike some people, I reckon. We better get moving."

Bess touched the spot on Joshua's forehead where that kiss had landed. "I know you're a friend."

"Gut."

Nothing more to be said. Aidan climbed in and set the buggy in motion. They rode in silence punctuated by the squeak of the wooden wheels against the axles and the rocks on the road and the steady thudding of the horse's hooves. Those sharp petals around her heart softened and brushed against her chest like a delicate tickle. She sighed.

"What's the matter?" Aidan glanced her way, then immediately back at the dirt road that led to the house that Caleb would never finish. "Do I need to stop?"

"Nothing. It's a nice day, that's all. It smells good."

"After all those dead birds, everything smells mighty good."

She was so selfish. She hadn't even asked. "How is that going? Will you be able to restock soon?"

"Inspectors were out yesterday." He shrugged. "They're still finding contamination. We'll start over cleaning and disinfecting again tomorrow."

"How long can you go on like this?"

The knuckles of the fingers wrapped around the reins were white. "I'm finding my way back, slow but sure." His voice dropped to a husky timbre that reminded her of Caleb when his groossmammi passed. "I have ideas, ways to raise the money needed to build a new flock. I'm raising hogs. It's slow going, but I'm hopeful."

"Hopeful is good." She could learn so much from Aidan's determined effort to persevere. "Everyone is praying Gott's will be done in this. Whatever we're to do — you're to do — will become clear."

His forehead wrinkled under the blunt cut of his blond hair. "Are you praying? Or do you simply believe Gott's will be done, our puny prayers or no?"

She couldn't tell him her faith walked on such shaky, spindly legs it surely would do no good for her to pray for anyone. How could Gott hear such a weak, distant whisper from a person who had professed her faith in front of her entire Gmay only three short years ago at Easter? "I'm a little low on prayers at the moment. I need to stock up."

"Hard times are when you most need to

draw closer." His hands loosened on the reins. He leaned back. "Without Him, we're lost. Trust in Him and you need nothing more."

"People keep telling me that."

"But you don't believe."

"My head wants to believe, but my heart asks how could a Gott so cruel as to take my Caleb be worthy of all praise and glory."

"He isn't cruel. To be in His presence is a far greater joy than any Caleb would have in this world."

"He had joy with me." She swallowed hard against the pain that had a stranglehold on her throat. "I had joy with him. I know that makes me selfish. I don't know how not to feel that way. I want to be an obedient and cheerful follower. I can't figure out how. All my life I've believed that Gott's will is sovereign, not to be questioned. I know suffering is to be expected. Scripture says so. In this world, we will have trouble. Why can't I accept that Caleb is in a better place and this is where I'm supposed to be? Why is suffering necessary?"

There, she'd said it. Aidan had a strong faith. Surely, he would have an answer.

"I don't know."

Disappointment skewered her. "But you believe."

"That doesn't mean I have the answers. No one has all the answers. Otherwise, we wouldn't need faith. Faith is believing despite not having all the answers."

She stared at the trees that lined the road and the pastures beyond them turning green with crops that would one day soon be harvested. "I want to believe."

"Then let it be. Gott is all knowing. He knows what's in your heart." Aidan smiled, his angular face lighting up. The painful regret that pestered him since avian flu invaded his flock faded, leaving the man she'd known forever. His pewter eyes were warm. "Stop squirming and let Him do his business."

"I'm trying."

"Spending time with an Englisch man is not trying. It's running away."

"It's only plants."

"Are you sure?"

His tone and his expression married in a quick ceremony that reflected a certain anxiety that surprised Bess. He feared for her.

She could not lie to him, any more than she could lie about the bruise. "I don't know."

"You know what is at stake?"

"I do."

The buggy rounded a deep bend in the road and the frame of what would have been her home came into view — forlorn and empty, its windows bereft of glass, the walls without paint or finish. Poor thing, still waiting for its family. For light and warmth. One day it would be finished and home to another family. That would be her prayer now.

Aidan jerked on the reins. The buggy stopped short of a pile of lumber and Sheetrock.

"I'm so sorry."

They spoke at the same time, their words in perfect sync. Aidan's eyes were bright in the sun that filtered through leaves of a nearby sycamore tree. "Gott knows your heart is broken. He will mend it for you with His own hands, with the tender touch of His fingers." Aidan's voice softened to a mere whisper, a silky balm to her sandpaper rough soul. "He will make you whole again. Don't run away to a world that doesn't conform. Let Gott work in you. He will. In His time, He will. You know He will."

She gritted her teeth, fearful sobs would spill out. "I know that. I will try."

He dropped the reins. His hand crept toward hers. Stopped within a mere inch. His fingers were long and lean, unlike Caleb's stubby, callused ones. He had a cut just about healed on his index finger and scratches on his palm. A rough, work-hewn hand. Instead of touching her, his fingers smoothed the tiny quilt that covered Joshua between them. The baby, who dozed, smiled in his sleep as if he knew Onkel Aidan watched over him.

Bess's fingers hurt with the effort to keep them still. She wanted — she desperately needed — the touch of another human being.

Everything about the rigid set of Aidan's shoulders and the fierce lines etched on his face said he needed that same touch.

From her? Or from simply someone? Anyone?

Aidan and Caleb had been inseparable from the time they were toddlers. She'd even been a bit jealous at times of their closeness. No one could penetrate it when they closed ranks. Until Caleb was old enough to see her as more than the skinny girl who followed her older brother Jasper around and pestered him to let her fish with the boys, he'd not given her the time of day. Or night.

She would not think of the nights. They would take her right back to the intersection of desperate for the touch of a human being and full of love with no one to receive it.

Not a pity hug from Aenti Sylvia or a chin-up hug from Uncle Ike.

A tight, rib-crushing, no-holds-barred, I-love-you-like-I've-never-loved-anyone hug.

Aidan's hands were strong and his arms strong. She'd seen that look before but never from him. It invited her in to a place she'd never imagined going.

"Aidan?"

He turned his back in one quick, jerky motion and hopped from the buggy. "I can always hire on to help other farmers in the meantime. The Englischers want hardworking farmhands."

The change in topic gave her whiplash. She inhaled, shoving the unspoken words between them into the farthest corner of her mind. "But it's not what you thought you'd be doing."

"A lot of things are not as I expected. Gott's way of telling me He's in charge of the plan, not me, I reckon."

A pointed reminder that she too must accept that Gott was still in charge of her life.

She tugged Joshua from the basket and tucked him in her arm. He was heavy and warm and solid. Unlike anything else in her life. He sighed in his sleep, a tiny bubble of spit forming on his pink rosebud lips. So sure someone else would care for him and provide for his every need. Her son would one day be in for a rude awakening.

She turned to get down. Aidan stood squarely in her path, his hands outstretched. "Let me help you."

His touch sent a tiny shiver up her arm, across her shoulder, to the nape of her neck. "Why don't I give you the baby and get myself down?"

He nodded and held out his arms.

For a fraction of a second, she considered what it would be like to be held by them. She shivered at a smidgen of jealousy for her son who would know the feeling.

Aidan smiled at her and took Joshua, shifting him to the crook of his arm. He cocked his head toward the clearing. "Look. They've arrived."

A dozen purple martins with their glossy, purple-blue bodies and blackish wings perched on the apartment house Caleb had constructed in the evenings after long days working on the house his growing family would occupy. The white apartment building made of cedar had four sides, one in each direction, each side three dwellings just the right size for the couples to make their nests and yet keep out the starlings and

343

sparrows.

Caleb had studied plans and mulled over his choices for days before building what he called the perfect colony. It stood on a flagpole some twenty feet off the ground with plenty of room for them to fly off in search of dragonflies, beetles, june bugs, cicadas, bees, grasshoppers, and other delicacies abundant in these parts.

"They're here." She clapped her hands together, allowing the confusion and uncertainty of only seconds earlier to drain away. Caleb would've loved his. Like she loved flowers and gardening, he loved playing host to all manner of birds. "Do you think they'll stay?"

"If the owls and the hawks leave them alone. And the snakes can't get up the pole." He carried Joshua a few feet closer to the birds who seemed enraptured over their new digs and not the least interested in visitors. "I added a stovepipe baffle to the pole. See it there, about four feet off the ground? It will wobble and keep the snakes from being able to shimmy up the pole."

He held Joshua up, his face close to the little one, talking as if the conversation was just between the two of them and the baby understood every word. "I added insulation to the apartments so it won't get too hot or

344

too cold in there. And I threw some pine needles into the compartments. I read something that it makes them think the houses have been occupied before. They like the idea that others came first."

"You did all that? Why?" Bess didn't remember Aidan having an interest in birds, other than to hunt turkeys at Thanksgiving. "I mean you have your hands full at the farm —"

"I did it for Caleb. He loved watching birds. Remember those binoculars he wanted so bad? We all pooled our money to buy them for his birthday two years ago."

"Three years ago. I remember." Caleb spent hours studying the skies. He even took them with him when he went out to work the fields. "He would come in for supper and report to us all the birds he'd seen until Solomon told him to stop chattering like a schoolgirl. Then he waited until later and we sat on the porch and he sketched pictures of the birds to show me."

She still had the sketches, carefully wrapped in dish towels and laid in the bottom of the cedar box that had been her hope chest. One day she would take them out and show them to Joshua.

Aidan smiled. "He sang to a different hymn."

"He did."

Silence filled the space, but it had a companionable quality she'd not felt with Aidan in a long time.

"It's ironic."

Bess studied Aidan's face. He looked so melancholy. "What is?"

"Caleb loved watching birds. He couldn't wait to see the birds passing through when they migrated. Remember that trip to Swan Lake National Wildlife Refuge two years ago?"

"It was fun." All their vacations were fun. Caleb's penchant for pranks and his love of a good tall tale ensured that no one was bored — or slept much. "We ate chocolate chip cookies and peanut butter and jelly sandwiches for breakfast."

"You remember the food. I remember how fascinated Caleb was with the Canadian geese, the mallards, the tanagers, the Northern pintails, and the teals." The names rolled off Aidan's lips as if he'd relived this memory a hundred times. "He wanted to go back in the summer so he could see the great blue herons and the egrets."

"But we never did."

"Nee. It's harder to go in the summer. More work here."

"Why is it ironic?"

Grimacing, Aidan shifted Joshua from one arm to the other. "Because that's how my flock got sick."

"Because of Swan Lake?"

"Because migratory birds are the main way bird flu is spread. Their droppings."

Ironic indeed. Caleb loved birds because they soared with such seeming ease. They traveled the earth seeing the sights from high above. He wanted to see so much. Like her parents, he had a wanderlust. He talked of visiting Yellowstone National Park and the Redwood Forest. The Grand Canyon. Time had been too short. They hadn't even had time for Swan Lake in the summer and it was a mere hour's drive by van. "If Caleb had known that, he might not have liked the birds so much."

"It's not the birds' fault. They're simply the creatures Gott made them to be. They do what they do by instinct. Not even understanding it themselves, I reckon." Aidan smiled, no hint of bitterness in his face. "We should go to Swan Lake when they do the bird count in the fall. Take Joshua. He would like it. We can introduce him to his daed's favorite pastime."

"That would be nice."

A light shone in her mind's eye, illuminating the future summer, a place where she could take a trip with a friend. To find herself looking forward to spending time with Aidan surprised Bess. She didn't want to wait until summer. That surprised her too.

And what of the possibility that he would be hit by a truck tomorrow? Or she could? To spend the rest of her life alone or to have joy in small, fleeting increments, those were her choices, it seemed.

Could she learn to trust again? She peeked at Aidan. How had she never noticed his eyes before? Or the way he looked at her as if he never wanted to lose sight of her?

She shook her head. *Stop it.* Loneliness and grief were no reason to go off the deep end. "We should go back." Her words sounded sure, but her heart wanted to stay put. Caleb's presence might permeate every piece of wood, every nail, every tool, but Aidan's presence tempered the pain, even caused it to dissipate. "They'll wonder where I've gone."

"Has Solomon said any more about your job?"

The sense that she might find peace at last fled. "He talked to Freeman. They left a message at the phone shack in Haven. I reckon my daed and mudder will come."

"They'll want you to go to Haven?"

"Jah."

Aidan tugged on his hat and bent his head so it hid his face. "Do you want to go?"

Joshua stirred and began to fuss. "Give him to me." Bess held out her arms. Aidan's fingers brushed hers. They were even warmer than they had been over the pork chops and cornbread. She closed her eyes, trying to block out the rush of tangled emotion. "We better go. He's getting hungry."

"You're right." But instead of moving toward the buggy, Aidan strode toward the opening that would've been the front door. "You didn't answer my question."

"I don't know. Sometimes I think they're right. I thought working at the B and B would make me feel better, but everyone acts as if I have gone daft. I seem to like it too much. I like working with Minerva. I like . . ."

She couldn't say the words aloud. Not to Aidan. Not to anyone. She liked the freedom. The time away from her crying baby. She could breathe. And then there was Dusty. Was her response simply that of a lonely woman who longed to connect with someone — not only physically, but in every other way?

"The B and B and those people are new and different. They take your mind off your troubles. They help you forget." His tone was gentle. "A man throws himself into his work. I know I did after my parents passed. I worked harder than ever. I reckon you're doing the same. Trying for a fresh start."

Like he did with the hogs. Finding a way to go on after losing his flock, his livelihood, so soon after losing his best friend. Not giving up. They had that in common. "It does feel that way. Only others might think that fresh start should not leave a bopli in the lurch."

"Joshua looks mighty well cared for to me." Aidan faced her. He moved toward her, his hand out. She thought he might touch her, but instead his fingers tugged at the blanket around Joshua. "Hazel has room in her arms and her heart for Joshua. He's in good hands for now."

His emphasis on the words *for now* could not be missed. *For now.* And later? What did he envision happening later? The feelings etched on his face couldn't be clearer. Aidan cared about Joshua. He cared about Bess.

The sun broke through the clouds. Leaves rustled on a spring breeze that wound through the sycamore's branches. The smell of wild honeysuckle wafted around her.

Aidan cared.

350

It couldn't be allowed to matter, could it? She couldn't dare love again, it would only end in devastation. Wouldn't it? Better to flee while she still could. "The bishop thinks I should go to Haven."

"Freeman is a wise man and he is the bishop." Aidan's tone turned neutral. The feelings that had been etched so clearly on his face only seconds before fled. "I reckon you'll do as you're told, in the end."

"My daed will say I should go too."

"Sometimes we have to do things we don't want to do." Aidan whirled and headed toward the buggy. "All of us."

He stopped, hand on the buggy's front wheel. His back was turned, his head down. "I don't want you to go."

His voice was so low, so hoarse, and rough, Bess couldn't be sure she'd heard right.

"What did you say?

"We better go. Joshua will want supper soon." He held out his arms. "Let me take him for you."

She wanted to step into those arms herself. Instead, she handed over her child.

Still, Aidan's words echoed in her ears. *For now.*

TWENTY-NINE

Bess sat straight up in bed. She gasped. The silence surprised her somehow. Something, some noise, had propelled her from sleep filled with uneasy images of Aidan, his face hidden in the shadows, his voice hoarse and full of an emotion even she could recognize in her grief and loss. Or maybe it was simply the dreams themselves. The dreams had eddied and swelled like a river flowing, first past Aidan and the farm, then Dusty and the B and B. Choices flowing by before she could grasp one or the other. She could only rock in her tiny boat, praying the waves didn't knock her into the raging water.

Another noise. It might have been a door. Or a whisper. She held her breath, head cocked, listening. When Joshua started crying, he didn't usually stop. She had to get to him before he woke the others. Aidan's words whirled in her brain. A gift from God. Joshua was her gift from God. *Please let this gift from God sleep through the night.* Exhaustion weighed down her entire body. She tugged leaden legs over the side of the bed and rested for a second.

Gott loved her just like she loved her child.

She sighed and bowed her head, her eyes burning with fatigue. Gott lost His child. Gave Him up for her. And all she did was whine and complain. *Gott, help me be the mudder I need to be.*

The darkness lightened.

A squeak like a door opening or a floorboard yielding to someone's weight traveled through the crack under her door. Someone was up and about. Digging out from under the quilt and sheet, Bess rubbed her eyes and stuck her bare feet on the wood floor. Her toes curled at the cold. She grabbed her shawl from the hook and wrapped it around her shoulders, then lit the kerosene lamp and dropped the match on the end table. Yawning, she trudged down the hallway, the shadows dancing as the lamp swayed in her hand. The door to the kinner's bedroom stood open. She had closed it after Rachel, Sarah, and Levi said their prayers and crawled into their beds. One of them surely decided to make the trek downstairs to the bathroom in the dark. Too much water at supper. She'd warned Levi about that. At least he no longer wet the bed.

Since she was up, she might as well check on him. She kept walking. A shadow bounced in front of her. Someone or something moved. Her heart pounded in an off-kilter rhythm, slow, then fast, then slow, making it hard to breathe.

"Who is it?" She fumbled with the lamp, holding it higher. The person seemed to shrink into the shadows. "What are you doing in the kinner's room?"

"Who are you?" Mattie stood in the doorway, blocking the entrance to the room. She held a bundle of blankets in her arms.

"What are you doing here? You should be asleep in the dawdy haus."

"Who are you to tell me what I should or shouldn't do?" Mattie's gray hair, streaked with white and an occasional black lock, hung down her back, but she wore the same burgundy dress she'd worn during the day. "This is my house."

It had been. Now it belonged to Isaac and Hazel because Solomon had chosen to retire and hand it over to his eldest child's husband. His own sons, including Caleb, had their farms already.

"I heard something. I came to check on Joshua."

"Joshua?" Mattie's features were etched by the lamp's light. She frowned. "I heard Caleb cry. I tended to him."

She'd heard the cry all the way from the dawdy haus? Nee. She'd imagined it. Her longing and grief had summoned a memory of a baby grown up long ago. Something reached in and clutched Bess's heart with a grip so hard it had no room to beat. "We talked about this —"

A baby wailed from the vicinity of those blankets in Mattie's arms.

Joshua.

"That's not Caleb. It's Joshua. My bopli."

"Nee, this is my suh Caleb. You think I don't know my own bopli?"

"I know you do."

"Then go about your business."

How could she make Mattie understand Joshua was her business? "Let me take him for you. You can go back to bed. No sense in both of us being up."

"I can take care of my suh."

"I know you can, but I'm young and I can do without sleep easier."

"I'm young. Every bit as young as you are."

The harsh wrinkles around her mouth and eyes said otherwise. This wasn't an argument that could be won with the truth. Mat-

355

tie walked in a strange nether land where she saw herself as a young mother caring for her baby.

Bess sought a way into that world that would allow her to take care of Joshua without hurting her mother-in-law's feelings. "You look tired, though. Getting up in the middle of the night, night after night, with a fussy baby can really take the steam out of a person."

Mattie's frown eased. "That's true."

Bess settled the lamp on the floor. She edged toward Mattie and held out her arms. "Let me take him for you."

Mattie drew back. "You don't know how to take care of him like I do. You'll leave him alone. I've seen you with your bopli."

More truth than Bess cared to concede. "I wouldn't. I don't."

"You can't have my baby."

"I'm sorry. I'm sorry for your loss. It was my loss too." Bess let her arms drop. "But that's not your baby. It's Joshua. My son. Caleb's son."

"How can that be?" Mattie shook her head. "He's not old enough to be a daed."

"He is. He was. Don't you remember what happened?"

"Leave her be." Heavy footsteps sounded on the stairs. Solomon emerged at the top.

"She doesn't want to remember."

"I don't blame her, but she's scaring me."

"She would never hurt him." Solomon eased between them and put his arm around his fraa's back. "She's sick, that's all."

"You take her and let me have the bopli."

His expression hidden in the shadows, Solomon turned to Mattie. "Fraa, you must give the bopli to her." His voice floated, disembodied, in the dark, barely a whisper yet laced with determination and regret. "I'm your mann. You must do as I tell you. Hand him over."

"Nee, don't make me." Mattie's body sagged against him. Her arms flopped. Joshua's small body dropped.

Bess jerked forward. Solomon beat her to it.

He caught Joshua before he hit the floor.

Bess's heart returned to her body, but her breathing came in gasps that echoed in the quiet night. Her arms stretched toward Mattie. She didn't remember raising them.

Solomon cradled Joshua in his arms, a soft *tut, tut* sound accompanying his gentle rocking. "There, there."

Joshua didn't seem to agree. His squalls gained momentum.

"Hush, hush."

"Give him to me." Mattie tugged at Sol-

357

omon's sleeve. "He only wants me. I'm the only one who can quiet him."

"Stand back, fraa."

Mattie ducked her head and edged away from Solomon. Bess dashed forward, then stopped, forcing herself not to snatch Joshua from his groossdaadi's arms. Solomon handed him over with the practiced hands of a man with six kinner.

Bess swallowed hot tears of thanksgiving. She turned to Mattie. "Danki for checking on him, Mattie."

"No need to get fancy." Mattie's lips quivered. She spun toward the stairs and marched away.

"She'll not be up here again." Solomon brushed past Bess. "But you should keep a better eye on him."

"I'll move his cradle back into my room."

"Nee. Don't spoil him because you're afraid."

Words of recrimination died a slow death in Bess's throat. He was hurting for his fraa. "Don't worry about us. I'll take care of him so you can take care of Mattie."

"Mattie's fine." The slope of his shoulders belied his bravado. "She's fine."

"I know."

"I'll take her to the doctor, get her checked out. Soon."

"Like you said, she'll be fine."

"Solomon, where are you?" Mattie's querulous voice floated up the stairs.

Solomon clomped down the first step. He looked back. "Get some sleep. Dawn will be here soon. Another day."

He sounded hopeful, but the lines around his mouth and eyes held something else. Fear.

Solomon feared the future, something no Plain person should ever do. Or admit to doing.

They had that in common.

THIRTY

Never disappoint an expecting woman. Bess found herself wedged between Hazel and the wagon, loaded down with quilts, canned goods, embroidered tablecloths, and a wealth of other items to be sold at the spring craft fair in downtown Jamesport.

"You have to come." Hazel's hands went to her stomach. Her white face and the hard swallow said it all. Morning sickness. "We need you to make change."

"I'm so sorry I have to work. I would love to be there to help you, but two couples are checking out and two more are arriving tomorrow. The rooms have to be shipshape. It can't wait until Monday. Ruth can make change. I'll ask Minerva if I can leave a little early so I can come by to help you pack up."

She heaved the pile of quilts into the back of the Weaver wagon. Exhausted after her middle-of-the-night encounter with Mattie and dreams punctuated with the scene with

360

Aidan outside her half-finished house, Bess could barely keep her eyes open. Aidan's strange declaration — *"I don't want you to go"* — so soon after Dusty's unexpected declaration — delivered in a beat-up old pickup truck — had filled dreams that made sleep fleeting.

They were friends. Both of them. She hadn't expected danger from either quarter. The danger of caring again. Loving again. So soon after losing Caleb. It didn't seem possible.

A friend's touch didn't send goose bumps scurrying up a woman's arms.

She had imagined it, such was her hunger for affection. What kind of woman loved one man her entire life and then found herself responding to the touch of another? Two men, at that. She couldn't ask. Not Hazel with her morning sickness.

The other widows. They lived in loneliness too. For much longer than she had. Perhaps Laura or Jennie or Mary Katherine. Or all three.

"Ruth gives people too much change because she doesn't know how to add and subtract in her head. It's a good thing most people are honest." Hazel grunted as she tugged a box of strawberry and blueberry jams out of the way. "And that means I'll have to entertain Joshua and Gracie while I'm trying to sell to the tourists."

"Sarah and Rachel will help. Even Levi entertains Joshua with his funny faces and sounds." Hazel had minded her own babies while manning the booth in the past. "Joshua will be like a magnet for the tourists. They'll all stop to coo at him and stay to buy something."

She prayed those words were true. The parade of festivals and craft fairs aimed at getting tourists to spend more of their hard-earned dollars in the small town meant added income for the Gmay. Most every family participated in some way. Solomon used to make rocking chairs and sell them, but his arthritic hands no long allowed it. Isaac had taken over the task, added coffee tables, end tables, desks, and lantern stands to the list. Mary Katherine and Laura sold knitted sweaters, caps, and scarves. Iris and her mother sold all manner of canned goods. The Grabers focused on homemade cookies and breads. Others sold homemade candles and leather goods.

Hazel put her hand to her lips. She took a deep breath and let it out in an audible swish. Her forehead was damp with sweat. "I hope so. It's been a long winter. We need to do well today. It's our first craft day of the season."

"Are you all right?" Bess studied her sister-in-law's face. Her complexion looked even pastier than usual. "Are you sure you should go? Your sisters could handle it without you."

"I've lost my breakfast five days in a row. Toast, crackers, broth — nothing seems to stay down." Hazel's mouth worked and her hand went to her lips again. "But it'll pass, it always does. Eventually, Gott willing. It's worth it in the end."

In the end, when she held her new baby in her arms. Envy wound its way around Bess's heart and squeezed like a hangman's noose. She focused on shoving the last box of canned peaches into the wagon. "Joshua should nap. He was up half the night fussing so he has to be tired."

She didn't mention Mattie's visit. Hazel had enough on her plate.

"There was a lot of onion and garlic in the spaghetti sauce. Next time stick to buttered noodles for supper."

Good advice, but a little late.

Truth be told, Bess hated to miss the bazaar. She liked talking to the tourists and visiting with the other women. She liked strolling among the booths and eyeing the wares of their competitors. She liked the idea of earning money for goods they'd made themselves. It couldn't be helped. Minerva had asked her to come in on a Saturday as a favor. Soon she would have to tell the B and B owner she couldn't come back at all. "If you're sure you're all right, I have to go. The sooner I go, the sooner I'm done."

"I'm fine. I'll be fine." Hazel took a deep breath and let it out. Then another. "Ruth and Sophie will be there by the time I get there."

Twenty minutes later Bess trotted into the B and B kitchen, her old apron slung over her shoulder, ready to work. She hummed a tune, thinking of the beds to be remade and the towels replaced, bathrooms scrubbed. She had her work cut out for her. She'd have to hustle to make it to the bazaar booth to help Hazel pack up. It was the least she could do after letting her sister-in-law watch Joshua all day. The aroma of bacon and sausage hung in the air. She sniffed and her stomach rumbled. She hadn't had time to eat breakfast.

"Guder mariye."

She plowed to a stop. "Mary Katherine, what are you doing here?"

"Same thing you are. Working." Mary Katherine applied elbow grease to a washcloth on the gas stove top with such vigor the burners rattled. "I came by this morning to apply and Minerva put me to work on the spot."

Bess's days at the B and B were truly numbered now. It was for the best. Everyone thought so, except Aidan. Aidan understood. She slipped that thought into a deep pocket to examine and revel in later. "You'll do the cooking and the cleaning then?"

"Yep. The doctor said you needed help. You're working day and night, between this job and Joshua. So I'm here to help. I cooked up a pile of pancakes, scrambled eggs, hash browns, sausage, and bacon for breakfast." Mary Katherine waved the washcloth in the general vicinity of the dishwasher. "The pots and pans are washed and the dishwasher loaded. I'm to make cinnamon rolls and coffee cake for tomorrow's continental breakfast since I won't be here. When I finish that I'm to help you with the bedrooms if need be, before I go."

Bess opened her mouth, then closed it. Truer friends couldn't be found than Mary Katherine, Laura, and Jennie. She would be done so much quicker now. And for Minerva to recognize the B and B needed this additional help, it was Gott's blessing. Mary Katherine had plenty to do already, no matter what she said. She sewed for the bazaars, acted as the Gmay's scribe for *The Budget*, scribbling stories and poems, and looked after grandbabies as needed. Now she cooked at the B and B. "I'll be back to help you put together the cinnamon rolls as soon as the dough finishes rising."

"That's my girl." Mary Katherine manhandled a glass measuring cup and pulled a huge glass canister of flour toward the ceramic mixing bowl. "A fine team we'll make. Run along. The clean sheets are on top of the washing machine in the utility room."

Indeed they were and still warm. Barely able to see over the top of the stack, Bess tottered up the stairs and into the Blue Room.

"Hey, watch where you're going."

Bess bounced back. The doorjamb dug into her shoulder. The pile of sheets plummeted to the floor. "Sorry, so sorry. I couldn't see —"

"No harm done, I suppose." A far too skinny woman dressed in tight jeans and a chartreuse sweater that matched her lipstick and the band in her black, shoulder-length hair bent to help Bess pick up the sheets. Her peeved expression belied the words. "You shouldn't try to carry so much at once. It's bad for your back."

"My back is strong." Bess rushed to pick up the sheets and back out of the room. She wasn't supposed to bother the guests. "I thought you were already gone. I'm so sorry. I'll come back."

"No, no, don't bother." The woman made a *pffft* sound and waved her hand in a dismissive gesture. A string of gold bracelets clanked on her slim wrist. "I missed a few things when I packed this morning. We're headed out as soon as we stop at the By-Gones Shop to buy a quilt."

"Oh, they have beautiful quilts. I'm sure it'll look nice on your bed." Her cheeks heated. She shouldn't be speaking of the guest's bed at home. "I mean —"

"We picked the Jacob's Ladder pattern. It matches the décor of our bedroom. I want a second one for the guest bedroom, but Craig says it's ridiculous how much they want for them. You folks are awful proud of your handiwork."

Jacob's Ladder reminded her of Dusty and the nursery. He'd been so kind that day. And every day since. It wasn't his fault she couldn't reciprocate. Her mind focused on the woman's words. Proud? Plain folks worked hard at humility. "We're not proud of anything."

The woman rummaged through a pile of magazines on the nightstand and picked up a slim gold case etched with roses. "There you are." She flipped it open, revealing a neat row of skinny cigarettes. "Good, I'm not out. I didn't mean to offend, but those prices are ridiculous."

"Every quilt is handmade and takes a long time to finish."

Every stitch lovingly made as the women talked about babies born, groossdaadis who died, the purple martins coming and going, the late frost that decimated the peas, and the hailstorm that ruined the barn roof. And the family off to Mexico to try an experimental treatment for cancer and all the other news that made life in the Gmay go round and round.

"I suppose so." The woman fingered the cigarettes as if contemplating lighting one up, despite the no Smoking sign over the door. She snapped it shut with a sigh. "So you're Amish."

"Yes, ma'am."

"Don't ma'am me. I'm only thirty-five." The woman frowned, which served to make her narrow, pinched face look older than her age. "You don't believe in using electricity or driving cars."

"That's right."

"Yet here you are working in a B and B using a vacuum and a dishwasher and who knows what else. How do you square that?"

Her tone was downright accusatory. What did it matter to her? "Well, we have a set of rules and it says we can use some electricity for work. Just not in our houses."

"Seems a little contradictory. Or convenient." The woman slid a mirror from her back pocket and proceeded to run a finger over her lips while staring at herself in the small rectangle. "What exactly is your problem with electricity? You think it's evil or something?"

"No, it's not evil in itself. But we take the Scripture that says to keep ourselves apart from the world very seriously." Her plan for the day was to make beds and clean bathrooms. She hadn't expected to defend her faith. Not that it needed defending. It was fine, thank you very much. The thought surprised her. The conversation with Aidan had turned her around, at least to the extent that she now knew she hadn't completely given up on Gott. "We don't want to connect to the grid, because we'll start acting like . . ."

Like you.

From the woman's expression, she too could finish the sentence. "You don't mind taking our money, though. Or judging us."

"I'm not judging. We don't —"

"It's all right. I don't mind you cleaning up after me in the bathroom, either." The woman plopped down on the overstuffed chair at the foot of the bed, stretched out her bony legs, and crossed them at the bare ankle above her flat shoes. "You don't seem to mind hanging out with our men, either."

Our men? What men? "I better get started on the bed." As uncomfortable as a kitten stuck in a litter of dirty, hungry piglets, Bess tossed the comforter aside and tugged at the sheets on the mattress of the cherry sleigh bed. "Lots of work to do."

"You're blushing! I'm right. I saw you flirting with that man, the son, what's his name?"

"Dusty? I was not —"

"Now you're beet red, girl. I saw you and him out in the front yard where the entire world could see you getting cozy over those pretty pansies." The woman tittered and tapped the mirror against manicured fingers. "I guess that's universal, even for people who belong to cults."

"Cults?"

"Sure, what else do you call a bunch of folks who dress like pilgrims and live like survivalists from another century? Do you

370

have some guy like James Jones who'll ask you to drink the Kool-Aid, or are you all going to sail away in flying saucers when the gods arrive from outer space to take you away?"

"I'm not sure what you're talking about." Bess had no idea. She only wanted to escape. She grabbed the dirty sheets and edged toward the door. "I'll come back when you're done."

"At least if you hook up with that Dusty fellow you can escape. You'd look good in jeans and a T-shirt. You've got the body for it. You just need some makeup on that white face and some bangs. You have a long forehead. Did you know that?"

"I'm not hooking up —"

"Hello, hello, I have the clean towels." Mary Katherine strode in, her arms full up to her chin. "I think your husband is looking for you downstairs, Mrs. Bitters. I wrapped up two biscuits with butter and strawberry jam for you to take with you. They're on the kitchen counter."

Bess heaved a sigh of relief. Mary Katherine to the rescue.

Mrs. Bitters scooped up a makeup bag from the dresser and dropped the gold cigarette case into it. "He's so impatient." She turned to Bess. "You should snuggle up

371

to the redhead. At least then you could get out of that long dress. You must get so hot in the summer."

With that ridiculous statement, the woman sauntered past them, makeup bag clutched in her thin fingers.

"Danki." Bess fought the urge to give her friend a big hug. "That was a very strange conversation."

"You won't thank me when you hear what I have to say." Mary Katherine's look could only be described as stern. "I heard quite an earful before I came to the rescue."

"She had a lot to say."

"She's not the only one saying it."

"That we're a cult? I'm not to blame for the silly ideas folks who don't really know us and don't care to get to know us have in their brains and decide to spout at the oddest moments."

"I'm not worried about what they may think of our faith, although it warms my heart to know you still have yours. Some have wondered of late if you were about to stray." Mary Katherine eased onto the end of the bed and patted the spot next to her on the mattress pad. "I'm not even worried about people with nothing better to do who engage in idle gossip."

Her tone said she was worried, however.

Bess had wanted to ask the widows about her quandary. Apparently, they had the same thought. This was more than the doctor's prescription. Was she ready to hear what this woman had to say? "We're taught to ignore idle gossip."

"It's not gossip, in this case, but concern."

"Concern for me? I've done nothing." Except ride around the countryside in a truck with Dusty. Consider and then wish for Aidan's touch. "I mean, I've tried to do the right thing."

"You're simply trying to earn an honest wage, help out your family, and move on with your life." Mary Katherine patted Bess's hand with warm fingers still damp from dishwater. "Laura, Jennie, and me, we understand how that is. We truly do. We're praying for you."

Her kind words eased the ache in Bess's chest where her heart had once been. "Your prayers are appreciated. I think I hear a *but* in there somewhere."

"We share Freeman's concern. Spending time with an Englisch man alone in his truck. That's cause for concern."

"Dusty is a kind man, a sweet man, really, who is trying to be nice to me, to be a friend." The words came out with far more ferocity than she intended. She liked Dusty a lot. How could she have all these feelings welling up in her for two different men? One she'd known all her life. One she hardly knew at all. No one could replace Caleb. "Dusty is a friend, nothing more."

"We Plain women don't get to have Englisch men as friends. I understand how lonely it is when you lose your mann." Sadness welled in Mary Katherine's face. "Don't mistake kindness for something else. We all want to grab on to something or someone to buoy us when we seem to be drowning in a well of loneliness. I know this. So do Laura and Jennie. Make sure you grab on to the right person."

"I'm not looking for anyone. I don't want to feel like this again when he's snatched away for no good reason. Besides, there is no one who can replace my Caleb."

"He's not your Caleb anymore. He belongs to Gott. And if Gott plans for you to love again, you best get on board, because the plan He has for you is always better than anything you can think up." Mary Katherine's smile said she knew how bittersweet those words fell on Bess's ears. "Now Aidan, he's another story. A story that could set you right again."

How could Mary Katherine possibly know? "I'm not ready."

"That's up to Gott, isn't it? Don't forget that." Her tone suddenly brisk, Mary Katherine popped up from the bed. "We better get these chores done. They're not paying us to sit around and boo-hoo over our circumstances."

She scooped up the dirty sheets. "I'll get the sheets off the other beds and get a load started. By that time the cinnamon rolls will have risen and I'll be able to get them in the oven."

Bess tugged the clean sheet down around the mattress corner and tucked it in. She straightened. "How do you know what Freeman is thinking? Did you talk to Solomon?"

"I talked to Freeman last night to make sure he had no qualms about me working here." Mary Katherine paused in the doorway. "He said he thought it was a good idea."

"Why?"

"To keep an eye on you."

They didn't trust her to make good decisions. They thought she needed a chaperone. "Nothing is going on here."

"By me working here it may make it possible for you to continue working here until your parents say otherwise." Mary Katherine smiled. "We'll have a cinnamon roll as a treat before we leave. They'll be hot and gooey, just the way I like them."

She was changing the subject, when all Bess wanted to do was talk about how kind and sweet she was. "You took this job for me?"

"Don't be silly. I needed something to do. The girls take care of the house and the garden and do the cooking. I had much too much free time on my hands. A woman needs to work."

Mary Katherine didn't have that much free time. "Right."

"Get a move on. Minerva will be back any minute and she'll wonder what we've been doing all this time."

"Mary Katherine?"

"What, child? We're burning daylight and I'd like to get home in time to make a nice chicken pot pie for supper. The kinner are coming and bringing my grandbabies."

"Danki."

"Don't be thanking me, you silly goose."

Daed might still drag her back to Haven, but she had a better chance now of convincing him to let her stay. She had Mary Katherine.

Friends made life more bearable.

She tried to think of nothing else as she made the bed. Friends.

Dusty, with his ragged beard and dirty boots and holey jeans, could only be a friend. Aidan, with his long fingers and lean body, who worked so hard on the land and had such faith that Gott could heal her pain and give her joy once again. One represented an escape from her present circumstances, the other a chance to live the life she'd thought she would have with Caleb.

Could she look at Aidan every day and not see Caleb?

Could she live her life without her family and her friends, only seeing them in passing on the streets of Jamesport?

Her stomach flopped. Her heart twisted.

Gott, are those my choices?

Or she could simply go to Haven with her parents.

THIRTY-ONE

The beautiful spring day brought out the sun and the tourists who crowded the streets of downtown Jamesport. They jostled for position at the quilt, jewelry, leather goods, and canned goods booths, their faces red with sunburn. Bess dodged between a couple sharing a sausage on a stick and a woman scolding a curly-headed toddler who'd spilled his red snow cone on a white T-shirt that read GRANDMA'S FAVORITE.

The Weavers always had their booth in front of the Kramer Family Restaurant where foot traffic was sure to be heavy. She shielded her eyes from the sun with one hand and craned her neck to see around two teenagers arguing over whether jalapeño jelly could be used as a dip or should be reserved for toast. Neither, in her opinion. Too spicy.

There. Hazel had Gracie on one hip and Joshua nestled in the crook of her other arm while she talked to a customer who held a jar of pickles against her chest as if afraid someone would snatch it from her. Both babies were fussing. Where were Ruth and Sophie? Rachel and Sarah should be helping too. Bess hustled to the table.

"We grow all our own vegetables and we can them ourselves. Fresh from the garden into the jars." Hazel's face flushed with heat. Joshua fussed louder. She began to sway as if to comfort him. "These were canned this year so they're fresh."

"You're sure you know what you're doing? I don't want my kids getting botulism with their hamburgers next week." The lady's orangey penciled eyebrows lifted and fell. "I ate at that Amish restaurant yesterday and I'm just sure I got food poisoning."

With her round belly that preceded her and a behind that kept up, the woman looked mighty healthy to Bess. "We've never had a complaint in all the years we've been selling here." She stepped into the fray as she held out her arms to Hazel. With a look of gratitude that went beyond simply relieving her of one of her burdens, Hazel handed Joshua over. "Canning is what we do. We can in the summer so we'll have plenty to eat all winter long."

"Sounds so much healthier than buying

from the supermarket." The woman's fluffy orange curls bounced as she nodded. "Fine. I'll take two of these and a jar of the strawberry jam — make that strawberry and peach. Harold loves peach."

Harold presumably was her husband. Bess lowered Joshua into the basket Hazel had brought for that purpose. His cries escalated. He sounded tired and hungry. "Hush, hush, just give me a minute." She fumbled with newspaper, wrapped the jars, and stuck them in a paper bag. "Here you go."

The woman held out a credit card.

"We don't take credit cards." Bess pointed at the sign Ruth had made with her neat block print. "Cash only."

"Seriously?" The woman's pudgy face pursed in a frown. "What kind of operation is this? I don't know of any place in the world where you can't use plastic."

Bess fought the urge to point out she did now. "Sorry, we don't have any way to process them."

"It's very simple. You just get one of those do-hickeys —"

"Ach, ach." Hazel gasped and slouched over. "Ach."

"What is it?" Bess tugged Gracie, who chose that moment to begin to howl, from her sister-in-law's arms. "Hush, hush, little one. Are you all right?"

Her face white as the sheets hanging on the line on laundry day, Hazel tucked her hands under her arms, tight around her chest, and nodded, but she didn't look fine. "I need to sit a minute, that's all."

"Where are Ruth and Sophie?" They never left one person alone in the booth. "And the kinner?"

"Jane didn't come today. William had a fever. Sophie had to leave early. Esther fell off the trampoline. They think her wrist is broken." Hazel grimaced and heaved a sigh. "Sarah and Rachel took Levi to get a funnel cake. They must've been lured into one of the games. They've been gone a while."

She gasped again, took two steps back, and plopped into the rickety lawn chair that served as their resting spot between customers. "It's okay. I'm fine."

Bess turned to the lady, who dug through her purse, her forehead wrinkled in concentration. "Here, here, just because I spent all this time picking them out and Harold loves homemade pickles." She handed Bess a ten and a five. "But you really should get with the times, you know. It's ridiculous. Who doesn't take plastic, seriously?" She scooped up her package and did a sharp about-face.

Bess shook her head. Get with the times?

Had the woman not noticed their dresses and their prayer kapps? It would be funny if it weren't so sad. "Hush, bopli, hush, you're fine." She hoisted Gracie higher on her hip and turned to commiserate with Hazel. "Can you believe her?"

Hazel stared at her lap, a look of horror on her face. "Something's not right. I can feel it." Her breathing sounded shallow, panicked. "I feel something . . . damp."

With a gasp, she leaned forward and began to rock. "Ach, ach, something's not right."

"You're hot and sweaty, that's all." One of them had to remain calm and it had to be Bess. "It's probably indigestion. You probably overdid it."

"Overdid it? I carried the boxes over to the table and set up the display." Hazel's features contorted in pain. "I carried both babies around, but it's no different than usual. You think I did something to the baby?"

"Nee, nee, I didn't mean that." Bess tried to keep her concern from her voice. "You probably just need to rest a bit."

Hazel stood and craned her neck so she could look at the back of her dress. "It's wet. It's wet!"

Indeed it was. Wet and a pinkish-red color.

Swallowing her rising apprehension, Bess put her hand on her sister-in-law's shoulder. "Sit and rest. I'll get Ellen to watch the kinner and then we'll get you some help. It'll be fine."

She shifted Gracie to her other hip and strode to Ellen Miller's table. Two customers stood in front of it, debating whether they should get the chocolate whoopie pies or the oatmeal. "You could get a dozen of each." Ellen winked at Bess. "They'll keep and they're good with a glass of cold milk."

"Hazel isn't feeling well." Bess sidled closer. "I think it might be the bopli."

Ellen's long nose wrinkled. "Take her home then. She probably needs to rest."

"I think it's more than that. She's . . . there's . . . it looks like blood on the back of her dress."

"Go on, take her to the emergency clinic. They'll call the baby-doctor, Dr. Jessup, to come in." Ellen made a shooing motion. "Hurry, I'll take care of your table. Give me Gracie and send the little ones to me. I'll take them home when I'm done here."

Bess turned and ran. To her relief, the other kinner had returned to the table, laughing and chattering about the cakewalk where they'd won two dozen cupcakes and a German chocolate cake. Bess instructed them to box up the remaining merchandise and then go directly to Ellen's table. "Where are you going?" Her face troubled, Sarah tucked a small hand under her mudder's arm. "How come we're not going home together?"

"I'm a little under the weather, Dochder." Hazel smoothed her daughter's kapp. "Bess is going to take me to the ER clinic, but we'll be home in no time. You do as Bess says and mind your bruder for me."

"Hurry home, Mudder. We want to make pizzas for supper. Can we make pizzas?"

Hazel nodded, but her chin trembled.

"Let's go, let's go." Bess tucked Joshua into Rachel's arms, helped Hazel from the chair, and paused while Hazel waved at the kinner and promised to be home in time to make pizza. "Careful with the baby. Walk slowly."

"I know how to take care of babies." Rachel frowned, looking like a miniature of her mother. "I do it all the time."

Indeed she did. Still, Bess glanced back more than once as she guided Hazel to the buggy. She would never take for granted the safety of a loved one, never again. A person never knew the last time she would see a mann. Why not a kinner? Gorge rose in her throat.

This was not about her. It was about Hazel. Hazel and the baby. The everlasting minutes ticked in one of the clinic's tiny curtained-off exam rooms with its smell of antiseptic and cleansers in a haze of comforting a tearful sister-in-law and waiting for the doctor, surely enjoying family time on his day off, to arrive.

Bess borrowed the phone in the reception area, called Freeman's phone shack, and left a message on the recorder, knowing it might be hours before someone thought to check it and then take the news to Isaac. The doctor arrived soon after, clad in jeans, T-shirt, and sneakers.

The nurse ushered her back to the waiting room for more waiting. Only minutes later Solomon and Isaac strode through the door as if the devil himself followed after. His gaze fierce, Isaac mopped his face with a faded bandana. "Where is she? What do they say?"

"Dr. Jessup has her in the back." Bess gestured in that general direction "They haven't said anything yet."

"What happened?" His accusatory tone sent a chill through Bess. "Ellen said Hazel had all the kinner and the booth by herself today."

385

"Ruth and Sophie couldn't be there today."

"One had a sick child, the other with a broken bone. Where were you?"

Working. Her bopli hadn't been sick. Nor had she been there to help. "She said she didn't feel well. Then she . . ." Bess swallowed against the lump in her throat. She couldn't explain what happened, not to two men. "It seems something happened with the bopli."

Isaac's hands went to his hips. A pulse jumped in his jaw. He shook his head and sat suddenly.

Solomon eased into a chair next to him. "It's in Gott's hands now."

As if he'd heard the discussion, Dr. Jessup appeared in the doorway, a clipboard in one hand, his wire-rimmed glasses in the other. "Ah, you're here. Good."

"What is it? How is she?" Isaac sprang from his seat. "The bopli?"

"Let's talk in the back." Dr. Jessup stuck the glasses in the sparse white hair on top of his head. "Your wife is asking for you."

They disappeared down the hallway. An uneasy silence reigned for a few minutes. Bess kept her fingers interlocked in her lap. She sought words of prayer for Hazel, for the unborn child, for Isaac. *Lord, don't take their baby. Take me. It's my fault. I shouldn't have burdened her with my baby on top of everything else. I knew she didn't feel good this morning, but I put myself first. Forgive me. Don't take their baby. Please don't take him.*

Time inched along. Ten minutes, twenty minutes, thirty minutes. Solomon said nothing. Absolutely nothing. His head remained bowed. He surely prayed. Bess wanted to scream. She wanted to cry. Instead she prayed. The same prayer over and over again.

Finally, after an eternity, Isaac emerged, his arm around Hazel's shoulders. She leaned against him, her head down, kapp askew.

Bess stood. Solomon followed. "Hazel, how are you? Are you all right? The bopli?"

Hazel raised her head. Her eyes were red in a face so pale, every freckle stood out in stark relief. Without her glasses, she looked so young and innocent. Tears trickled down her face. She shook her head and kept walking.

Isaac shot Bess a venomous look. "You take your buggy. I'll get her home. Me and Solomon will."

Make no mistake, his look said. This was somehow her fault.

"I'm sorry," she whispered. "So sorry."
So much for answered prayers.

THIRTY-TWO

Bess wasn't a coward. She wanted to run far away from the Weaver farm. Even Haven wouldn't be far enough to escape accusing gazes. Her fault. All this was her fault for being selfish. Now, Hazel would need help. Her help. A day late and a dollar short, but still she would do everything she could to help. No two weeks' notice at the B and B. Hazel would need someone to help around the house. Minerva had Mary Katherine now and she could hire another maid. Hazel wouldn't be able to lift anything for a few days. She would need to rest. Resolute, Bess tugged open the door and marched in.

Isaac stood in the front room, Solomon at his side. The two men looked at her as if she were a stranger who'd barged into their home unannounced and uninvited. No matter. "How is she?"

Isaac's Adam's apple bobbed, but his face remained etched in stone. "Dr. Jessup said she's to stay in bed and rest for now. Tomorrow, she'll be up and around, like always. Laura and Mattie are with her now."

"I'm sorry."

"You should consider whether it is right for a mudder to run around working for the Englisch when her bopli is at home cared for by another."

Solomon grunted and put his hand on Isaac's shoulder. "Suh, Gott's will be done."

Isaac's eyes reddened. "Jah, Gott's will be done. Do you think it is Gott's will for Bess to spend time with an Englisch man while my fraa cares for her bopli?"

"Now's not the time." Solomon's voice was surprisingly tender. "We'll have Ruth make tea. You might want to get a bite to eat. You'll feel better."

As if putting food in a body could fill the gaping hole left by the passing of an unborn child. All the possibilities of that child's life. What he would look like, when he would take his first step, what his first word would be, who his first love would be.

He or she. Even that question would remain a mystery until eternity came to pass.

Isaac was right about the baby, but an Englisch man? Dusty. It was innocent. That didn't matter. Only Hazel mattered right now. "I won't be going back."

"Not now." Solomon's command cut through her. "See if you can make yourself useful. We'll speak of this later."

He did an about-face, then paused in the doorway to the kitchen and looked back. "Sarah and Rachel are watching the boplin."

"I'll go to Hazel then." She trudged up the stairs, stopping only long enough to check on Joshua.

She found Sarah entertaining him with a rattle he grasped in his fat little hand, a gaping grin on his face so like Caleb's. She planted a kiss on his curly hair and squeezed Sarah's shoulder. The little girl had no idea what her mudder was going through. She would make a good mudder herself one day. Gott willing, she would never go through what Hazel now experienced.

Girding herself to face her sister-in-law, Bess paused outside Hazel's bedroom. She inhaled, exhaled, listening to the sound of her own breathing. *Gott, forgive me. Please forgive me.*

She'd been jealous of her sister-in-law, not wanting to watch her belly swell and another baby come into the world. Now she wouldn't have to do that. Instead, she would watch Hazel mourn her unborn child while trying to maintain a stoic face, just as Bess had tried to do and failed after Caleb's death.

Gott, make her strong. Give her peace, knowing her baby is with You. Give her comfort knowing her baby will never suffer a moment on this earth.

Bess opened the door to the bedroom. The scent of sweat and regret wafted from the room. Laura sat in a rocker next to the bed, while Mattie lingered at the foot of the bed, as if standing guard over her daughter. Hazel lay curled up in a ball, her long chestnut hair scattered over her shoulder, her eyes closed, glasses missing. She looked small and frail, not old enough to be a mother of four.

Laura put a finger to her lips and then stood. They tiptoed over to the open window. A dog barked in the distance. Birds chattered in the backyard. Ordinary sounds that should dissipate into sad silence.

"She'll be glad you're here," Laura whispered. "She's trying to be strong, but she's beside herself, poor thing."

Mattie's *harrumph* broke the silence. She lifted her chin, her frown etching lines around her mouth. Without uttering a word, she marched past Bess and left the room.

Laura shrugged and smiled. "Mattie's had

a hard time of it."

"She's right. Are you sure Hazel will want me? I shouldn't have left Joshua with her. She had her hands full with her own four and the customers. I knew she didn't feel good this morning, but I went to the B and B anyway."

"It had nothing to do with kinner or craft fairs or work. This would've happened regardless. Sometimes something goes wrong in the womb. It can't be helped or fixed."

"It breaks my heart. She's made to mother."

"You have such a soft heart. She'll have more, Gott willing. He has a plan, never forget that." Laura squeezed Bess's hand. "We are honed by the fire. Nowhere in Scripture are we promised a life without pain or heartache or problems. This life will be full of problems. The one guarantee we have is that Gott knows and He sees. He watches and waits to see how we will react. Will we fuss and whine or put our shoulder into the burden and carry on?"

She had fussed and whined. Gott surely saw that. How disappointed He must be in her. "I should never have left her alone. I should've shared the burden. She needed to rest."

"You didn't know." Grimacing, Laura rubbed her gnarled hands together. "Don't take on that which is not yours to bear."

Bess shivered despite the humid heat of the room. No breeze lifted the faded white curtain. The air seemed to hang heavy on her shoulders, full of loss and grief and despair. "The truth is I am to blame. If I were a better mother, I would never have left Joshua with her."

Laura leaned against the windowsill and pointed to the rocker. "Sit, child. Whatever are you talking about? To me, Joshua doesn't look to lack for anything. He's healthy, happy, chunky. I could cuddle him all day."

"But I couldn't."

The words sallied forth on their own. She wanted them back. What mother admitted to not wanting to hold her child all day? She hung her head, waiting for Laura's judgment.

"You're not the first mother to have mixed feelings."

"They're not mixed. He reminds me, painfully so, of Caleb."

"When a joyous occasion happens so close to such a grievous event as the death of a beloved, the two mix together and one can hardly be separated from the other. It's only human."

"Others might see the child as a wonderful way of keeping their husband close, even in death." Bess gripped her hands so hard her fingers hurt. "Why can't I?"

"We are only human. As much as we bow our heads and determine that we will accept what life brings, accept every event, every loss, every bump in the road as Gott's plan, sometimes, we simply falter because we are human."

"Is that how you felt when Eli passed?"

"I wanted to throw myself off the barn roof."

"But you didn't."

"Gott would've frowned on it, I reckon. I know Freeman would." Laura chuckled. "With every day, it gets easier. It seems like a betrayal of the man you love, but it's the only way to go forward. Caleb would want that. He would want you to be a faithful follower. He'd want you to find a way to accept that Joshua is a gift Gott has given you to help you through this moment in life. It is only a moment. This life is only a fraction of a second in all of eternity. You will laugh again. You will find reason to laugh again. You may even love again."

The image of Aidan cuddling Joshua close as he showed him the purple martins Caleb had so loved danced in her mind's eye. Followed ever so quickly by one of Dusty patting the dirt around Jacob's Ladder with a loving touch. Both images fluttered and dissipated, replaced by a faded portrait of Caleb. The edges were peeling and torn. The color of his eyes unclear, the way his lips curved in a smile almost indiscernible. "Is it really possible?"

"To laugh again? I already do. My grandbabies make me laugh almost every day."

"I mean love. Will you love again?"

"I'm old. Too old to start a new season. For me, the moment had passed."

Sadness blurred the lines around the other woman's face. She said the words with a matter-of-fact air, but her face said she felt the sting of this truth. Loneliness served as her companion in old age. It shouldn't be so for such a kind, thoughtful, loving woman. Despite her age — or perhaps because of it — Laura still had much to give to a companion, a mann.

How did Gott decide who received the gift of a lifelong love and who did not?

It didn't matter. Neither Laura nor Bess had received that gift. Bess wasn't too old to try again, but fear tied her hands. "Being a mother is the only important thing now, not foolishness over love. I'll be fine."

"I know you will. Jennie and Mary Katherine and I are around to make sure of it. Remember that. You're not alone. You're never alone. Gott is with you." Laura eased from her perch on the windowsill. "Sit with Hazel a bit while I get some tea, will you? I'm parched."

"Danki."

"No need to get fancy about it." Laura moved to the door with a step much lighter than that of most women her age. "It's what friends do."

Bess settled back into the rocking chair and watched the rise and fall of Hazel's chest. She looked so peaceful in her sleep. To sleep sometimes offered the only respite from the pain of grief and loss. Bess understood that. She sought sleep like she sought water when she was thirsty. Until this business with Aidan and Dusty, sleep gave her the only peace she'd known in months. Now, fully awake and painfully aware, she rocked and prayed, prayed and rocked, for Hazel's physical healing, for her sore heart, for the baby that would remain with Gott rather than suffering the ills of a broken world.

"You're here."

She looked up to find Hazel watching her. "You're awake."

Hazel pushed herself up into a sitting

position and brushed hair from her face. "I can't believe it."

"I'm sorry for your loss."

"Gott's will."

"Jah, that's what everyone says."

Hazel wiped at her face with her sleeve and sniffed. "You don't believe it?"

"I do, but I have trouble finding solace in it. I know this is my failing. Freeman would say pray and ask forgiveness for my weakness. And I do. Do you?"

"I try, but right now all I feel is empty."

"I should've been there. I shouldn't have left you with Joshua on top of your own kinner and the booth."

"I love Joshua like he's my own. I thought I could carry them both."

Hazel's unspoken words hung in the air. She loved Joshua. She couldn't carry them both. It had been too much and now she was bereft of her own baby.

"He reminds me of Caleb."

"Isn't that a good thing?"

"Some days it is. Other days it hurts my heart."

"I thought losing Caleb was enough. We shouldn't have to bear any more losses." Bitterness wrapped itself around Hazel's words, making them low and hoarse. "I guess I was wrong. I can't understand it."

Her true feelings bared for Bess only. Hazel had given her the gift of trusting her to understand. "I think we're like Job. We remain faithful through trials and tribulations. We're being refined by the fire."

"I don't feel refined. I feel tired and sad and empty."

"They say it will pass."

"They should hoe our rows."

Their backs bent, heads aching, hearts heavy. "We can't outwalk our grief. We have to turn and face it."

Hazel sighed and closed her eyes. She had the right idea. Bess leaned back in the rocking chair and closed her own eyes. They would rest first and face the battle when they were stronger.

Some day. Soon.

THIRTY-THREE

Pulling weeds offered its own brand of satisfaction. If left to their own devices, weeds suffocated the tomato plants and all the other vegetables that represented sustenance year around for Bess's family. Weeds were like negative thoughts. If allowed to remain and grow unencumbered, negative thoughts ran rampant, blocking out the sun, sucking up needed nutrients until darkness overcame the light.

Bess sat back on her haunches and wiped at her face with her sleeve. She inhaled the heady scent of earth and grass fresh cut by Sarah, who sang at the top of her lungs as she shoved the push mower forward. *Focus on the blessings.* Family, a roof overhead, food on the table, little girls who ran about laughing and playing and loving life. A good Gott who loved her and took care of her. Joshua, who slept a solid five hours without eating the previous night.

To her everlasting regret, none of it kept her from missing the B and B. Or Minerva. Or Dusty.

Not at all.

The April sun warmed her face. It felt good to be out of the house. Hazel had embarked on a cleaning frenzy that had the girls beating rugs on the clothesline in the backyard and Hazel mopping the floors until they shone. Even little Levi had been given a task, to dust every piece of furniture in the front room.

Heat flamed up her neck and across her cheeks. What kind of thought was that for a Plain woman? She could no more miss an Englisch man than she could miss a movie or a TV series. A Plain woman, mother, and a widow. She closed her eyes and strained to see Caleb's face. His features had faded even more. She longed for a picture. Nee, pictures were graven images and wrong. Hadn't she been told that her whole life? She squinted against the dark, trying to discern his cheekbones, his nose, his smile. The details escaped her. His laugh, surely she could hear his laugh. Silence bellowed in her ears.

Ach, Caleb.

She bent over her task with renewed zeal. She would keep busy. Work was the best medicine. Not laughter, work. Her days of working in town were over. Her days of learning about plants from Dusty were over. Hazel needed her. Joshua needed her. Her place was at home.

The sound of an engine revving and gear grinding forced her to look up. A beat-up pickup truck, once blue, now rusty, puttered up the road toward the house. The B and B delivery truck did not belong here, but it gave her a warm feeling to think a member of the Lake family had come to check on her. They were kind people.

She stood, trowel in one hand, and brushed dirt from her apron and skirt. The truck jerked to a stop a few yards from the garden. Dusty emerged. He shut the truck door with a gentle nudge and started forward.

"There you are." His flushed face blazed with a multitude of tangled emotions. "You didn't come to work today. I — we — were worried."

"Didn't Solomon stop by to tell you I wouldn't be coming anymore?"

"He did, but I — we — had to know if you agreed with that course of action." He halted at the first row of tomato plants. No matter how perturbed, he would take care not to trample plants. "If you were all right."

"I'm all right. I need to be here. My sister-in-law needs me."

"We need you too." His expression, his tone, the way he hunched his shoulders as he walked told Bess the *we* was still an *I*. "Minerva is beside herself."

"Tell Minerva I'm sorry."

"You should tell her yourself. Come by and talk to her. She's willing to rearrange your hours, do whatever is necessary to accommodate your needs, your family's needs."

"I can't keep working."

"Why?" He edged his way between the rows of cucumbers, green peppers, and leaf lettuce. "You're a grown woman capable of doing more than one thing. You came into town and got yourself a job. Don't back down now."

The fact that he didn't understand only served to illustrate why she couldn't continue to spend time with him. "It's a family thing. My sister-in-law —"

"I heard. I'm sorry for her loss. It's very sad. I can't imagine how she must feel." His Adam's apple bobbed. "Take a week. Take two weeks or a month, but come back."

His descent on her finally stopped, but he stood so close she could see the tiny drops of perspiration on his forehead and the way his chest heaved under his thin cotton T-shirt. She could smell his man sweat. "I can't."

"You don't want to? I thought you liked working there." He ducked his head and kicked at a clod of dirt. "I thought you liked me."

His plaintive tone reminded her of Levi when Sarah or Rachel took the last pancake at breakfast. "I do. I do."

"Then come back. The pansies and the impatiens and the morning glories miss you." He couldn't seem to look at her, instead studying the horizon. "I miss you."

"I haven't been gone a day."

"I look forward to seeing you in the mornings. Seeing you around the house, it's almost like we're . . ." His red face grew darker. He sought her hand in his big paws and clasped it with a gentle touch as if she were fragile. Goose bumps prickled her arm and raced up the nape of her neck. "Don't tell me you don't feel it too."

"I don't." She whispered the words. "I can't."

He sighed, an infinitely sad sound. "That day in the truck, I was sure you were thinking about it, considering the idea."

His powers of observation were great. Everything about this was unfair to him.

"I'm a mother with a baby. A Plain woman. We don't . . . date men who aren't Amish. Besides, my husband . . . He's the one I love."

"You're so young, though. Life can't be over for you. You have to go on."

"I will, but not with you." It hurt to say those words. It hurt to see the pain they caused him. "It's not that I don't like you. If I choose someone outside the community, I lose everything. My family won't be able to talk to me. I won't be able to see them."

"What kind of religion is that?" He shook his head so hard his shaggy hair bounced. "That punishes a girl for loving someone?"

She didn't love Dusty. She couldn't. No matter what happened, she loved her family. Even though her husband, on the brink of becoming a father, died on the icy asphalt on a cold, snowy January day, she still had her faith. "It's not punishment. In this world, we'll have trouble, but Gott will see us through it. In His time."

"Just give me a chance. I can see you through this trouble."

Movement in the distance caught the corner of Bess's eye. A dirty gray van approached, a plume of dust following like a dog's tail wagging. "I can't. I'm sorry. It's time for you to go."

"You won't come back to the B and B then?"

"I can't."

He stomped down the path between the rows. At the garden's edge he turned back. "Come with me. Bring the baby. We'll plant our own garden with all the vegetables you can imagine and then flowers, lots of flowers in every color. It'll make you happy. You'll smile. I love your smile."

"I'm so sorry, I truly am." The van drew closer. "You have to go now."

He swiveled and lifted his hand to his forehead to shield his eyes from the sun. "Who is it?"

The van jerked to a halt next to the pickup truck. Too late.

"My father."

THIRTY-FOUR

The van's back door slid open with a high-pitched squeal. Daed's head, covered by a straw hat, emerged first. His work boots hit the ground. He straightened. Bess still couldn't see his expression. He strode toward them. His head came up. His face held thunderclouds, the likes of which she'd never seen in the Missouri sky. She tried to draw a breath but felt no air in her lungs.

Dusty drew himself up to his six-foot-plus stature and held out his hand. "You're Bess's father. I'm Dusty Lake."

Daed ignored the hand. "We've come more than three hundred miles this morning to see our daughter and grandson. You'll understand if I ask you to take your leave."

"I do." Dusty's hand dropped. He turned toward Bess. "Talk to you soon."

They wouldn't talk — not soon or anytime. "Tell Minerva I'm sorry."

"She'll ask Mary Katherine to take on

more duties." Dusty side-stepped Daed and tromped toward his truck. "She'll put another ad in the paper. That doesn't mean she'll give up on getting you back. She loves you."

Like I do. The unspoken words shimmered in the air, so bright they hurt Bess's eyes.

Mary Katherine would be happy to work more hours, if it meant keeping Bess out of trouble.

Bess in trouble. The thought seemed ludicrous. She'd had scrapes before, crawling out her window to go ice skating when Mudder had forbidden it. Child's play.

Dusty was simply a case of wanting to escape to the forbidden. To escape this existence that only reminded her of Caleb. It wouldn't work. There was no escaping.

The look on her daed's face told her this was no longer child's play. His disappointment hurt more than anger would've. Bess wanted to wrap her arms around him in a hug, but she didn't. A show of affection would never do. He stood before her, not speaking, hands hanging at his side, simply staring as if trying to see inside his daughter to that thing that had caused her to veer from the path. She swallowed and willed herself not to look away. She had done nothing wrong.

Mudder hopped from the van and trudged toward them. Surely Mudder would hug her. Nee, she stopped next to Daed. Neither spoke for a long moment. Daed looked tired. He should be back in Haven helping her brothers with the planting, not here checking on his wayward daughter.

"You didn't have to come —"

"Freeman felt differently." His voice roughened with contained emotion. "He made that clear when he called. We were to come as soon as we could."

"I've done nothing except get a job and earn my keep."

Daed jerked his thumb toward the pickup truck that putted down the road, black exhaust fumes unfurling behind it. "That didn't look like nothing."

"He's the son of the B and B owners."

"An Englisch man who comes out here to visit you?"

"Shouldn't he be working?" Mudder posed the question. "What reason would he have to drive out here on a workday?"

"He wanted to convince me to return to work. I left them in the lurch."

"You did what is best for you and your bopli."

"I did it because Hazel needs my help now." She inhaled, working to keep her voice steady. "I shouldn't have left her to carry the load at home. I only worry that it was wrong to make a commitment and not keep it."

"Your eternal salvation is more important than any commitment to an Englisch hotel." Daed's fingers tightened around his suspenders. "It's best if you come to Haven with us. A fresh start will do you good."

"Hazel needs me here."

"Hazel has been caring for your child."

"Now I will help her with her little ones. That's only fair."

"It was a long drive." Mudder touched Daed's arm. "Let's go inside. Get something to eat, drink, and then talk."

Daed grunted. He pivoted and brushed past his fraa without another word.

Mudder stared at the ground. "It was hard for him. Getting that call from Freeman."

"I'm sorry."

"We don't expect it from a married woman, a mother, a baptized member of the church. We raised you better."

"It was innocent." The remembered feel of Dusty's hand on hers only a few moments before warmed her cheeks. "He's a nice man. They're nice people. They make me feel . . . useful. I cleaned bedrooms and did laundry."

They didn't look at me with pitying, watching eyes.

"You're a grown woman, a member of this Gmay. You know the Ordnung. You know what's expected of you."

True words. "I didn't encourage him."

"You didn't keep to yourself, either. You embraced his worldly ways."

"I planted flowers with him."

"You did something you love with him. Something he loves."

Indeed. Mudder saw so much without even being in the same town. To be so wise. Bess had shared a moment without even meaning to do it. "It meant nothing."

"From the look on his face, I reckon it meant something to him. A lot."

Again, she was right. Mudder was always right. "I didn't think —"

"Nee, you didn't. So now you must come home with us."

"Haven isn't my home."

"It will be."

"I need to help Hazel."

"You've done enough to Hazel."

Bess's breath caught in her throat. Mudder might as well have said Bess killed the baby. She bowed her head, stealing herself against tears that burned her eyes. "I'll do whatever you want."

411

Mother's hand squeezed her shoulder. "Gott forgives you. So do we."

Bess nodded, mouth clamped shut to keep the sobs corralled.

Still, moving to Haven seemed wrong. She cleared her throat. "Shouldn't I be here to make amends? Running away to Haven only serves me, not her."

Mudder pursed her lips, her face troubled. "We only want to do what is right. Your daed fears for you here."

"If I'm no longer at the B and B —"

"But that man came here."

"He won't come again."

"I'll talk to your daed, but he has the last word."

Of course he did. "I will do better."

THIRTY-FIVE

The auctioneer's low, rumbled cadence, "Two, two, now who'll give me two, now two, two, give me two fifty," mesmerized Aidan. Horses whinnied and neighed in time, their thoughts flung in the air one after the other. Harnesses jingled and hooves thudded against dirt. A concert of sounds. The pungent smell of horse manure, sweat, and fresh-cut hay mixed in an enticing, earthy aroma. A sea of straw hats with black bands surrounded him, a steady murmur of *Deutsch* mixed with Englisch.

He inhaled and a tight knot inside him loosened. He liked a good horse auction, even if he couldn't afford to buy a horse anytime soon. Watching the enormous, beautiful beasts traipse up and down, their regal heads dipping, tails swishing, strengthened his sense of God being present. He created these magnificent animals. They were beautiful and utilitarian. Hard workers and loyal to their masters. One of Gott's great gifts.

Timothy's invitation to attend and help him buy another set of work horses had been just what the doctor ordered. It took Aidan's mind off the farm and Bess. The farm, anyway. A cluster of young boys shot past him, jostling for position against the railing. He stumbled toward Timothy, who leaned against the bars, a piece of hay stuck between his teeth. His brother removed the hay and pointed with it. "What do you think of that one?"

Elmer Zimmerman trotted up and down the enclosure with a handsome blue roan Belgian. "He'll go for a pretty penny. A little thin through the shoulders and quarters."

Timothy sniffed, the expression on his chubby face philosophic. He might ought to eat fewer slices of his wife's shoofly pie. "She's leaving, you know?"

"Who's leaving?"

"Don't play dumb with me, Bruder."

A cheer went up. Joseph Borntrager waved at the crowd as the auctioneer declared him the new owner of the blue roan. A pretty penny indeed.

"I've been at the farm birthing two more litters of piglets for the last two days." Twenty more to add to his stock. With time, he would have his hog farm. With the income, he'd be able to invest in a new flock of chickens. Gott willing. "I have no idea what you're talking about."

"Josephina talked to Sophie who talked to Isaac, and Bess's parents came to fetch her to Haven." Timothy paused to suck in a breath. The grapevine writhed its way through Jamesport with its usual vigor. "Freeman called them because he's concerned over the time she's spending with the son of the B and B owners."

Aidan didn't bother to respond. Freeman should be concerned. A man who drove so recklessly, he let Bess get hurt in his company. A man who showed up at her house to beg her to come back. The grapevine brought news to Aidan as much as the next person.

He should've been more forthright with her that night with the purple martins. He had meant to speak his mind, but he hadn't. He'd come so close. In the end the most he could utter after so many years of silence was a whispered, *"Don't go."* If he couldn't gather his courage and tell her how he felt, why should she stay? *Give her a reason to stay.* To see if she could learn to feel the same way about him. He was no Caleb.

No one could replace Caleb. Aidan didn't

want to replace anyone. He wanted his own spot by Bess's side.

Roy Miller trotted out a pair of tawny chestnut Belgians, their flaxen manes bouncing. At two thousand pounds apiece, they stood at sixteen hands and were experienced in the field. They still had a good ten years of work in them. These were the two Timothy had his heart set on. "You're up."

"Bruder, don't look at me that way." Timothy had the audacity to appear hurt. "I'm not one to gossip and you know it. I only tell you because you need to know."

"Pay attention."

Timothy grimaced and turned back to the enclosure. "You're sure these are the two?"

"You asked for my opinion and I gave it."

"You always were the best judge of horse-flesh in the family." Timothy stuck his hand in the air and hollered. The auctioneer's assistant noted his bid. The competing bids flew fast and furious. His face red with excitement, Timothy held his ground but to no avail. The price crept up beyond his limit of a thousand apiece. Kicking at clods of dirt with his work boot, he stuck his hands in his armpits as if to ensure they didn't pop up and bid again of their own volition. He looked like a little boy denied a puppy.

"It wasn't meant to be."

"There are a few others that might work. Let's go look in the barn again." He squeezed through the crowd, smiling and nodding to acquaintances. Timothy wasn't one to nurse his wounds. At the barn he turned. "Aren't you going to do something?"

He was like a cat with a mouse.

"Let it go."

"You're the one letting her go."

What chance would he have with Bess if they took her to Haven? Not that geography had much to do with it. She was close now and he hadn't made his intentions known. That day with the purple martins he'd felt a moment when her heart had seemed open to him. Just a scant second when her face had softened and she'd looked young and sweet and happy the way she had before she'd married Caleb. "What makes you think she's mine to let go?"

"I can see it. Josie can see it. Even Iris saw it."

"Saw what?"

Timothy blew out air in an exaggerated huff. "Bruder, you are the most stubborn man alive. Go to her. Make your case."

"She's Caleb's widow." The words came out against his better judgment. "I'm responsible for him dying."

"Nee. A truck did that."

"I sent him out there."

"She doesn't hold you responsible."

"How do you know?"

"I can tell by the way she studies you when you're not looking. Like she's trying to figure something out."

"You're seeing things."

"Nee. You're both too stubborn to admit you have feelings."

"It doesn't feel right."

"If you don't do something now, you'll never have a chance. You waited too long to speak up before and she married another man." Timothy's face grew redder as he gathered steam. Aidan had never seen his brother so worked up. "Now there's this Englischer. Now we're talking about her losing her eternal soul and her life in this community. Will you let that happen?"

Nee. He'd send her away himself before he let her do that. "If she goes to Haven, she'll not be tempted by the Englischer."

"If she goes to Haven, you'll never be able to give her the second chance you both deserve."

"I have nothing to offer her." A farmer he'd met once or twice from Seymour walked by and threw them a curious look.

418

Aidan lowered his voice. "A chicken farm with no chickens."

"You have hogs."

He did. Not a hog farm, but a start. "It'll take time to build the operation."

"It'll take time to build something between her and you. You have time for both. If ever there are two people who should stop being miserable and follow Gott's plan . . ."

"You claim to know Gott's plan?"

"It's plain as the nose on your face."

Aidan opened his mouth and shut it. The giant, red-haired man walked through the barn door with another man. His gaze met Aidan's.

Dusty Lake smiled, waved, and made a beeline straight for Aidan.

THIRTY-SIX

Why would an Englischer who worked in a nursery and lived in town at a bed-and-breakfast be at a horse auction? Aidan didn't need to see him ever again. The man charged toward him, face split by a wide smile. Sweat stained his green T-shirt, which featured what looked like catsup and mustard stains. The knees of his jeans were missing. He held out one massive hand.

"Remember me? I'm Dusty Lake." His handshake nearly crushed Aidan's fingers. He caught himself before he shook them out. Dusty jabbed a thumb toward the other man. "This is my father, Gavin. It's serendipity that we ran into you right at this moment. It really is."

Aidan didn't know what that meant. Politeness demanded he find out. He introduced Timothy. More handshakes ensued. His brother grimaced and rubbed his fingers. Aidan fought the urge to elbow him.

"Why serendipity?"

"We need a horse. You know horses, I'm sure. I bet you know everything there is to know about horses. Amish men would."

"You gentlemen talk horses." Gavin mopped at his face with a huge, startling white handkerchief. "Dusty, find out how much we should spend on a decent horse. Not an expensive one, just whatever it takes. I need to find the facilities. Can you point me in the right direction?"

"I'm headed that direction myself." Timothy grinned at Aidan. "I reckon my brother can tell Dusty all about horses. He does know just about everything there is to know. He's a good judge of horseflesh."

"Perfect. Perfect." Gavin stuck the handkerchief in the pocket of his beige linen pants, wiped his hands on his red, long-sleeved shirt with its gold cufflinks, and trotted after Timothy in his black pants, blue shirt, and suspenders, a mismatched pair if ever Aidan had seen one. He turned to Dusty.

"I thought your parents operated a B and B."

"They do."

Images of Dusty giving the tourists' children rides on a mini pony appeared. Or a petting zoo? "Why do you need a horse?"

"We have a buggy but not a horse. Dad wants to give the boarders tours of Jamesport Amish spots like schools and the cemeteries and such in the buggy. He heard the other owners did it and it was another revenue stream."

Revenue stream. Fancy talk for making money off the Plain. The Amish on display. The people who flowed around them now at the auction, their Deutsch language a familiar, calming sound in Aidan's ears. His people. Yet they couldn't complain. They needed the income from their stores and the fairs and markets. He nodded. "Are you talking about the buggy that sits in the front yard? It doesn't look too sturdy."

"No, no. It's bigger and it's an open carriage, really, not a buggy so much." Dusty's hands flew about as he gained momentum. He raised his voice to be heard over the good-natured shouts and laughter of men who enjoyed bidding wars on good horseflesh but harbored no ill will toward the winner of the battle. "It's in the shed in the back. Very nice. There's tack and such. Not that we exactly know how to hitch up a horse."

"Something you'd have to learn." People who bought animals and then didn't take care of them — whether because of ignorance or laziness — got Aidan's goat. "There's a lot to learn. Animals depend on their owners."

"Yeah, and we need to know how much to spend on a good horse. They seem pretty expensive."

"It's not just how much you pay at auction. There's the feed, the farrier, the vet bills, a trailer, the tack. Will you keep it on your property or board it elsewhere?"

"The shed in back has stalls. They must've kept a horse there before."

"Animals are a lot of responsibility. Everyday responsibility." Aidan inhaled the familiar, homey scents of horse manure and dirt, mingled with the barbecue plates sold in booths nearby. "The stalls need to be mucked every day. Horses need room to roam. Pasture. Grass to eat. Company. Medical care."

Dusty looked nonplussed. "Company?"

"You can't park a horse in the garage like you do a car."

"Right. Right." Dusty chewed on his lower lip. His hands went to his hips, jutting out so the crowd passing by had to adjust its flow to give him wider berth. "I'm so glad I ran into you. How's Bess?"

"Pardon?"

"Bess? I've been worried about her."

He had no right to ask. Aidan had no right to speak on her behalf. "She's at home where she belongs."

"She seemed happy working at the B and B." Dusty cleared his throat. "She seemed happy."

"She's happy at home with family and her baby." Aidan raised his face to the brilliant sun that beat down in a shimmering blue sky and let its heat warm the icy spot where his heart should be. She was happy, wasn't she? "She doesn't miss the job."

She didn't miss Dusty.

"Are you sure?" His concern seemed genuine.

Aidan understood it, but it couldn't be allowed. "The best thing you can do for Bess is to leave her alone."

"I'm trying."

Aidan saw something familiar in Dusty's face. Longing. A sense of loss. A wanting. He recognized those symptoms. "You know Plain folks keep to themselves for a reason."

"I know. She told me."

"Then you know what happens if we don't. Do you want her to lose everything?"

"No, no, but I can't believe people would be that cruel. To shut someone out because they loved someone."

"What makes you think she loves you?"

"I didn't mean to imply that." His face reddened. "She likes me, though, I can tell."

But she hadn't said as much. She hadn't crossed that line. Maybe she didn't feel that way about Dusty. Maybe she was trying not to hurt his feelings. Maybe Aidan still had a chance. He hadn't lost again because of his own inability to act. He pivoted to walk away. "I think you should ask someone else about the horses."

"Wait, I didn't mean to offend you." Dusty tromped alongside him. "I'm sorry."

"No offense taken."

"You're mad, I can tell."

"I'm not mad." He walked faster. "I need to go."

Dusty plowed to a stop. "You like her too. Don't you?"

Aidan forced himself to stop and face the man. "Plain folks don't talk about such things."

"You do. I can see it in your face."

Aidan turned his back and moved away. *Keep moving. Keep going. Don't speak of it.*

Dusty's long legs had no trouble keeping up. "Someday she's gonna marry me."

Aidan's gut clenched. Purple dots danced in front of his eyes. He sought to inhale, but no oxygen flowed into his lungs. *Breathe.* With great care, he unclenched his fists.

"You would do that to her?"

"I can make her happy. We can make a life together with Joshua. A fresh start."

"You mean you can make you happy." The image of Dusty holding Caleb's baby in his arms propelled Aidan to stop and face him once again. The man behind him did a two-step and grumbled as he adjusted course. "You would take her away from the life she's meant to live for your own selfish reasons."

"Love isn't selfish."

Aidan stood eye to eye, toe to toe with the man. "If you really love her, you'll stay away from her."

He brushed past him, moving in the other direction, any direction away from a future that included Bess marrying another man — again.

THIRTY-SEVEN

Bess didn't like sneaking around. That gray chasm stretched wider between fraa-turned-widow and daughter-who-answered-to-parents. She needed to make her plea to Laura before Mudder and Daed realized she slipped out of the house after cleaning up from the noonday meal. They'd been watching her with eagle eyes for three days now. They had decided to return to Haven the following day.

She was supposed to be packing her belongings, not tracking down Laura to plead for her help in staying in Jamesport. She had to stay. It was the only way she could figure out the path she needed to take. She needed time to discern her future. The only thing she knew for certain was that future needed to happen in Jamesport.

Someone had parked a buggy at the hitching post in front of Laura's small dawdy haus. Bess chewed on her lip, contemplating. This couldn't wait. She clambered from her buggy and went to the door.

"It's open," came the warbled response to her knock. Of course it would be. Laura's simple abode was a magnet for an endless stream of grandchildren and great-grandchildren. She had the best cookies and pies in the district. Everyone knew that. "Don't be shy. Come on in."

Bess gathered up her courage and marched through the front room to the kitchen from which the words emanated.

"It's me, Bess."

She stopped. Iris stood at the kitchen table, packing something into a straw bag.

"We're just restocking." She smiled and cocked her head toward the bag. "Emily Hisler is due any day and so is Lavina Kemp. We want to be ready."

"I'm surprised to see you here." Laura brandished a dish towel. "Have a seat. We're having coffee and leftover biscuits with strawberry jelly. Help yourself."

"I'm fine." Bess sank onto the bench at Laura's pine table. The aroma of baking cookies — gingersnaps if her nose served — made her mouth water. "I needed to ask you a big favor. A question."

"You don't want to go to Haven." Laura opened the oven door and peeked at her

428

cookies. The sweet yet piquant aroma of ginger, cinnamon, cloves, and molasses wafted in the air. "Because of Aidan."

How could this be so obvious to everyone? What did they see that she didn't? "Jah. Nee. This isn't about Aidan."

"Ach, you two are a stubborn lot." Laura glanced at Iris as if to commiserate. "Aren't they?"

"They are."

"He was Caleb's best friend." Bess traced small nicks and scars in the table's wood, each representing memories of time Laura had spent preparing meals with her daughters. "You think he suddenly decided he had a hankering for his widow?"

"Not suddenly. For that reason, he stepped aside and Caleb married the woman he loved." Laura grabbed a pot holder that looked like the homemade ones her grandkinner wove with brightly colored cloth loops on small metal looms. "His is a true, unselfish, noble love."

The kind that would last forever. Bess had known that love once. To have it again would be a precious gift. But how could she trust it wouldn't be ripped from her a second time? She couldn't bear that. "How do you know this?"

"We have eyes in our heads, don't we, Iris?"

"I didn't —"

"It's all right. I promise." Iris snapped the bag shut. "I'm not still mooning over what I can't have. I wasted enough time on that. I'm waiting for Gott's plan to unfold. I have faith it will. Aidan is all yours."

"I didn't mean for any of this to happen. I'm not even sure it has happened."

"None of this is your fault." Iris poured coffee into a huge mug and brought it to Bess. "I can't fathom what you must be going through, losing Caleb. You didn't ask to be in this position. Now you are. Gott, in His infinite wisdom, will figure it out for both of us. Milk, sugar?"

Her crisp, matter-of-fact statement was a balm to Bess's sore heart. To be so wise and so kind at such an early age. Bess longed for that. If Laura let her stay with her, Bess could figure it out.

What would her role be here in Jamesport? If only she knew what was going on in Aidan's head. Every time he looked at her she saw an unasked question on his face. "I don't know what to think about Aidan. He hasn't made his feelings clear. Not at all."

"Because he has to sort them out first." Laura set a plate of warm cookies on the table in front of Bess. "You know how hard this is for you, to lay aside your feelings for Caleb. To let go of the life you had with him. Imagine how confusing and difficult this must be for Aidan."

"He takes one step forward and two steps back."

"Give him time to figure it out. You need time to heal. So does he."

Which meant staying in Jamesport. Bess wanted to see as clearly. Memories of Caleb and years of relegating Aidan to friend stature kept those feelings at a distance that made them almost impossible to see. She had laughed with him, shared most of her childhood memories with him, Christmas, birthdays, rumspringa, baptism. Always there, always ready to be a part of her life. She could trust and accept this gift, or she could remain alone for the rest of her life. The choice was hers. If she went to Haven, she would never know which road to take. "I wondered . . ."

"Don't wander too far. You'll get lost."

"Laura!"

The older woman's chuckle floated on the air like feathers hijacked on a fitful breeze. "Ask away."

"My parents want me to go back to Haven with them."

"And you don't want to go."

"It seems like running away."

"If they decide you must go, you must go." Laura sipped her coffee and plunked the mug on the table. "You may be a widow with a child, but you're still their daughter. And you have no mann to provide for you."

"Neither did you."

"My parents had passed by the time I lost my Eli. My kinner were grown. They think it's their place to tell me how to live my life now. Don't worry, there's no escaping the multitude of people who think they know what's best for you." Laura rubbed her swollen knuckles absently. "They only do it because they care for you. That's the thing we must remember. They meddle because they care, not because they think we're not capable of caring for ourselves. Leastways, that's what I tell myself."

"I know. But what if I stayed with you?" Bess wiggled on the bench. "Mudder has known you since she was a girl, and you were best friends with Groossmammi. If you invited me to stay with you, they wouldn't worry so much. I'd be out of Hazel's hair and I wouldn't be there to remind Mattie every day of what she's lost. She's taken to wandering in the house at night and picking up Joshua for no reason."

"She is lost, that poor woman."

"She is. Even Solomon is ready to admit it. At least, he's said he will take her to the doctor." Yet he'd gone out to the fields every day instead, his gaze avoiding hers before he slammed the door behind him. "So let me stay with you and give her peace."

Laura's forehead wrinkled. "If your daed agrees to it."

"Will you come with me to talk to him?"

"You want me to plead your case?"

"Mudder and Daed will listen to you. They don't seem to hear anything I say."

"I'll meet you there after Iris and I check on Emily. Then we can talk with your parents about what is best." Laura stood. "In the meantime, pray. Pray that you discern Gott's will for you. Pray that you learn to trust Him. Know that His will doesn't involve leaving your family or your faith. That should be clear to you from the get-go."

How did this woman know everything? "Nothing is clear to me."

"Gott would never give you leave to do something that goes against His Word, against Scripture."

"He doesn't want me to be happy?"

"He delights in our happiness, but He never said there would be no troubles in

433

this world. He said He would carry us through. This is momentary suffering. If you can even call it suffering. Persevere. You have family. You have your son. You have friends. Count your blessings."

"I do."

"Gut. Remember that perseverance leads to hope and hope does not fail. Get home to your bopli. I'll see you there later."

Her throat dry, Bess pasted on a smile and followed the two women out to the buggies. She wanted their sense of direction. Without her job at the B and B, without her mann, she had one focus left. Joshua. Being his mudder. What came next was up to Gott.

And Laura.

THIRTY-EIGHT

The expression on Mudder's face said it all. Bess straightened her shoulders and met her gaze head-on. Mudder's frown stretched from Kansas to Missouri and then some. She shoved her glasses up her nose and laid the Burpee seed catalog on the table next to her rocking chair. "We were looking for you."

"I went to see Laura." Bess smoothed her wrinkled apron with damp palms. "She'll be over after a bit."

"You left without saying anything." *Again,* her tone added.

"Rachel and Sarah knew. They're keeping an eye on Joshua for me."

"Better than nothing." Mudder's tone argued with her words.

"I'll go check on him."

"Why is Laura coming over?"

"To visit. We'll talk when she gets here." Bess fled up the stairs. The bedroom Joshua shared with baby Gracie, Levi, and the girls was empty. His crib, crammed up against one wall, held only a scrabble of blankets and a soiled diaper. The girls knew better than that. She picked it up and headed back down the hallway. "Rachel? Sarah!"

No answer. She hustled down the stairs and past her mudder, who had gone back to perusing the catalog. "They're not up there. Did they say where they were going?"

"Hmm, nee."

Bess dumped the diaper in the pail in the laundry room and did a quick look-see through the house. No girls. No chubby babies with faces wet with drool and gowns decorated with spit-up. Maybe they took him for a walk. She headed out the back door. "Sarah, Rachel!"

Sarah's head popped up from behind the sprawling tomato plants in the vegetable garden. "You're back. Aenti Judith was looking for you."

"I found her. Where's Joshua?"

Rachel popped up next to her sister. She held Gracie in her arms. The baby crowed and flapped her arms as if she expected to fly. "Groossmammi took him."

Mattie? A wave of unease lapped over Bess. She backed away from it, trying to keep her footing on solid ground. "Took

436

him where?"

"She didn't say." Sarah shrugged and held up a plump tomato bigger than her two hands folded together. "Look, we're getting ripe tomatoes already. This will be *wunderbarr* sliced up for supper with a little salt and pepper. Yum."

"When did your groossmammi take Joshua?"

Rachel and Sarah looked at each other. This time the shrug was simultaneous. Sarah stared at the sky, her neck craned, head cocked, nose wrinkled. "The sun hasn't moved much. Maybe an hour."

Mattie could go far in an hour.

Bess whirled and rushed up the porch steps. Her skirt caught on the railing and tore. "Ach." She tugged it loose with trembling fingers. Mattie raised six children. She knew how to care for Joshua. Nee, she hadn't been herself. Not in a long time. Not since Caleb . . .

Bess sped through the open screen door, through the kitchen, into the front room, peering into corners as she went, as if Mattie had made herself small and curled into the shadows on purpose.

"The girls say Mattie has Joshua. Did you see them leave?"

"I thought the girls had him." Mudder

stood, her knees creaking and popping louder than the joints of the rocking chair. "She probably took him for a walk to put him down for a nap. He's been so fussy."

If Mudder only knew. "Laura will be here any minute. Will you visit with her while I catch up with Mattie?"

"Joshua is fine with Mattie. She may be cantankerous, but she knows how to care for a bopli. Why are you in such a dither about it?"

"She's not been herself in a while. Not since . . ."

"Surely she's beyond that by now."

Spoken like the faithful, strong servant she was. Mudder had lost boplin, but she'd never lost her faith. Bess hoped to be like her one day. But not today. "Neither of us are beyond it." The force of the painful empathy that roared through Bess nearly knocked her back a step. In as few words as possible, she described Mattie's strange behavior. How could she judge Mattie when she had exhibited her own lack of faith daily? *Gott, forgive me.* "Solomon doesn't want to see it, but it's getting worse. He said he would take her to see Dr. Lowe, but he hasn't."

"Gott will watch over them. Go look for her. I'll wait for Laura. She can take me out to the fields to tell Solomon and your daed if you haven't found her by then."

Bess headed to the dawdy haus first. The Weaver dawdy haus was different from Laura's. The squat, wooden structure with its white exterior and gray roof looked like an extension of the main house. It was small enough to be a shed, just big enough for two people who spent most of their time elsewhere. This time, she didn't bother to knock. Family didn't. She shoved open the door and peered inside. Neat as a pin, as to be expected. Mattie's darning lay in a basket on the table next to a hickory rocker. Reading glasses lay on top of a German Bible, still open to somewhere in the middle. The two surely sat together every evening in companionable silence born of nearly fifty years of marriage. The faint aroma of pie — apple pie — baking hung in the air. Solomon's favorite.

"Mattie, are you here?"

A bird's irritated screech sounded through the open window. As much as it reminded her of Mattie it wasn't the answer Bess sought. She padded into the tiny kitchen. The pie sat on the windowsill. She touched it. Still warm. The tub on the counter held two dirty mugs, a mixing bowl, measuring cups and spoons. Mattie had left in the middle of cleaning up.

"Where are you?" She said the words aloud even though the silence told her no one would hear.

Mattie had left in a hurry.

Bess whirled and trotted back out the front door. She quickened her pace, around the empty chicken coop, by the toolshed, through the barn, behind the barn, along the path down to the pond. The minutes ticked by, accompanied by the chirp of birds, cricket song, frogs, and Bess's own increasingly frantic breathing.

Mattie wouldn't hurt Joshua, but what if she dropped him again or fell with him in her arms? If she decided to take him somewhere in the buggy, the possibilities were even scarier. She didn't have the strength to stop an out-of-control horse spooked by a passing eighteen-wheeler or tractor.

Stop. Stop looking for trouble before it finds you.

Think. Think.

Trust. Trust in Gott.

Bess stared at the stalls in the dark, cool barn interior. Solomon's buggy was gone, along with Nellie, their sorrel. Where would she go? Visiting with "her" bopli? Into town? She had at least an hour's head start. Bess harnessed a horse to Isaac's buggy, climbed in, and snapped the reins. She had to find them.

Did she still believe Joshua was Caleb, or had she decided to take her grandson to his father?

The cemetery first. In some strange way, it might make sense to Mattie. The drive took twenty long minutes. The gate stood open. She leaned forward in the seat and put her free hand to her forehead to shield her eyes from the sun's glare. Nothing. "Mattie, where are you?"

A horse whinnied in the distance. Rusty responded in kind. Bess guided the buggy to the left, toward the sound, along the dirt path that served as the cemetery road. It took her to the place she hadn't been since January when the ground was covered with snow, the trees barren of leaves, and the sky a leaden color that promised more snow. A man knelt on the plot that was home to Caleb's remains.

Aidan.

He held a trowel in one hand and a clump of weeds, dirt clinging to their roots, in the other. He looked up. The dreamy contemplation on his face faded, replaced with a burnt-red blush that tore across his cheeks. He dropped the weeds and stood. "What are you doing here?"

She wanted to ask the same question of him, but there was no time. "Looking for Mattie. She disappeared this morning with Joshua."

"What do you mean disappeared? Surely, she took him for a walk."

"I looked everywhere. She's gone. Almost two hours now." Bess breathed, working to control the tremor in her voice. "I thought maybe she brought him here to be close to Caleb."

Aidan came here to be close to his friend. Bess, Caleb's own fraa, had not come.

"Caleb's not here. I come here because it's quiet and it's the last place we were together." He worked mud off the end of the trowel with long fingers, his expression troubled. "What does Solomon say about his fraa?"

"He's working in the fields. Mudder went to get him." Working, not pulling weeds in the cemetery. Bess looked beyond Aidan. A riot of colors burst all around Caleb's grave. Flowers. Shades of pink, purple, red, golden yellow. "What are you doing here, besides enjoying the quiet?"

"I planted the flowers you never did."

"I never did?"

"I gave you a bunch of packets of seeds the day of the funeral. You probably don't

442

remember."

The image of his face full of misery and the shaking of his hand when he held out the packets accosted her. She hadn't been able to raise her arm. Her own misery had weighed too much. "So you took it upon yourself?"

"He's not here, but somehow I feel like he sees. It's a flight of fancy, I know." His face turned a deeper shade of crimson and his jaw jutted, but he pointed at the sprawling rows of flowers in a half-dozen colors. "They're all perennials and hardy. Pink coneflowers. Butterfly weed — it's not really a weed — the hummingbirds and butterflies will visit them and him. The Virginia bluebells are great too. The geraniums make a good border and they smell like apples. Black-eyed Susans will bloom later in August to keep the colors going into fall. The hydrangeas look like clouds, don't they?"

The multitude of words flowed from his embarrassment, but also from his enthusiasm. It made her think of Dusty. No scientific names here, just a Plain man's love of the earth and all the beauty Gott had created. Simple, with no plans for buying and selling. Only showing his love and remembering a good man gone too soon. His way

443

of honoring Caleb. Dusty wouldn't understand their ways. Her ways.

Bess longed to slip from the buggy and sink onto the ground so she could run her fingers through the soft petals and inhale the healing scents. She longed to share in Aidan's enthusiastic embrace of Gott's creation. But she couldn't, not now. "This is wunderbarr, but I have to go."

"Another time. I'd like to . . . talk." He scooped up his tools and slid them into a saddlebag, then moved toward the horse that stood nibbling at grass a few feet away, tossing his head now and again as if to invite Rusty to join in the repast. "I'll come with you. I'll help you find Mattie. She couldn't have gone far."

The crushing weight on Bess's shoulder's eased. She wasn't alone in her search. Aidan's nearby presence helped her stay calm as they searched in vain.

It seemed Mattie had gone farther than either of them thought possible. They searched the roads around the cemetery and all the way into Jamesport. No sign of an elderly lady and a baby. After two more hours of fruitless stops at each of the Weaver kinners' houses and then the houses of friends, they returned to Solomon's.

A cluster of men milled about in front of

the house. Freeman stood talking to Solomon, who tugged at his beard with one hand, his glasses perched precariously close to the end of his nose, the usual forgotten pencil stuck behind one ear.

"They haven't found her either," Bess called to Aidan, who rode abreast of the buggy. "Why are they standing around then?"

A siren blipped and bleated behind her. She looked back. A Daviess County sheriff's car sped along the road, dirt and exhaust billowing. The driver flashed his red-and-blue rooftop lights at her. She pulled to the far right side of the road, Aidan just ahead of her. The sheriff roared by.

They'd called in the cavalry.

THIRTY-NINE

They had searched every nook and cranny themselves. That was the only reason Freeman would allow the Englisch law enforcement folks to be called to Solomon's farm. Bess's heart raced, making it hard to think. Her hands shook and the horizon wavered in her sight They couldn't find Mattie. Or Joshua. Solomon must be truly worried. And Freeman as well. Otherwise, they wouldn't have moved so quickly.

She swallowed hot tears. She'd lost Caleb. Not Joshua too. *Please Gott, not Joshua too. Trust. Trust in Me. Trust Me with everything.*

She had no choice but to trust. Nowhere else to turn. *Gott, he's only a baby. Protect and keep him.*

"Let me help you."

She started, realizing that Aidan stood looking up at her, hand outstretched, waiting for her to get down from the buggy. Given that her legs felt like wet noodles, she was relieved to accept his offer. His fingers were strong and sure. She fought the urge to lean on him. His hand tightened and he nodded at her, as if reading her mind. "It'll be fine. Joshua and Mattie are in Gott's hands."

She inhaled. *Just breathe.* "I know."

"We'll find them." His gaze burned through her with a promise that went beyond his spoken words. He offered her something precious. She need only reach out and accept it. "I know you will."

He nodded and turned to the men who had circled around the deputy, one Thomas T. MacGregor, according to the pin on his pocket. He took notes with a flourish, glancing at Solomon, now and again as if to assure him he still listened.

"And this baby Mrs. Weaver has with her?" His forehead wrinkled over bushy, auburn eyebrows that looked like skeins of wool. "Who does the baby belong to?"

"To us, to my daughter-in-law —"

"To me." Bess spoke up. The men turned to look at her. Freeman frowned. Bess raised her chin, refusing to look away. "I was searching for them. Aidan helped. We've been to all the nearby farms, the cemetery, the pond. She's gone."

"We've also searched." Freeman's tone

suggested he took umbrage at Bess striking out on her own. "Mattie isn't here."

"Where were you when the baby was taken?" Deputy MacGregor didn't look up from his pad so he couldn't see what Bess saw. The looks exchanged by Freeman, Solomon, and her father. They wanted an answer to that question too. "Did you give Mrs. Weaver permission to take the baby or ask her to take care of him?"

"I went to visit a friend. My nieces were watching him." She hesitated. "Mattie has been . . . She hasn't been herself. I wouldn't leave Joshua with her."

The deputy looked directly at her for the first time. "What do you mean — ?"

"She's been a bit under the weather." Solomon jumped in. "She gets confused sometimes."

"Dementia? Alzheimer's?" Deputy Mac-Gregor's eyebrows disappeared under his hat and reappeared. "Do we need an Endangered Person Advisory?"

"I don't know exactly. She's not in her right mind." Solomon's shoulders sagged. "I thought to take her to the doctor, but she just gets confused sometimes, that's all."

Freeman put his hand on the other man's shoulder and stepped between them. "What is this advisory?"

"We send the information to the SHP — Missouri State Highway Patrol. They send the alert to all law enforcement in the state as well as the media. Of course, it usually includes a description of the car and a license plate number. In this case, we could describe her. An elderly lady in a bonnet with a baby wouldn't be all that helpful in these parts."

The media. Freeman's face reflected Bess's quandary. They almost never wanted the world involved in their dilemmas. They took care of their own, solved their own problems, and steered clear of the world's.

"We don't need the entire state involved." Freeman put his hands on his hips, his expression fierce. "She's one woman in a buggy. She can't have traveled far."

"You called us, sir." Deputy MacGregor pursed lips that played hide-and-seek in a shaggy, rust-colored handlebar mustache. "The sheriff's department doesn't have the resources to search this entire county. By involving other law enforcement agencies, it's likely we can find her sooner."

"We have to let them do whatever is necessary. Joshua will be hungry soon." Bess put her hands to her face, trying to stop the words. It wasn't her place to speak. She turned, looking for support. His expression

449

neutral, Daed stood on the porch with his arms crossed over his chest. Laura and Mudder gathered nearby, their hands clasped as if in prayer. Bess faced the deputy. "We need to start looking before it gets dark."

"I'll call in the advisory." Deputy Mac-Gregor spun on the thick soles of his shiny black boots and headed back to his car.

"You have forgotten your place." Freeman's glare singed Bess's face. "We'll decide what is best. Go in the house and wait there. The men will search again."

Bess opened her mouth. Aidan shook his head ever so slightly. She closed her mouth and forced herself to trudge up the steps to the porch. The screen door didn't slam behind her.

"Bess, wait." Laura caught at her sleeve. "Wait. The first thing we must always do is pray. People will say when all else fails, pray, but they're wrong. Pray first, pray always, pray for everything."

She halted. It took every ounce of strength not to sink to her knees and wail. Without turning to face Laura, she bowed her head. "It's my fault. All this is my fault."

Laura tugged on her sleeve again. "Look at me, child."

"I'm not a child. I only acted like one. I

450

wanted my way and when I couldn't get it, I sought relief by running away, by getting a job in town."

"You see the error in your ways and you correct it. You repent and ask forgiveness. Gott forgives. His grace is sufficient for all your sins. Yours, mine, and the rest of the world."

"He must be so peeved with me."

"Nee, so pleased that you are growing." Laura's tone was kind. "You are honed by the fire, your character refined. These are the plans He has for you."

"For how long must I be refined?"

"For however long it takes."

FORTY

Refinement took time, it seemed. Cooking for the search party did nothing to take Bess's mind off Joshua. Day turned to night, and then to day again. The men had gone to their homes to sleep when darkness fell and then gone out again at first dawn, the search widening to other districts and into Jamesport itself. The sheriff's department deputies fanned out across the county. The Missouri Highway Patrol issued an Endangered Person Advisory. Still, no sign of a small, old, cantankerous lady with a questionable memory, hurting heart, and a baby. Scrambling eggs and toasting bread did not banish her worries. Was Joshua hungry? Wet, tired, cold, alone? Had Mattie abandoned him? Did he cry out for his mudder?

She slipped another loaf of bread from the oven and placed the pan gently on the counter. In her heart of hearts, she wanted to throw it across the room. Such a childish thought. Still, how could she be making sandwiches while her son was missing? *Gott, he's only a baby.*

Shedding the oven mitts, she closed her eyes. They burned, as always. Would she never be able to smell baking bread again without being reminded of that day in January when her world tilted and never righted itself? The image of another casket, this one tiny, filled her vision. Another funeral. Another black hole in the ground.

Nee. Her throat closed, the ache in her chest so fierce, her legs threatened to collapse under her.

Thy will be done. Keep him safe. Keep him close. Keep him in Your arms. He's better off there than with me. I understand that. I bend to Your will, not mine.

The irony of her agony was not lost on her. She'd been so quick to foist him off on Hazel. Anything to put distance between her and the pain of looking at his face and seeing Caleb. God had given her a special gift and she had rejected it.

Gott, forgive me. He's lost his daed already. If You decide to let me be his mudder, I'll care for him and watch over him. I'll never let him out of my sight. That's a promise, Gott.

She was his mother. She had to find him.

Glancing around, she contemplated her

escape. Mudder sliced ham for sandwiches. Hazel sat at the table, her eyes red rimmed, hands occupied with snapping green beans for supper. The other women were doing laundry and taking care of the house, helping the way Plain folks did during times such as this. She wiped her hands on her apron and angled toward the back door. If she didn't look back, they wouldn't see her go.

"Where're you going?"

Her mother's voice caught her at the door, hand on the knob.

"To get a breath of fresh air."

True. Not the whole truth. Shame burned her cheeks.

"Are you all right?"

Mudder's tone was so sweet, so caring, Bess swiped at her face. She didn't turn around. She'd never be able to hide her true feelings if her mother saw her face. *Don't cry. Don't cry.* "I'm fine." She managed to keep the wobble from her voice. "I just need to get out and walk around for a bit."

"Take all the time you need. We can handle the food. Bring in a couple of tomatoes from the garden when you come back. We'll slice them up to go on the sandwiches later. Sarah can bring up another jar of pickles from the basement."

"I will."

She would, as soon as she found Mattie and Joshua.

The bright sun blinded her for a second. She lowered her head and breathed, letting the morning air cool her face. The scent of honeysuckle and fresh-cut grass calmed her. *Now what, Lord, now what?*

First, she needed a buggy. Mudder and Daed had borrowed one from Laura's daughter. It would still be in the barn. Daed had left with Solomon at dawn in his buggy. Isaac had his. She darted across the yard, feeling like a runaway, and squeezed through the barn door without opening it all the way. Minutes later she headed out on the open road at a steady clip.

Laura's words accompanied her in rhythm with the *clip-clop* of the horse's hooves against the asphalt. *"Pray. In all things pray. Pray first. Pray always."*

Where, Gott, where? Show me the way.

A horse appeared in the distance, headed her direction. Not Daed or Freeman, they rode in buggies. If it were one of the other men, they would surely send her back to the house. No escaping the encounter. She'd come this far. She sucked in air and straightened. She would do what she needed to do, what any mother would do.

The horse drew closer. Aidan waved. Resigned, she slowed and stopped. Aidan pulled up alongside the buggy. He was a good man but still a man. He would send her back to the house because that is what the bishop would want. No matter, she would not go easily. "What are you doing out here?"

"I was going to ask you that." He shoved his straw hat back on his head. Dark circles hung heavy under his bloodshot eyes. "I was up most of the night with another sow farrowing so I got a late start, but I'm here to help now."

"All the men are out searching already."

"Nothing new this morning, then?"

"Nee."

"Then where are you going?"

"To find my suh." Defiance colored her words. She struggled to subdue it. "I mean, I couldn't stay in the house anymore. I couldn't take it. I'm his mudder."

"I understand."

She almost dropped the reins. "You do?"

"I'm a man, but I'm not that thick-headed."

She couldn't contain the snort. "I didn't mean it like that."

"It's all right." He turned the horse so he faced the same direction as the buggy. "So

456

where do we go from here?"

"We?"

"We'll look together. They can't complain if you don't go off on your own. They only worry about having another woman to look for."

"I'm not Mattie. I can take care of —"

"I know. It's only because they care that they make you stay back. They care."

"I know."

"So where were you going?"

Chewing her lip, Bess studied the horizon, hoping against hope that Mattie's wiry figure would appear, a wiggling bundle of boy in her arms. She closed her eyes and folded herself inside the mind of a heartsore mudder who sought relief from unrelenting grief. Disoriented, confused, overwhelmed by loss, she'd fled. She'd want to go someplace where she'd been happy. Someplace with good memories. A place where bad memories wouldn't intrude. Stockton Lake. The wildlife refuge. They were too far away to travel in a buggy. Someplace closer.

The image of a neat two-story, white, wood-frame house barreled into her mind's eye. Tangled roses crept up a trellis on the front porch. A swing set and trampoline filled the space between a clothesline full of sheets and the back porch where blackberry and shoofly pies cooled on the windowsill, their scents mouthwatering. Groossdaadi Shoop gutted and cleaned fish — the smell less inviting — on a stump in the shade of an elm tree. "Remember how we used to go to Caleb's groossmammi's house the weekend after school got out in April?"

"Every year, like clockwork. Caleb disliked school so much. Knowing we were going to his groossmammi's right after the school picnic kept him going through that last day."

Caleb did dislike school. He wanted to spend his days helping his daed in the field. He saw no importance in geography or essay writing. The trip to groossmammi's house out by Trenton was a reward for sticking it out one more year. "Caleb was born there."

"I know. By accident."

If having a baby while visiting family could be called an accident. Caleb had come a few weeks early, but he was still a Jamesport Weaver. "I think Mattie liked it there too. I think she got homesick sometimes for her family. All of Solomon's family are in Jamesport, but her mudder and daed were up in Trenton."

"They visited back and forth all the time. It's a stone's throw. Not even that."

"Still, she's confused. She thinks Joshua is

Caleb. Maybe she took him home for a visit."

"Her mudder passed a couple of years ago. They put the farm up for sale since everyone else was down by Jamesport."

"She might not remember that. Not in the state she's in."

Aidan's horse tossed his head and snorted. He sidestepped, forcing Aidan to focus on the road for a few seconds. "We should let them know where we're going."

"Going back to the farm will waste time. It'll take almost two hours to get there as it is."

"You're determined, I see that. I'll ride up to Timothy's house and let his fraa know. She can send one of the boys to tell your mudder. You don't want to give her more to worry about." Aidan began moving toward the dirt road just beyond the buggy. "I can leave my horse in Timothy's pasture. Just don't leave without me."

"I won't, but hurry. We have to get Joshua and Mattie back. Safe and sound."

"We will."

Now or never? Aidan picked up the reins, snapped them, and clucked. The horse tossed his head and leaned into his load. The opportunity to talk to Bess alone had

459

presented itself so unexpectedly, Aidan wasn't sure how to proceed. Exhaustion muddied his mind. He had much to tell her, much to say, but Mattie and Joshua were missing. He would spend the next two hours in a buggy with Bess, but was this the time? Would there ever be a time? He hazarded a peek at her. She leaned forward as if willing the buggy to go faster and get to Trenton sooner.

This wasn't the time or the place. He would keep her safe and help her find her son. That was his job today, not to make this situation harder for her.

She leaned back against the seat and sighed. "You always know the right thing to do."

Her words needed deciphering, like the words spoken by the foreign family who'd opened the convenience store near the highway outside Jamesport. "I do?"

"You helped Caleb with his schoolwork back when we were scholars. You went for help went I fell out of the tree. Caleb just stood there, his mouth open, but you ran to get Mattie." A soft smile graced her face, then fled. "You have been like a father to Joshua in Caleb's absence. You came for me today, and you didn't send me back to the house like the other men would've."

"I came to help search for Mattie and Joshua." He did what everyone in their community did — come together in a moment of crisis. "I think you're right about them being in Trenton. You're his mudder. He'll need you if he is there."

"The others would've made me stay home while they went. They would bring him back to me. I'd be expected to accept that. I know why you didn't."

"You do?"

Her eyes were brilliant blue in the sunlight. She nodded. "I reckon you were waiting for me to figure it all out. You're a patient man, Aidan Graber. Far more patient than I deserve."

He swallowed. *Gott, let the horse lead the way and forgive such a strange prayer.* "You've had a long row to hoe."

"I took a job in town. I let Hazel care for Joshua. I spent time with an Englisch man." Tears welled in her eyes, but none fell. "I've made it harder for myself."

"You had to find your own way. We all do. No one faults you for that."

"Everyone does. Solomon. My parents. Isaac. Even Hazel, poor, sweet woman, as much as she doesn't want to." Bess kneaded her apron with both hands, her voice tremulous. "Gott forgive me."

461

"He does."

"I pray it is so." She cleared her throat. "Danki."

"For what?" He stole a glance at her. Her cheeks blazed crimson. Her hands were clasped so tight her knuckles were white. "In some ways, I've made it harder."

"Being patient. Understanding. Not judging. Waiting. No else would."

"I talked to Dusty at the horse auction this week." If they were getting things off their chests, he might as well confess too. "He still thinks he has a chance."

"He's a good man."

"But he's not the man for you."

She shook her head. "Nee, he's not."

"Gut."

"What does that mean?"

"It means I'm glad you see it."

She might not understand his full meaning, but she would. Soon. As soon as they had Joshua safe in their arms. "Together, we'll find Joshua." And then they would start again.

She nodded. "Together."

He liked the sound of that.

FORTY-ONE

The sun blazed overhead by the time they reached the tiny hamlet of Trenton. The closer they traveled, the more Bess's throat tightened. If she was wrong, they'd wasted most of the day. If she was right, they would soon know if Mattie had managed to keep Joshua safe in her strange, disoriented state. She knew one thing for sure. She would not take Joshua from his home and family. She could not. Nor could she take him from Aidan.

That realization led her down a road she feared and welcomed at the same time. Everything about his words and actions told her he traveled that same road. They had to find Joshua and then find each other. The latter might take time, but Aidan had waited for her before. Everything about his actions said he would still wait.

Fortunately for her, Aidan had a better recollection of the back roads that led to the farm that had been Mattie's childhood home. The hand-printed sign that read HOMEGROWN TOMATOES still hung on the pasture fence at the last left turn onto the dirt road, even though no one had farmed the land in at least two years. Hanging next to it was a larger, preprinted FOR SALE sign with a telephone number. Someone had drawn a smiley face on it.

With a soft but firm "Whoa," Aidan halted the buggy under a massive oak tree. Tall grass and weeds choked the front yard all the way from the wood frame house with its peeling paint to the faded red barn. Quiet reigned. No voices called to each other. No dogs barked. No chickens chirped.

"It doesn't look like they're here." Her stomach roiling with disappointment, Bess hopped from the buggy and paced. "I'm sorry I made you drive all the way out here."

"Let's look around before you get all wound up." Aidan slid from the other side and patted the horse's broad rump. "There's a lot of ground to cover out here. She could be anywhere."

Bess practiced breathing. *Gott, help us know where to look. Please, Lord, bring Joshua back to me safely. Protect and keep him and Mattie.*

She'd prayed continuously on the slow

trek to Trenton, thankful for Aidan's silence. He seemed to know she could no more carry on a conversation than she could fly. Her entire focus had to be on the other end of the road. This spot here and now.

She halted, faced the house, and cupped her hands to her mouth. "Mattie? Mattie! Are you here?"

No answer.

"You go up to the house. I'll check the barn." Striding backward so he still faced her, Aidan threw her a reassuring smile. "We'll find them, you'll see."

"Danki."

"For what?"

"For being patient with me."

"You've always had a mind of your own. You take your sweet time making it up, but when you do, you never look back." His smile deepened as he turned. "It's one of the things I most like about you."

He stumbled on the word *like.* It sounded as if he might use another one-syllable word that began with *l* and ended with *e.* Bess halted but Aidan kept going. "Aidan?"

"Find Joshua."

His words wafted on the breeze. *"Find Joshua."*

She focused on the house. The screen door on the back porch sagged. A broken window had been patched with duct tape. The house had that lonely, unlived-in look. She slipped up the steps and peeked in the window. The kitchen was empty. She tried the doorknob. The door opened without protest. Plain families were like that.

"Mattie, please, if you're here, answer me."

Nothing.

Nothing in the front room. She took the stairs two at a time to the second floor. The first bedroom was utterly and completely empty. *Mattie, where are you?* The next room held the first ray of hope. It reeked of dirty diapers. A horse blanket was laid out on the floor with a second, smaller blanket rolled up tight at the top, like a pillow. A canvas bag held diapers. An empty baby bottle lay on its side on the floor.

They were here. They'd been here.

She flew down the stairs and out the front door. "They're here. Aidan, they're here."

He didn't answer. She raced across the yard and to the barn. The door stood open. He'd already searched and moved on. She peeked in. Mattie's buggy and horse were present and accounted for, but no Mattie.

Her lungs ached and her throat hurt as she ran from the barn and turned toward the woods that blanketed the land between the barn and the fields. "Mattie, Mattie,

466

please answer me!"

She remembered this path. It led to the pond where they'd cooled their feet, caught tadpoles, and the occasional small fish. A blue jay scolded her from above. Her breathing grew louder in her ears. The trees parted and opened up into a clearing. The pond.

A baby cried.

Blinded by the sun, Bess halted. She gasped for air and threw her hand to her forehead to shield her eyes.

Mattie stood, waist deep in the water. She clutched Joshua, naked and wiggling, in her arms. "Hold still, child." The pale-blue material of her skirt had turned a dark blue and brown with mud. It seemed to weigh her down. "You're dirty, Caleb. Stop wriggling."

"Mattie, what are you doing?"

She swiveled and squinted at Bess, her frown deep and wide. "Go away."

Bess put her hand to her chest as if it could quiet her pounding heart. "It's me, Bess. I came to take you home."

"Me and Caleb are home." She tussled Joshua under one arm and flung the other out in a wide arc. Water glistened on his pale-pink skin. He wailed, his small legs churning as if he pedaled a bicycle. "This is my home. Not yours. Mine."

467

Bess inhaled. Mattie held the person most dear to Bess's heart. She held her future as a mudder. *Please Gott, forgive me for neglecting this most precious task You have given me. Never again. Help me reach her.* "You're right. But Solomon wants you to come back to Jamesport. So do your kinner."

"Solomon? Jah, jah, Solomon." Mattie's forehead wrinkled. She pursued her lips. "He should be here. My mudder always said we would do better here. Too much tourist business in Jamesport. Keep yourself apart from those people. That's what she always said."

"I remember your mudder. She made gut gingersnaps. Solomon likes gingersnaps. We could make some for him." Bess moved a few steps closer. "Why don't you come up here and put Joshua's clothes on? He must be cold."

"He's dirty. There's no water in the house and I needed to bathe him." Mattie turned back to the pond. She slogged deeper into the water. "I can't let a child of mine go around dirty."

"Nee, that's enough. The water is too deep. The bottom drops off. The rocks are slick."

The words were no sooner spoken when Mattie's arm flew into the air. She screeched and flailed. She fell back and disappeared into the water, Joshua with her.

Two seconds as long as eternity itself later, she reappeared, coughing, gasping, and shrieking. "Caleb! Caleb!"

Bess flung herself forward, her long skirts hindering her headlong dash into the water. It rose to meet her, cold and dark. The murkiness yielded nothing. She whirled, hands wide, grasping, reaching.

The seconds went on and on, her future as dark and cold as the water. Frantic, she plunged deeper into the water, again and again. Nothing. No squalling, wiggling reminder of Gott's goodness and His grace in the face of terrible loss and tragedy. *Nee, Gott, please. Don't take him. Take me, not him.*

Her hands collided with a small, solid form.

Joshua. She heaved him up over her head and stood, frantic to keep a grip on the wet, slippery butterball. She struggled to hang on. Her feet slipped in the mud and flew out from under her. She went under again. Pond water, thick and green, filled her mouth. She sputtered. Joshua flopped and escaped her grasp.

Nee, nee. Lord, help me.

Her arms circled his waist and pulled him

up again.

She scrambled to her feet, slipping and sliding, her wet dress dragging her back as she struggled to reach the shore.

Air, sweet air, filled her lungs.

She clutched Joshua to her chest and held on. He screamed in her ear, face red, curls sopping.

"You're okay. You're okay." She grabbed Mattie and led her, sobbing, toward the shore. "We're okay. We're fine."

"Bess! Bess!" Aidan erupted into the clearing, long legs pumping. His straw hat flew off. He skidded to a stop at the waterline and held out his arms. "What happened?"

"We took a bath." She inhaled sweet air, exhaled. "Mattie thought we needed a bath."

Aidan waded into the water. He guided Mattie to dry land where she collapsed in a heap on the ground. He turned to Bess. His arm went around her shoulders. "I heard a scream. I thought . . . I don't know what I thought."

He hugged her to his chest, Joshua between them. His arms were warm and strong. She never wanted to leave that circle. "She slipped and fell in the water." Bess's heart raced at the images that would haunt her dreams for years to come. "Joshua went under. I couldn't find him."

"He's safe." Aidan's arm tightened. He leaned closer, his face full of an emotion even Bess could identify. "I thank Gott. You're safe and he's safe."

Bess rested her forehead on his broad chest. "We'll be fine as long as we stay together."

"I'll stay with you as long as I can, as long as Gott sees fit." His jaw worked and his Adam's apple bobbed. "I don't want to lose you. Or Joshua."

"You didn't."

"I want to talk. There's some things I have to say. Some things I want you to know."

She wanted that too. "As soon as this is over."

Aidan glanced back at Mattie, who began to scrub at the dirt on her dress. "She needs a doctor."

"Can you get to the phone shack at the next farm over? We need to call Solomon. He can let the others know the search is over."

"They'll have towels and blankets." Aidan grabbed a tiny gown and diaper from the boulder where Mattie had left them. He handed them to Bess. "We'll all go."

She nodded. "Together."

"Together."

FORTY-TWO

Joshua smiled at her. Bess wrapped a warm, dry blanket around his clean clothes and then stopped to study his pudgy face. He smiled a content, full-tummy smile. No doubt about it. Not at Aidan. Not at his groossmammi. At her. She picked him up and cuddled him close to her body. Despite her own dry clothes and a shawl donned over them, she still felt chilled to the bone. Her legs were wet noodles under her. Better to sit.

She sank into a chair in the front room, near the ones occupied by Laura and her father. Solomon had taken Mattie to the dawdy haus to rest after Freeman convinced the sheriff's deputies everyone was fine. As fine as could be under the circumstances. Everyone had gone home or gone to bed, the excitement done.

Except Aidan and Laura. He stood, looking out the window, a faraway expression

473

on his face. He'd been quiet when they'd finally made that drive home. In the raucous joy at their arrival back at Solomon's house, she hadn't had the opportunity to speak to him again. But he was still here. Still waiting for her.

Mudder trotted into the room, a tray filled with cups brimming with coffee in her hands. "I reckon you could use a hot drink to warm you up." She placed the mug on the end table next to Bess's chair. "Just don't spill it on the baby. He's been through enough."

"He's asleep." Indeed, he was. Without crying and without spitting up. "He's tuckered out. Which is good, because there's something I want to ask you about."

Laura nodded in encouragement. Aidan turned from the window, his expression expectant.

"It's been a long day." Daed looked as worn out as his grandson. "It's time we all turned in."

"I've asked Laura if I could stay with her instead of going to Haven with you." Bess would make her own case. She no longer needed others to stand up for her. "It's best for me and for Joshua."

"You'll not work at the B and B. I thought you understood that." Daed's frown etched lines around his mouth and eyes. "Others cannot care for your bopli. That's how we got to where we were today."

"I will care for Joshua. I'll help Jennie with her kinner and help Mary Katherine make baked goods and jams and jellies for the market. I'll help Laura and Iris with their work, if I'm needed."

Mudder sat on the couch next to Daed. "Jamesport has always been her home."

"It'd be easier on Mattie for me to live in another house but still close by. I can come to visit so she can see Joshua, but not have him right here where she's tempted to take him for a ride again."

"It's a good plan, Jeb." Laura rocked as if to punctuate her words. Her head inclined toward Aidan, who hadn't moved. He looked as if he barely breathed. "For everyone."

"I know better than to take on three women." Daed snorted. "Stay, Dochder. But know this, you can always come to Haven. We'll always have a place for you."

His gruff words and woebegone face told Bess what he couldn't say aloud. He missed her and wanted her close. "I will never forget that." Careful not to jostle her sleeping child, she rose and went to him. She planted a kiss on his cheek. "I'll bring

Joshua to visit often."

He would know both sets of grandparents.

"I reckon I should get home." Aidan edged toward the door. "Let you folks get your rest."

Without explanation, Bess followed him out the door. She didn't look back to gauge Daed and Mudder's expressions. She was a grown widow with a child.

At the porch steps Aidan turned. "I'm glad you're staying."

"Me too."

"I have livestock to feed. I best get to it."

"Eliza and Clara will have the house."

"The house Caleb was building for you."

"I won't be needing it." Would he understand? His sudden smile said he did. She smiled back. "I'll never forget Caleb. He will always be a part of my life. But he's gone. I'm here and I need to figure out what to do next."

"That's good."

"See you soon, then." The words were her promise to him.

"See you soon."

A promise shared.

EPILOGUE

One Year Later

The breeze held the first tantalizing hint of spring. Bess raised her face to it and closed her eyes. Another winter's end. Dark days banished. Light abundant. Contentment flowed over her. The buggy rides with Aidan over recent months always brought that same feeling of something she could find nowhere else. Sometimes they talked. Sometimes they didn't, the silence full of unspoken words allowed to lie fallow because there would be time for them later.

The buggy hit a rut and she opened her eyes. They'd turned onto the road that led to Aidan's farm. His home came into view. In all their travels, he'd never brought her here. She peered into the dusk. Ram scrambled to his feet in front of the pullet barn. A cat rose and stretched in a more leisurely fashion. Aidan's welcoming committee.

"What are we doing here?"

477

"I have something I want to show you."

"A surprise?"

He grinned. "You sound like little Sarah."

"Everyone likes surprises, even grown-up women."

"I don't like surprises." He pulled his lips down in a mock frown. "They're not always good."

"Is this one good?"

"I think so." The humor faded from his pewter eyes. "I hope so."

"I trust you."

He ducked his head. "That's good to know."

A few minutes later he helped her from the buggy. Instead of letting go of her arm the way he usually did, his fingers slid down her arm and became entwined with hers. She looked up at him. His grip tightened. "Is this all right?"

"It is."

"Gut."

He tugged and she fell into step next to him. To her surprise, they headed away from the house, toward the pullet sheds that had sat empty for more than a year. Ram ran circles around them with an occasional soft, welcoming *woof*. The no-name cat lost interest and wandered over to a spot under the buggy.

At the shed door Aidan stopped. "A lot of water under the bridge in the last year."

She paused next to him, seeing in her mind's eye what he saw.

She had moved in with Laura and spent her evenings walking, talking, sewing, and reading with her and the other widows. The healing had come in fits and starts. Wounds healed, scars formed and then faded. Not gone, but almost smooth to the touch. Memories became lovely spots to be visited on occasion, rather than miry pits to be avoided. Aidan had waited for her with a restful patience. He'd given her the precious gift of time.

Mattie never really recovered. She passed one autumn night. The doctor said her heart simply gave out. Solomon never wavered, trudged onward. Hazel bore another son. Daed had a second stroke but recovered by sheer stubbornness.

Joshua learned to sit up, then crawl, and walk, his journey so like Bess's. Every day he looked more like Caleb. She held this miniature portrait close to her heart at night and sang him to sleep in the rocking chair. He snuggled close, trusting her as she trusted Gott to raise him in the way Caleb would've wanted.

His first word had been *mudder,* followed

closely by *aenti*. Laura spent as much time with him as his other aunts, she deserved the title. Sharing Joshua with Laura gave the other woman a balm for her loneliness. Together, they learned to go on in this strange unexpected season in their lives.

The evenings spent with Laura, Jennie, and Mary Katherine had given way to long rides with Aidan. Bess had become accustomed to Laura's sly glances in the morning and chuckles over her appearances at breakfast, yawning and sleepy-eyed. She thanked Gott for Laura and her willingness to watch over Joshua so that something new could grow and take shape.

"It's been a good year." Even as she said the words she knew they weren't enough to describe her feelings. "I wouldn't have thought it possible."

"All things are possible with Gott."

"I had to learn that the hard way."

"If I could've spared you that journey, I would've. But Gott's will be done."

Bess had no doubt that he spoke the truth. He'd put her happiness ahead of his before. "Danki."

"For what?"

"For waiting for me."

"Healing takes time and you are worth waiting for." He let go of her hand, opened

480

the door, and waved her through. "After you."

The sound hit her first. *Cheep, cheep, cheep,* multiplied hundreds of times. The chirping of chickens. Many chickens. The white, ventilated cardboard boxes with their peaked roofs like little houses sat along one wall. The baby chicks filled the pens, tiny white balls of fluff with pink beaks. They seemed to be in perpetual motion. They hopped, they stumbled, they dug in the straw, they ran into each other, all the while, chattering incessantly.

"You did it!"

Aidan grinned, a full-out grin that stretched across his face. "I did."

"How?"

He scooped up two chicks and handed one to her. Its nubby fur felt soft on her palm. It pecked and chirped its way across the expanse as if hunting for something or someone. "By raising hogs. It's called diversifying. I saved enough from selling hogs to buy six thousand chicks. They arrived yesterday."

"You're back in business." She studied his face. The lines had relaxed around his mouth and eyes. The dark circles that spoke of sleepless nights had disappeared. "This is what you want?"

"I always thought I raised chickens because Daed did." He smoothed the chick in his hand with gentle fingers. "But I missed the rhythm of it. I missed the sound. I missed them."

"They're cute."

"They'll end up on someone's table."

"I know, but in the meantime, you care for them and they're in good hands here."

He shrugged. "I'm a farmer."

"I'm happy you're happy."

He took the chicks and settled them back into the pen. "I wanted you to see that I'm able to support a family again."

The importance of his words settled around her. She nodded. "I see that."

He took a step closer. She inhaled his scent and held on to it. He touched her cheek. "But do you see why I wanted you to know?"

She gazed up at him, trying to make sure. She couldn't afford to misinterpret. "We've spent a lot of time together in the last year."

"I'm not Caleb."

Bess breathed. Now or never. She took a trembling step toward him. "I don't want you to be Caleb."

"Are you sure?" His fingers caressed her cheek and slid across the material of her dress above her collarbone. "I stepped back

482

once. I would do it again. Caleb was like a brother to me. I wanted him to be happy. I was happy for him. Now I'm stepping forward. For my own happiness. I need to know there's no one standing between us, living or dead."

"No one." The words came out in a whisper. She cleared her throat. "No one."

He leaned down. His lips brushed hers, then fled before she could kiss him back. "I'm asking you to marry me this summer."

"I'm saying jah." No whisper this time. She would shout it in the middle of Jamesport if she could. Aidan loved her. She loved him. Gott loved them both and He'd led them down this path to a new beginning, a second chance she little deserved but desired more than she would ever have thought possible. She'd been given the gift of two great loves in a single lifetime. Gott's grace was endless. She had no qualms. Gott would give them whatever days He saw fit. She wanted those days. And she wanted Aidan to kiss her again. "Jah, jah, jah."

He sighed, a soft sound of relief mingled with joy. "I guess that means you're sure."

"Very."

His arms slipped around her waist. He lifted her off the ground in that long-awaited, tight, rib-crushing, no-holds-

483

barred, I-love-you-like-I've-never-loved-anyone hug. It went on and on. His lips nuzzled her neck, sending goose bumps scurrying in all directions. He dropped tiny kisses on her cheeks and nose.

Finally, his lips sought hers again. The wait was worth it. Pain fell away. Loneliness fled. The future appeared, whole and filled with possibility. It wouldn't always be like this. Experience had taught her that. She might love and lose again, but she wanted the possibilities. She wanted the bright, sunny days and everything that arrived on a spring breeze. Together, they would sow seeds and grow as one. They would share a life given to them by a Gott who knew what was best for them and for how long.

When she was certain she would collapse under the sheer weight of the joy, he pulled away. "I love you, Bess. I have always loved you." He set her on her feet again. She swayed. His hands stayed on her waist. "The right to say those words gives me great joy."

"I love you too. I will always love you."

"Greater joy still."

Together, hand in hand, they turned to face their future.

DISCUSSION QUESTIONS

1. Bess's husband, Caleb, is killed in an accident after only one year of marriage. She's twenty, pregnant, and a widow. In the beginning, she blames God. Do you think bad things come from God? How do you explain it when bad things happen to good people like Bess and Caleb?
2. The Amish believe God has a plan for each of His children. Scripture says He has plans to prosper, not harm us. Yet we still suffer. Why do you think that is?
3. What do you think it means for our character to be "refined like silver"?
4. Has there ever been something that happened in your life that you couldn't understand at the time, that hurt and caused you pain, but now you look back and see a benefit you couldn't see before?
5. Bess doesn't believe she will ever love again the way she loved Caleb. Yet she does. Do you think it's possible to truly

and equally love more than one person in a lifetime? Why or why not?

6. The Amish believe that our days on earth are numbered and we're only passing through, so death is not something to be feared but rather a stepping stone to a better, eternal life. As Christians, we believe Jesus Christ died on the cross for our sins, so we could be forgiven and receive eternal life. Yet most of us are fearful of death. Does that fear reflect a lack of faith? How do you overcome it?

7. Some people believe they have a right to a pain-free, happy life. Some preachers promise it to their congregations, if only they believe. What does Scripture say about suffering in this life? How do you feel about that?

8. When something bad happens to you, is your first inclination to be joyful about it? Can you give examples of how you have matured and been "made complete" by the difficult times in your life?

9. In the beginning Aidan was determined to marry Iris and "learn" to love her. In some cultures, marriages are arranged and couples don't know each other well before they are wed. Do you think it is possible to "learn" to love someone, or was Iris right to decline his offer even though she

loved him?

10. If Caleb hadn't died, Aidan would never have realized his dream to be with Bess. He chose never to act on his feelings for her while Caleb was alive. Do you think it's right for him to be with her now that his best friend has died? Why or why not?

ACKNOWLEDGMENTS

Every time I write a novel, I have a honeymoon period with the story. I think up all these great conflicts and hurdles I want to make my characters suffer through and overcome. Then I sit down to write and it hits me: I don't know anything about any of this stuff. Fortunately, other people do.

In this case, I want to thank Sharee Stover of Norfolk, Nebraska, who offered her husband's expertise on how avian flu outbreaks are handled by law enforcement. She didn't share his name and I didn't want to pry, but I appreciate his e-mail help and the links to newspaper articles that were attached. A big thank-you also goes to Jordan Bednar, owner/farmer of Tandem Farm Company, outside of Austin, Texas. Justin took the time to talk with me by phone about raising chickens. He offered his sage advice on how to make my story more realistic. The original contact with Justin came via my good friend Eileen Key, who tracked down his information through her family. Eileen was also so kind as to read my first draft in all its sloppy glory and give me her invaluable feedback on the story and characters.

As always, any mistakes in this story are totally mine. I know a little about a lot, it seems, but I'm an expert on almost nothing.

It's important to note that, while this story takes place in Jamesport, Missouri, where there is a large Amish population, the characters in this book are figments of my imagination as are the businesses described, which have fictitious names. I have used poetic license in my description of several places in my story, so please remember that above all else, this is fiction.

I dedicated this book to my agent and friend Mary Sue Seymour, who passed away in 2016 as I was finishing this story. I would be remiss not to acknowledge here how much her guidance and support meant in making it possible for me to get my books published. She was known as the "Amish Romance" agent and had a huge role in making Amish fiction its own genre. She had an unerring eye for good stories and represented some of the best Christian fiction writers of the genre. She was also a strong Christian woman who was unfailingly kind, gracious, encouraging, and when need be, unflinchingly honest. I wouldn't be a published author today if it weren't for Mary Sue. I just know she's correcting someone's grammar in heaven right this minute.

Writing as a full-time occupation would not be possible for me if it weren't for the support and encouragement of my husband, Tim. He's been my rock through a myriad of health issues. The seriousness with which he views his marriage vows never ceases to astound me. He maintains my website, takes my photo portraits, orders my swag, and gives me social media advice. He also cooks, buys groceries, and does laundry! Without him, I couldn't do this.

Finally, my deepest appreciation goes out to the readers who buy these books and make it possible for me to continue to write them. God bless you.

ABOUT THE AUTHOR

Kelly Irvin is the author of several Amish series including the Bliss Creek Amish series, the New Hope Amish series, and the Amish of Bee County series. She has also penned two romantic suspense novels, *A Deadly Wilderness* and *No Child of Mine.* The Kansas native is a graduate of the University of Kansas School of Journalism. She has been writing nonfiction professionally for more than thirty years, including ten years as a newspaper reporter, mostly in Texas-Mexico border towns. A retired public relations professional, Kelly has been married to photographer Tim Irvin for twenty-nine years. They have two children, two grandchildren, and two cats. In her spare time, she likes to write short stories and read books by her favorite authors.

Twitter: @Kelly_S_Irvin
Facebook: Kelly.Irvin.Author

The employees of Thorndike Press hope you have enjoyed this Large Print book. All our Thorndike, Wheeler, and Kennebec Large Print titles are designed for easy reading, and all our books are made to last. Other Thorndike Press Large Print books are available at your library, through selected bookstores, or directly from us.

For information about titles, please call:
(800) 223-1244

or visit our website at:
gale.com/thorndike

To share your comments, please write:
Publisher
Thorndike Press
10 Water St., Suite 310
Waterville, ME 04901